Blood on the Walls

WILLIE HAMILTON

·

Blood on the Walls

BLOOMSBURY

Picture section: page 4, bottom right © Popperfoto;
page 5 top © Hulton-Deutsch.

While every effort has been made to contact the copyright holders of
illustrations, and to make acknowledgement for their use, if any errors
or omissions have occurred, please contact the publishers who will
correct these in any subsequent edition.

Frist published 1992 by Bloomsbury Publishing Limited,
2 Soho Square, London W1V 5DE

Copyright © 1992 by Willie Hamilton
The moral right of the author has been asserted

A CIP record for this book is available from the British Library

ISBN 0 7475 1116 0

10 9 8 7 6 5 4 3 2 1

Designed by Geoff Green
Typeset by Hewer Text Composition Services, Edinburgh
Printed by Clays Ltd, St Ives PLC

Contents

Introduction | 1
1 Childhood, Windsor, Muck, and Revolution | 7
2 The 1926 General Strike: Workers of the World Unite | 14
3 Cockroaches, Lops, Head Lice and Chamber Pots | 18
4 Spreading My Wings | 22
5 University, Conscientious Objection and War | 30
6 Armed Service. For King and Country | 40
7 1945 and All That | 49
8 The 1950 Election: Victory and Defeat | 61
9 New Member at the Palace of Westminster | 64
10 The 1951 Election | 71
11 The Long Haul | 74
12 Two More Elections, Two More Labour Defeats | 79
13 A Trip to the USSR | 90
14 Sixty Days in the USA | 93
15 Lord Home and Mr Wilson: Aristocrat Versus Academic | 100
16 CADCO, or This Little Piggy Went to Market | 108
17 War Damage Bill | 114
18 1966 to 1979, or Joy to Disaster | 118
19 The Four Margarets in My Life | 148
20 A Grantham Grocer's Daughter | 156
21 Sovereignty, Europe and the European Parliament | 166
22 1987 and After | 171
23 Miracle or Mirage? | 176
24 What is Your Member of Parliament Worth? | 185
25 Prince Charles, and Other Things | 197
26 An Urgent Message to Her Majesty the Queen | 204
Index | 212

Introduction

Autobiographies are unreliable sources for historians in search of the whole truth, and those written by senior politicians or statesmen are probably the most barren of all. To engage in self-justification, to be wise after the event, to sidle alongside the truth, or be miserly with it, to practise the art of protective omission – these are but a few of the artifices in the armoury of the old political lag when he puts pen to paper. Not only this. Many of these tales are evidence of a degree of conceit, of an urge to massage the ego, and a temptation to scratch one's own back.

On all these counts, I may be just as guilty as anyone else. I *have* written in self-justification. I freely confess it is *not* the *whole* story. I also plead guilty to the charge that what I have written is at least in part an expression of conceit. I do not perch on a 'holier than thou' pedestal, nor do I pretend to be a purveyor of the unabridged truth. Nobody, anywhere, will ever tell the unexpurgated story of their own private life, and certainly no politician. Indeed, why should they? All of us have, locked within ourselves, secrets that will never be revealed, not only because revelation might be embarrassing or shameful, but because it could often be trivial, uninteresting, or hurtful to others.

Nevertheless, I plead mitigating circumstances. I was a Member of Parliament for thirty-seven years. I never held any high office. I was never in a position to be called on to make any momentous decisions. I have, therefore, no temptation to lie, no incentive to distort or exaggerate.

I was seldom sufficiently energetic to keep a diary, except as a desultory record of meetings to be attended, engagements to be kept, birthdays to be remembered and other such trivia. Right until I became an MP I had regarded a diary as an unnecessary luxury. Thus it was that my memory of my early life, clear though much of it is, often goes awry when I seek to record it in strict chronological sequence. Nevertheless, the overall picture is accurate, and I have sought to record it because I think it may be of some interest to social historians, politicians, and psychiatrists. It may also promote a better understanding, especially among younger generations, of what it meant, and what it still means,

to be born and bred in a society rapidly rotting with inequalities – in
wealth, education and environment – which make a mockery of all the
prattle about personal freedom, democracy, choice, and all the other
'buzz' words currently in vogue.

As the second of four sons of a Durham coalminer, born in a colliery
hovel tied to the job, in a community where women and children died
meanly, where the only unifying bond was grinding poverty, I never felt
any need to *prove* my working-class credentials, nor any urge to assert
my political virility by seeking to hide my family origins or to deny my
educational background. I wasn't particularly *proud* of my origins, but
was never *ashamed* of them either.

What I have written is a potted version of life as I remember it,
underpinned by colourful and amusing conversations with my two
younger brothers, Jack and Arthur, still alive in Durham, and not least
by a number of taped recordings which I made a few years ago with
old Durham miners, all of whom remembered my father as a miner
and as a local Labour Party politician. But a tape cannot convey the
richness of the Durham accent, nor the facial expressions of those men
as they described their horrific ordeals in the coalmines of seventy years
ago.

The early chapters, naturally, deal with my days as a child and
youth in a mining village. I have tried to describe as accurately and
as amusingly as I can that environment, and my education up to entry
to Sheffield University in 1936. Though my lavatorial stories can be
laughed at *now*, they were no laughing matter *then*. When I recall
them to my prosperous daughter, Sheila, and to my brilliant grand-
daughter, Joanne, they listen with a mixture of amusement and disgust,
disbelief and disapproval. They do not care to be reminded of the
origins of 'the old man'. So the book is written for the likes of them.
If they and others find it coarse and rude, it is because my life was
brutal and almost empty of any of the good things which are now
taken for granted. We sometimes laughed, but there was little to laugh
about.

The second part of my story is concerned with my higher education
at university and the Second World War. Wars are cruel, crude and ugly
blots on the long story of man's inhumanity to man. War can never
be ennobling, although it can produce brave and courageous deeds of
valour and sacrifice in the name of 'patriotism'. But in the twentieth
century, nobody ever *wins* a war. After the 1939–45 holocaust, the
Germans and Japanese were the undoubted military losers. The Soviet
Union, with twenty million corpses to prove it, was deemed to be on
the winning side. So, too, were we. In the light of what has happened in
the last forty-five years, that tabulation of winners and losers is scarcely
credible. No acceptable balance sheet of those terrible events can ever be
drawn up. With all his ingenuity, surely Man must find more civilised

ways of resolving international disputes than a crude resort to the law of the jungle.

By far the greater part of my book is devoted to marriage, fatherhood and politics at a national level. A recurring political theme is my abiding suspicion, if not contempt, of what I loosely call the Establishment. It has included everybody, from my own father, to headmasters I knew, to Party Whips, unelected appointees in Parliament, the monarchy, petty tyrants at local government level, Ministers of the Crown, top civil servants, and the aristocracy. I wore with fortitude a comprehensive list of shoulder-chips, with a mix of anger and amusement.

If much of what I have written sounds prejudiced or bitter, it is because *all* Party politicians are, by definition, prejudiced. They are elected – to the parish council or to Parliament – *because* they are prejudiced. There is nothing sinister or bad about that. Those men and women have strong and sincerely held views about everything that affects our daily lives. I myself entered Parliament with no experience of either local government or industry. Nor did I have that veneer of self-assurance that goes with a public school education and family affluence. My inferiority complex, such as it was, disappeared very quickly when I saw Tory MPs who had been blessed, or cursed, with those advantages. Many of them I soon found to be thick, suave, and completely unscrupulous when their interests were threatened.

Looking back over fifty years, I have often wondered how we escaped bloody revolution. The folk I lived among had nothing to lose but their chains. Yet they kept on wearing them. Perhaps they had no *choice*. There was 'no alternative', to coin a phrase. Whatever the reasons for their acceptance of their miserable lot, it had nothing to do with the absurd claim that something called the *monarchy* was a 'unifying force', something which bound us all together in one big happy family. Very early on in my life I was taught that it, the monarchy, was the very apex of something evil, of that pyramid of wealth, privilege and exploitation, at the bottom of which writhed coalminers, dockers, textile workers and the toiling masses everywhere. The monarchy was, and still remains, the ermine cloak hiding the rotting body.

I wrote about those things in *My Queen and I* in 1975. Much of the factual material in that book is now out of date, although the opinions I expressed have probably hardened. An updated version may soon be on the stocks.

Since I did not belong to any part of the Establishment, I never felt the need to genuflect to it. In parenthesis, I recall with great sadness that many years ago, before he was our Party Leader, but when he was a Minister of Her Majesty's Government, Michael Foot was almost forced to make an apology to the House of Commons for having openly expressed his republican views.

I paid a price for my anarchical views, and have given some account of that, I hope with no impression of sour grapes. Far abler men and women have failed to achieve ministerial office. The highest positions in Parliamentary life are attained by a combination of luck and ability – and the greater of these is luck.

The story here recounted is not so much autobiographical as a backbencher's commentary on his perpetual struggle against the odds to balance conflicting interests and resolve the multiplicity of problems which poured daily on to his desk, all of which had to be faced with financial and material resources more limited than those available to any clerk of a small town.

Nevertheless, the back-bench MP need not be a cypher. He can make his mark in a variety of ways, and not the least important is the help he can give to his constituents. To be described as 'a good constituency Member' is no mean compliment, and I like to think I earned that accolade. I regarded West Fife – later renamed Central Fife – as *my* parish, and the people there as *my* responsibility. I never felt aloof from them, and I hope they never felt remote from me. An MP has several loyalties: first of all to the national interest, secondly to his or her constituents' welfare, thirdly to his or her own conscience, and lastly to his or her Party. That should be the order of priorities.

I have said a little on MPs' pay. It often disgusted me. As someone with no other income, apart from occasional TV and radio fees, plus the odd fee from journalism, I had to live on my pay at Westminster. I did not retire a rich man. Fortunately, I made quite a handy profit from selling my London home in 1987, when Mrs Thatcher's gravy train stopped to let me get on.

One important omission is any lengthy reference to a rapidly increasing scandal, namely, the alarming increase in the number of outside financial interests which many Members have, and especially *Conservative* Members. They all claim that although they might be very well paid for such service as they give to their private employers, it does not influence their behaviour in Parliament. Frankly, I do not believe that. The rules of the House on these matters are so loose as to be almost useless. This scandal has been escalating for some time, yet under present rules it is all perfectly legal. I am glad I can claim that I never at any time engaged in that kind of dubious behaviour. I was never invited by any outside pressure group to be their paid Parliamentary front man.

I have singled out CADCO, the War Damage Bill and the Oman Affair for separate comment because each contains lessons to be learned about how grossly inefficient the control of public spending really is. These cases also show how Parliament can be used for dubious purposes, and how Governments can deceive Parliament by refusing to tell the truth, and even by refusing to say anything at all on matters of legitimate public interest, on the often specious argument that national security could be threatened. We are all far too complacent about the ease with which

Prime Ministers and Governments can literally get away with murder, whether in Gibraltar, Northern Ireland, or nearer to home.

Four 'Margarets' have intruded themselves at various stages in my life. They went in 'pairs' – and one pair couldn't have been more different from the other. The Margarets Windsor and Thatcher were influences as baneful as the Margarets Stevenson and McKay/Cogle were wholly blissful. A much longer and separate assessment is made of the Thatcher legacy.

I couldn't conclude before making a few comments on my last Parliamentary Election foray in beautiful Devon in 1987. I lost my first in Fife in 1945, and my last in Devon in 1987.

My account is little more than that of a very humble Member of Parliament. Like hundreds of others, I had a ringside seat in the greatest theatre of political debate in the UK, where lack of knowledge was never a good reason for not speaking. During that time I watched the unfolding of earth-shaking events over which I had little influence or control. That same lack of influence or control applied to the actions of our own Government. The idea that Parliament is 'sovereign', that *it* alone decides the UK's actions and policies, is now seen to be an outdated concept.

When, as PM, Mrs Thatcher used to rail about our Parliamentary sovereignty being threatened by Brussels, what she was really angry about was the threat to *her own* control of the House of Commons. The 'elective despotism' which she sought to impose was the prime cause of her downfall.

Now I can only reminisce, and regret. Perhaps I was wrong to content myself with being so parochial in that Westminster hothouse. It may have been a life wasted. I have since thought – too late – that there must have been more rewarding ways of spending my life than being screwed down to those green-leather benches of the House of Commons. However, what has been done cannot now be undone. For good or ill, the record must speak for itself. I cannot be the impartial judge of its worth.

1

Childhood, Windsor, Muck, and Revolution

'A Good Riddance: The King has done a popular act in abolishing the German titles held by the members of his Majesty's family.'

Punch, 27 June 1917

At a stroke, King George V absorbed the German titles of Teck and Battenberg into the English peerage. The family's links with the names of Guelph and Wetton, Saxe-Coburg-Gotha, Hanover and Brunswick, were pushed down the toilets of history. And so we got the squeaky-new Royal House of Windsor. Good old George V planted seeds in 1917 which flourished with hardly a hiccup ever after.

More terrible events were happening elsewhere. Millions of young lives were being lost in the holocaust of war. And the Russian Revolution was beginning the nightmare of Leninist-Stalinist terror and repression which was to endure for another seventy years.

In the light of these historic events, it was not surprising that nobody noticed the birth of Willie Hamilton in the middle of that momentous year. On 26 June, Mrs Jennie Hamilton gave birth to the son of Joe Hamilton in the mining village of Herrington in the county of Durham. No church bells were rung. No flags were hoisted. I was the second son of Joe and Jennie – just another mouth to feed out of a coalminer's pittance.

Joe had several things in common with our present Queen. Firstly, he never paid income tax. Secondly, he lived in a tied house. That is to say, it went with the job, and no rent was paid. Then Joe never had a holiday. And that, I was told in 1971 by Sir Michael Adeane, then Her Majesty's Private Secretary, was a burden Her Majesty had to bear. Nor could she, 'like other hard-working people, look forward to a period of retirement at the end of her life'. Poor royal soul. My father was lucky. He *could* look forward to his retirement – and expect to be kicked out of his house. The fourth thing Joe had in common with Her Majesty was that he had four children.

And there the similarities ended. Joe Hamilton and Queen Elizabeth might have been living on different planets. Their lifestyles were those of affluence and privilege for royalty, deprivation and squalor for the miner.

The assertion that all men are born equal is a patent lie, perpetuated by the well-off and suffered by the lower orders.

Herrington is about five miles inland from the port of Sunderland. That town was busy exporting coal and building ships in the nineteenth and early twentieth centuries. Our village bordered on other mining communities like Philadelphia and Shiney Row, spreading like an invasive cancer towards Newbottle and Houghton-le-Spring to the south, and Penshaw and Fatfield to the north.

Coalmining, preaching and teaching were the main sources of work. Miners' sons were as sure to go down the pits as princes were to become kings. My father worked in the Dorothea Pit – the Dolly – less than half a mile from our terraced house in Herrington. All miners lived within walking distance of the Dolly. You could hear it, see it, smell it and taste it every day. The reek, the dust, the sight of the colliery's big winding wheels at the pit-head, all were constant reminders of the treadmill to which those men and their families were tied, prisoners of the avaricious private mine-owners just as surely as the Negro slaves had been of the plantation-owners.

The mines around us were owned by the Lambton, Hetton and Joicey Collieries Company. Years later, as a Member of Parliament, I met a very wealthy Tory MP, young Lord Lambton, one of the main beneficiaries of the bloody labour of men like my father. On one occasion, he and I were invited to take part in a televised debate at Cambridge University's debating society. It was to be in formal dress of bow tie and black jacket. The subject was to be based on the motion 'That the class system in Britain is now dead.' I think that was it. Lord Lambton kindly asked me if I would like to be driven up to Cambridge by him. I readily agreed. The alternative would have been a tedious train journey, carrying my little case containing Moss Bros's hired togs for the evening. 'Then come to my house in town to meet me,' said His Lordship. On arrival, I was ushered in by a butler with a Geordie accent. 'Can I get you a drink?' he asked. 'His Lordship will be a little while.' So I had my drink, followed by a soak in a bath as big as a swimming pool whilst His Lordship was changing, and then I waited, marvelling at the opulence. My father must have worked bloody hard and long to provide all this, I thought. And so to Cambridge in our chauffeur-driven limousine. On the way, Lambton chatted with me, like good friends should. By the time we got to Cambridge, he knew a lot about my family, and especially about my father, whose home address he insisted I should give him.

The debate went quite well. I suggested the class system was epitomised by the two protagonists that evening: 'The owner and the slave, the wealthy exploiter and his victim'. Lambton took it all very well. The privileged are very nice and considerate, so long as their wealth is not threatened!

As a result of that encounter, and for every Christmas until he died, my father received a brace of pheasants from the Lambton estates. Joe was furious. He didn't want any of the mineowners' crumbs. So he never touched those pheasants. My brothers weren't so squeamish and devoured the birds – every year. I don't know the end of that story. But it didn't bankrupt Lord Lambton. As of now (1990), he lives in sunny Italy, far away from the pits that made him rich.

The Hamiltons struggled on among the coal heaps of Durham. Our family life showed no outward display of warmth of any kind. We never addressed our parents as 'Dad' or 'Mum'. They were 'cissy' words. It was always 'Father' and 'Mother'. Ostentatious affection, expressed in hugging or kissing, was definitely out. It was expressed in other, more practical ways, like greasing the pit boots, fetching in the buckets of coal to bank up the fire at night, and helping to wash up the dishes after the Sunday dinner.

My mother was from a 100 per cent mining family called Chicken. Her father was a kindly, bearded old gentleman. He played the old pedal organ at the local Methodist chapel. And he used to visit us, to play our very own pedal organ. It was always hymns he played, and he encouraged us to sing along. As a young miner he had carried his own sons back from their work in that same Dolly pit to their colliery house in Philadelphia. There were four sons: Willie, Tom, Jack and Ralph. All were miners. And the three daughters – Mary, Annie, and my own mother, Jennie – all married coalminers. Like the royals, miners' families rarely wed outside their own class. But Mary did step a bit out of line. She married a 'gaffer' – one of the pit officials. They lived in a posh, flat-roofed tied house. Their concessionary coal was 'roundy' – big shiny pieces of best-quality stuff – not like our 'nuts', the inferior-quality product. We hardly ever spoke to the gaffer husband of Aunt Mary. He wasn't one of 'us'. He was a bosses' man. He wore a glossy steel hat, and carried a big stick.

We all lived within spitting distance of the pit. And when the family moved from Herrington to a tiny community called Spring Gardens, we were even closer to the pit-head – about 200 yards away.

That move came before I started school. I have no clear recollection of those early years. I couldn't then know of the thousands of young British lives being destroyed daily in that dreadful European war. Our own horror wasn't as bloody. But our struggle to survive was no less real, and arguably, work in the bowels of the earth was as dangerous as any soldier's life in the trenches.

Spring Gardens is a sweet-sounding name for a handful of miners' hovels. Our house had a backyard about ten feet square. In it there was a coal-house, and a 'netty' – a dry toilet or midden. And it was a two-seater! That puzzled me. I asked my Uncle Ralph about this luxury. Ralph was a droll, lonely man. Very kind and jolly, and nearly always drunk, though I never knew where he got the money to pay for his beer. But he knew what those two holes were for. 'There's one hole for each leg,' he explained. That was it. My social education was off to a good start.

We had two bedrooms upstairs, one for my parents and the other for my brother Tom and me. Tom was two years older, and we slept in the one double bed. Downstairs we had a small scullery where we washed in an enamel basin of cold water. There was no bathroom or hot-water supply. Lighting was by a paraffin lamp, and heating by one coal fire.

A small front garden gave enough room for us to keep a few hens. Each year – at Christmas and Easter – we killed one or two. Sometimes, Father would buy a box of chickens, which always seemed to come by rail to Penshaw Station, about two miles away. The chicks travelled in cardboard boxes with ventilation holes. When I collected them there were always a few dead ones. The family investment must have been worthwhile, because it went on for some years – like the wee shop which my parents started in a wooden hut in our backyard. There were about fifty houses at Spring Gardens, and no shop within a mile. So the Hamiltons became little capitalists. We sold cigarettes, matches and candles, soap, yeast and flour, sweets, chocolates and sugar. In the scullery we had a paraffin tank from which we sold the oil for the village lamps. It couldn't have made a fortune, but with miners' wages at about £1 a week, the margin between poverty and starvation was measured in pennies. We were a rag-and-bone community. I have a miner's 'Pay Note' for 1931 in my possession. For four days' work, the pay was £1.6s.2d – 131 new pennies in today's money.

Spring Gardens was on the road to nowhere – like all the folk living there. It was part of the pit, just like the little power station nearby, the railway workshops, the coal mountains, the heaps of pit waste and the ponds of putrid pit water. The noise, the grime, and the smells of oil and coal were all-pervasive even when the pit wasn't working. That was often. The blowing of the dreaded pit buzzer at 5 p.m. was the notice that the pit would not be working tomorrow. Nobody ever knew why. Various rumours would go about. The coal boats couldn't get either into or out of Sunderland docks, or coal orders were slack.

There were no family benefits then; no National Health Service; no free school meals or milk. Of course nobody paid income tax, or even National Insurance. My father was covered for health purposes by the Lloyd George scheme. In this scheme, workers earning less than £3 a year paid 4d to cover medical treatment for themselves, but not their families, whilst the bosses contributed a further 3d, and the State 2d. The rest of us – mother and boys – were covered by paying a shilling a week to a local doctor. A woman came round our houses every week to collect it. If we were unwell we went to the doctor's surgery, where you *always* got a bottle of 'tonic' or a few pills. The surgery was shelved all round with scores of bottles, each containing a different-coloured concoction. The prize to win was a tonic. The worse the brew tasted, the greater the conviction that it was doing you good. Faith-healing was the doctor's trick. It was at its height, or depths, in my childhood days. It still exists. Only the coloured bottles have gone.

TB and heart disease were certain killers. When I was a young teenager, a friend at my school had a knee in which TB was diagnosed. The cure then was to isolate him and his fellow sufferers in a remote hospital in north-west Durham, and subject the sufferers to freezing fresh air. Whatever the weather – and winters in the hills of Durham could be like blasts of ice – the windows were kept open at all times. After his spell there, my friend was sent home with a leg calliper. He was fifteen. He committed suicide by throwing himself over the cliffs at Seaburn, just outside Sunderland.

And I vividly remember how when my pals and I used to play football at our street-end in Spring Gardens, a wee lass called May used quietly to sit, cold and miserable, on her 'hunkers', her knees drawn up closely to her little chest, as blue in complexion as a bluebell. Nobody spoke to her. We watched her die before she was ten. Nobody seemed to care. These were 'the good old days'.

SCHOOL

Paddock Stile Infants and Primary School was about half a mile from our house. To walk to it, I went on a rough footpath past the cooling towers of the power station. Through the railings, I liked to watch local men swimming in the warm water from the towers. It was the nearest thing we had to a heated swimming pool. But it could be dangerous. Warning notices were ignored. The local policeman used to prowl about, but I don't know if he ever caught anybody. More likely he would have had a dip himself. We had to take our pleasures as we could find them, and to hell with the law.

For me, school was a great adventure. Books were scarce at home. Radio and TV for the masses were unknown. All our spare time was spent sitting at home in winter talking to our parents, or larking about in the cold streets playing with our friends. In the summer we played among the railway sidings, climbing into and out of the empty coal wagons. In the large colliery-owned field at the end of our street we had great fun feeding the pit ponies and trying to ride them. The schoolboy's unnecessary and painful trick of squeezing the stings out of bees had to be learned the hard way. A particularly vicious little bee was the 'red arsety'. It had a pretty, copper-coloured rear. When I asked

my mother if she had ever come across red arseties she was amused and
shocked. Her son's vocabulary seemed to be widening alarmingly.

Those summer days were happy times. We had wide, open spaces.
Our field was speckled with buttercups and daisies, thistles, clover and
the richest green grass, all fertilised by the pit ponies. It was a great thrill
to watch a lark rising vertically into the clear blue sky, trilling ecstatically
against the background din of the pit and the railway engines.

This sweet innocence of childhood is one of our Creator's priceless
gifts to mankind; a treasure all too soon destroyed and lost for ever.
There are no barriers between children. They know no prejudices of
colour, religion, or class. All those evils are conjured up by grown men
and women.

The wickednesses of our times are all man-made. Too often the main
victims are our innocent children.

School was like going on a voyage of discovery; an exciting jump into
another magical world. I used to get there early so that I could ring the
bell. It made me feel important, if only for a few minutes.

We learned our alphabet and letters by using flat tin trays filled with
wet sand. We also used little grey slates and slate pencils. I remember
one young lady teacher who had a strange effect on me. Miss Robinson
had a luscious chest. She also came to school on a motorbike. That was
greatly daring in those days. A young lady in a hurry. I often wondered
what happened to her. I hope she got everything she deserved!

I loved school, but I was glad to run home for dinner and tell my story
to my parents. When my father was on the back shift he came up the pit
at 6 p.m. I would just have time to get my tea before I ran across the
railway lines to the pit yard to wait for those winding wheels to turn.
That meant my father and his mates were 'riding', or coming up in the
cage. Even though all the men were black, it was easy to spot my father,
with his pit lamp gleaming in his ebony-coloured hand. The miners didn't
then wear safety helmets, and their lamps were not electric. Everybody
walked home to the nearby villages. Our walk only took five minutes.
My mother had the zinc bath on the living-room floor, with boiling hot
water in a big cast-iron pan ready on the fire. Then our house became
a little sweatshop, Dad getting his bath kneeling on the floor, the boys
washing his back, and Mother getting the meal ready. We also had the
pit boots to grease, and the pit clothes to shake and dry. Then the bath
had to be emptied outside and put away in the scullery.

The rest of the family didn't get baths too often. We never had
toothbrushes, and toilet paper was unknown. Torn up papers of any
kind were used for wiping ourselves. They were dirty, grubby, unhygienic
days. And I was just a grubby, but happy, mischievous brat.

I was happy partly because at school I saw boys and girls who were
much worse clothed and shod and less well fed than I was. One poor
little girl called Mary Orr used to arrive barefoot, dirty, with a sad,

haggard face even at the age of eight or nine, wearing, literally, a few dirty black rags. They always seemed to be black – and Mary always seemed to be late for school. She would be scolded and caned for her unpunctuality. I learned later that Mary's mother had died young, and the poor little soul had to try to get out to school another brother and sister. Mary probably died young too. Another victim of the system.

I was also content because I could do my lessons without much difficulty. I was able to read well at an early age. My handwriting was, and still is, awful, but I could put sentences together. And my facility for doing mental arithmetic thrilled me, my teacher, and my parents. This penchant for mathematics was short-lived and perished at an early age.

I became a 'teacher's pet'. I liked that. More books were put in my way, and I won one or two book prizes. I felt on top of the world.

Then my teachers decided I could jump a class, that is, leave out the next class up altogether. That was cruel. I lost touch with my friends. I had to learn a lot of new things quickly. But my parents, and especially my father, were becoming visibly excited by the promise of their son William.

2

The 1926 General Strike:
Workers of the World Unite

'All the workers in this country have got to face a reduction in wages . . . to help put industry on its feet.'

Stanley Baldwin, *Daily Herald*, 31 July 1925

I was only eight when the 1926 strike began on 4 May. I can't remember much about it. I was still happy at Paddock Stile School. Our parents must have protected us from the near-starvation inflicted on the miners by the avaricious owners. They were determined to impose an immediate and savage cut in the already pitifully low wages of their workers, while protecting their own profits.

My younger brother Arthur was born in 1926 and named after Arthur Cook, the militant and bonny fighter who was Secretary of the then Miners' Federation of Great Britain. So, what with Jack having been born four years behind me, in 1921, there were now four hungry young Hamiltons – and no income.

In my later studies of history – at both grammar school and university – I was taught more about the Battle of Hastings and the British Empire than I ever learned about the 1926 strike. And even today little blank faces would stare back at anybody questioning them on that blot on our social history.

Sixty years later, another Tory Prime Minister was to repeat similar sentiments to those of Mr Baldwin quoted above. The workers, and especially the miners, have long been regarded by the Tories as 'the enemy within'.

In early May of 1926, hopes were high that victory through working-class solidarity would come. Those hopes were shattered in days. Months later, the miners were literally starved into submission.

Yet throughout those long months, none of the Hamilton boys ever went barefooted to school. Not one of us ever went to the soup kitchens organised by the miners in every village to feed their children. In a fierce display of pride and independence, our parents somehow kept us fed and clothed. Neither of them ever smoked or drank. I remember my father telling me later that they had saved a bit of money – in a toy drum with a slit in it – and that it was all spent during the strike. It couldn't have been much.

As young ragamuffins, we tried to help in the struggle as best we could. As little boys – Tom was eleven, I was nine, and Jack was five – we couldn't do much. But we raided that big mountain of coal lying on the surface at the Dolly Pit. We weren't alone. It was *our* coal. *Our* fathers had dug it. So if it was theft, it was thieving in a good cause. We felt no guilt.

Despite our efforts, our coal-house was soon empty. Our 'free' coal had been stopped. But miners are a very resourceful, independent and hard-working lot of men. They knew there was a lot of coal in the so-called waste heaps lying around every pit. So the men dug their own holes in those heaps. They organised themselves into gangs, working round the clock on a shift system. At home, our mother made tea and sandwiches, and brother Tom and I took them to the men in the holes. In the blackness of the night that could be very dangerous. The holes were often twenty or thirty feet deep. The miners were lowered into them by means of a bucket on a rope. We could easily have fallen in, but we never did. God must have been on our side. From somewhere the men got the use of a horse and cart to carry the coal back to the houses.

As boys we too went digging. We took buckets and scratched among the waste heaps for any little bits we could find. Every little helped to keep the home fires burning.

That summer was a good one. We could play in the colliery field. The pit ponies had been brought to the surface when the strike started, and they were as pleased to be there as we were to play with them. We played in and among the empty coal wagons. I took to stealing packets of Woodbine cigarettes from our shop, smoking them with our 'gang' in an empty goods van standing idle less than 200 yards from our house. Some tell-tale reported us back to my mother, and I was given a belting – literally. My father's pit belt had a buckle at one end. I greatly feared the use of that evil weapon on my back or bottom. I became a non-smoker overnight – and have never smoked since! Who says corporal punishment is not a deterrent?

The General Strike ended on 12 May, less than ten days after the declarations of loyalty and solidarity. The miners fought on, alone, until the end of November. And it was just after that – it might have been early in 1927 – that I first became aware of the existence of another world.

I was ten years old, and compelled to stand outside my school gates, along with all the other children, and wave at some royal personage who was going to pass by in a car. To this day I do not know who it was. I just felt cold and miserable, and we seemed to stand for hours. Maybe we did. The car flashed past, and that was that. That day, a little revolutionary was born. When I went home for dinner, I told my father and mother what had happened. And so I got my first little talk on the politics and economics of the 'haves' and the 'have-nots'. From that day to this I have harboured a hatred – no, not a hatred, but a contempt and detestation – for all those who enjoy, without effort or obvious merit, the wealth created by men and women like my parents. And especially did I – and still do – associate that injustice, that intolerable economic and social evil, with the royal family.

In that winter of 1926–7, seed was sown which has grown and flourished ever since, nurtured by steadily more frequent little talks with my parents, but mostly with my father, about the injustices of the economic system in which we were the unwilling victims. It was a nightmare world, of which I was slowly being made aware by the slavery of my mother at her oven, kitchen sink, and her little shop, and by the articulate aggression of my father. He was quick to anger. There were frequent quarrels at home which made us frightened, especially when there were long periods of hostile silence between my mother and father. Times were harsh. My mother's health was never robust. She had frequent bilious bouts which may have been the warning symptoms of the cancer from which she died at an early age. My father had to leave school when he was nine, after his father died. At that tender age, he had to get out onto the roads with the family's horse and cart, selling paraffin oil to keep his widowed mother and younger brother, Tom. With no formal education, he wrote in a beautiful hand and used the spoken word like a skilled craftsman. Had he been politically ambitious, he could have been the Nye Bevan of Durham – a brilliant, self-educated orator, and one of the bonniest fighters for his class and family that was ever born. Unfortunately, like thousands of other working people of his time, he had limited horizons, and the inferiority complex which for so long has bedevilled the ordinary folk of our land and has resulted in the loss to the nation of so much talent and ability. I will be forever grateful to my parents, and especially to my father for having pushed me even beyond my ability.

It was he who impressed on me the vital importance of passing what was then called the 'eleven-plus' examination. That, he told me, would get me a place into a bigger and much better school, where I would learn a whole lot of new things, and would keep me out of the coal pits when I grew up. He often said that he would rather bury his sons than send them down those hell-holes, and he was as good as his word. He kept the four of us out. Only my younger brother Arthur worked in the coalmines, and he only opted to do so instead of going into the armed forces during the war. Later he bitterly wished he had gone into one of the forces.

THE ELEVEN-PLUS, OR THE LUCKY DIP

The exam was in three parts, and everybody could take it after attaining the age of eleven. The first part consisted of written tests in arithmetic and English, prepared and marked in our own school. That must have been the weeding-out process. The second stage was similar, except that the questions were set and marked by an outside body. I think it was the staff of the school to which we would go if we passed. The final hurdle was the most frightening. Parts 1 and 2 were sat at our own school, in familiar surroundings. Part 3 was held at the Big New School in Washington, about four miles away. My parents took me by bus. An expensive journey. I was terrified. What with the awakening of strange sex urges, plus exam jitters, I didn't know which end of my anatomy was the greatest embarrassment. Solids and liquids came perilously near to the spillage stage.

I survived the ordeal – of the exams. When I got home one day from school, my father asked innocently if I had been told the exam results yet. No, I hadn't. 'Well,' he said, 'a letter came this morning, and you've passed!' I'd never seen my parents look happier. It was the proudest moment of their lives. I was so happy and proud to see *them* so happy and proud. They knew what I didn't appreciate at the time, that this was the beginning of the possibility of my escape from the poverty and slavery of a lifetime in the coal pits. Only a small number could escape by this means. I was the only one of about thirty from Paddock Stile School who managed to jump the eleven-plus hurdle. I am certain that many more should have done so.

3

Cockroaches, Lops, Head Lice and Chamber Pots

In the middle of all this turmoil we moved again. This time to Shiney Row, about a mile away from Spring Gardens. Seven Barrack Row, Shiney Row, Philadelphia, Co. Durham, was the full postal address. Barrack Row got its name from the time when soldiers were in barracks there, ready to deal with striking miners in earlier years. Things hadn't changed much by the time we moved in.

From the outside the two-storey house looked good. It was built of nice-looking brick, in a street of thirty houses, and in a village of about 2,000 people. There was a sizeable co-operative shop, which sold everything from bacon to draperies. We had a wee bakery where we could buy rock buns for a ha'penny each, and cream horns for tuppence. We had a pub, a church, a Methodist chapel, a Roman Catholic church, and the Masonic Hall, and buses which ran from our door to Sunderland and Newcastle. To me it was slap bang in the middle of the world. The family was clearly climbing – and all because I had passed that eleven-plus.

The house had electric lights. That, apparently, was the main reason for the move. And it was still a colliery house, so the rent was paid by the mineowners – out of my father's sweat.

We had two rooms downstairs, and two up. The living room was about ten feet square, and the adjacent scullery a bit smaller. The four boys slept two in a bed in one bedroom, and our parents had the posh one at the front.

Cheap oilcloth – linoleum – was laid on all the floors and the stairs, and we had another square of it for our one table, which was about four feet by four feet – just big enough to seat the six of us when we had our Sunday dinner. The living room had the usual open coal fire, with a round oven on one side, and a long cupboard next to the oven in which we kept the pots and pans and plates and cups.

We already had one or two 'clippy' mats. These were made by friends and relations out of old clothes which were cut up into strips and woven into mats on a coarse jute backing. I think it was jute.

In the scullery was a cold tap and a sink, and off it was a small pantry. At the front we had a small garden. The back was more interesting. Across the unmade road we had a dry netty – a one-seater crap-hole. It was shared by three neighbours, and happened to be at an angle of about ten o'clock from our back door. When we left the house, we just had to hope that nobody had got there before us. In the middle of a cold winter that netty was a strong incentive to constipation. A trek across there, groping in the dark, and with the fear that a cat might be sitting on the seat or, worse, lying in wait among the ashes and excreta, ready to attack from the rear, was no joke. Diarrhoea was an embarrassing hazard in those days. It was then that the pail or 'po' (chamber pot to the posh) came into its own. We were well off for pos. We had three, one under each of the boys' beds, and a flowery one for our parents. Years later they became collectors' pieces, and in the eighties we bought two in Durham, and now have them for plant pots!

The pos were emptied each morning by our patient mother. Upstairs the 'milkmaid' went with her pail, and down she came with the family's pee, through the living room and out of the back door, where it was emptied into a drain.

That was the least of our problems. Very soon we found that the Hamiltons were not the only occupants of Number 7. We had armies of others, upstairs and down. In the bedrooms, in the living room, in the scullery. Upstairs, there were bugs, which we called 'lops'. Not fleas that jump, but brownish beasts, round and flattish, about an eighth of an inch in diameter, and slow-moving. They must have bred faster than rabbits. They were everywhere. In the beds, and on the walls. They moved as if they were in slow motion. Tom and I slept together. I was on the outside, Tom on the side next to the wall, so that I had the po just underneath my side of the bed. When I felt the lops crawling over me, I would get one between forefinger and thumb, lean out of bed, and hurl them into the po. They each died a violent death, either by crushing or drowning in pee. We crushed them on the walls with our thumbnails, so that the bedroom looked like a slaughterhouse, with bug blood splashed all over as if a crazy painter had been let loose. We tried to get rid of the loathsome things by burning sulphur candles after sealing up the window and doors; we tried various insect-killing powders; nothing worked. The carnage count was more than matched by the reproduction rate.

Downstairs, the wildlife was different. There we had another species – big black beetles. Polite folk called them cockroaches. We called them blacklocks. They were oval-shaped, about one inch long and half an inch across the back. They were jet black and glossy. They thrived on the heat from our big coal fire, which was never allowed to go out, so that the fireplace and its surrounds were the ideal breeding ground for these gruesome crawlies. They even got into the oven. My mother could never store any food safely unless it was in tightly enclosed containers. One day she decided to fight back. She called in the colliery workman, a Mr Bob Cummings, to pull out the cupboard adjacent to the fire. Bob was a personal friend. He told my mother to get a big pan of boiling water ready for when he pulled out that cupboard. He set about tearing off the wood panelling, and – dear God! Behind that wood was a solid sheet of what looked like black velvet, about eight feet by three feet. Bob poured boiling water over it, and those beetles never moved faster in their lives. It was a massacre. But only a partial Hamilton victory. Many of the black-velvet army survived, scurrying under the mat and into any crevice they could find – there to multiply and plague us like the bugs on our upper deck. The blessing was that none of our livestock bit. Maybe they were all vegetarians!

To complete the family zoo, we had head lice. Tom and I used to delouse one another on a weekly basis. Tom would hold his head over the upturned lid of a small cardboard cigarette box from our shop. I would hunt through his hair with a small-toothed comb – and out would fall the squirming little brutes, about the size of a pinhead. There weren't many. Perhaps four or five per capita. We flung them on the fire, or slaughtered them in the box. That way we kept them at bay. Other children had them too, so we didn't feel privileged! Everybody was scratching. As with the sulphur candles upstairs, various remedies were tried, from coal-tar soap for washing and strong carbolic soap which nearly skinned you, to rubbing in useless powders and other concoctions. But it was an uphill battle, and I can't remember when or how it ended.

We had few delights. Not much to be really happy about. One of them was to eat home-baked bread. Sliced bought bread was unknown to us. My mother baked every week – at least a dozen loaves at a time. Home-baked, crusty warm bread is a luxury few enjoy today.

We had a dough bowl the size of a brass-band drum. The Hamilton brothers used to help with the kneading. We watched the dough rise like magic. Then Mother cut it up for the separate loaf tins, and into the hot oven they went. At the end of the baking we had a golden harvest to feast on for the next week. On the evening of baking day, my mother's 'luxury' was to slump down in the family's only 'easy' chair – a wickerwork job, with arms – and sit like a queen while we knelt at her feet, cleaning the dry dough from her fingernails with a pair of scissors. That was domestic bliss for all of us.

Another developing pleasure for me was reading. We didn't have many books at home. We couldn't afford to buy them, and if we could, we had no place to keep them. Early in my childhood, though, my father had given me a copy of *Macbeth*. It was, he said, one of the best plays written by William Shakespeare, and he was our most famous playwright. But I found it hard going, the language strange, and the whole thing boring. Later, my pin-up teacher at Washington, Mrs Boyd, was to make my acquaintance with Shakespeare much more acceptable and enjoyable.

We had no public library at Shiney Row, but every week we did have a sort of lending library. A big van laden with books was unloaded at the local council school, put onto trestle-tables in the school hall, and we were free to borrow two or three each week. One of my favourite authors then was J. S. Fletcher. He wrote thrillers and bloodthirsty mysteries. One I vividly recall – *The Diamonds* – had a grisly murder in every chapter. I also liked all the G. A. Henty historical stories, such as *With Clive in India*, and *With Wolfe in Quebec*. Sometimes my father would give me a Penguin book (then 6d apiece) like *Three Men in a Boat*, *Silas Marner*, and, a great favourite, *Robinson Crusoe*.

We also used to have the *Daily Herald*. It was about the only Labour paper in existence in the 1920s and '30s. With the *Reynolds News* on Sundays, the *Herald* was the only regular daily reading we could afford.

4

Spreading My Wings

'Human history becomes more and more a race between education and catastrophe.'

H. G. Wells, *The Outline of History* (1951 edition)

I began my adventure at the Washington Secondary School in the autumn of 1928. My parents had taken me to a special shop in Washington to buy my uniform – a green and cream tie, a green cap with a yellow badge, a satchel, a grey jersey, and two pairs of grey stockings. They couldn't afford a blazer, nor a pair of new shoes or boots, nor any new short trousers. They would have to wait; my brothers were also in the queue. I never knew where the money came from, and I never asked.

The school was about four miles away, on the road to Newcastle. I travelled by school bus, with a free pass provided by the Labour County Council. All the 300 boys and girls there had passed that eleven-plus exam. They had been selected as the 'cream' of the area, and came from all the surrounding mining villages of Shiney Row, Penshaw, Fatfield, Usworth and Castletown, Washington itself, and Boldon near Sunderland. By modern standards, it was not a big school. But to me it was like a big new city, and frightening. The masters and mistresses terrified me. They all wore flowing black gowns, and looked like giant bats hovering over their victims.

We were allocated classrooms, each pupil with his or her own separate lidded desk, and a whole library of textbooks – on English, mathematics, physics, chemistry, history, geography, French – as well as a supply of pens, pencils and exercise books, plus a jotter. I felt as if I had my own Aladdin's cave. I was delirious with joy. I needed no encouragement to get a little lock and key to secure my new-found treasure from any possible thief.

There were thirty in our class – fifteen boys and fifteen girls. The girls all seemed bright-eyed and pretty in their shiny black shoes, long black stockings, green tunics and primrose blouses, with the boys in short grey trousers, grey stockings and jerseys and green and yellow ties. The boys sat on one side of the classroom, the girls on the other. Thus was launched probably the most formative part of my whole life.

The grammar school, as it was commonly called in other parts of the country, was a unique educational institution. In terms of content and opportunity, no one in my social class thought he had a right to expect anything better. Or so we thought at the time. But it was based too much on luck. It was socially divisive. It separated one child from another in too arbitrary a fashion. The system built up a sense of élitism and a strange feeling of superiority and snobbishness over those who had fallen by the wayside in that hit-and-miss process of the eleven-plus, which was so final in its assessment of success and failure.

The new school was for me a great culture shock. To be flung into a strange world of physics and chemistry, algebra, geometry and trigonometry, French, Latin and English literature, all the time mixing with adults wearing black academic gowns and strange chattering boys and girls, was bewildering and exciting. To be friendless and in a building that looked like a factory at such an impressionable age made me feel very vulnerable, and frightened. The headmaster and all his staff looked old and ashen, forbidding in their witches' garb and shiny shoes. And there was poor me, in my little armour-plated boots, straight from the bug-infested home of a humble miner. *He* knew the value of what I was embarking on. He could see the opportunities that were now opened before his second son. I could not. I was to let him down, I fear.

Those boots of mine deserve a special mention. All working-class boys wore boots. Shoes were for toffs. The soles and heels of my boots were shod with steel 'protectors' – heel plates like horseshoes, toe plates, and steel 'studs' hammered into every square centimetre of the soles. They were ideal for sliding on the winter ice, perfect for kicking tins and balls and stones in the streets, or for playing football at street corners. Pa used to buy cards of these protectors, at 2d each. It was surprising how quickly the steel wore away. Father tried his hand at cobbling. He bought odd bits of leather cheaply. He was a bit cack-handed, but with a sharp knife, a hammer and a last, he kept our boots in fairly good nick. But what a drag they were.

More immediate problems were raising themselves – not least my short trousers. Strange things began to happen whenever I gazed at those lovely peaches-and-cream girls. I desperately hoped my thin trousers would be up to the job. Those fifteen delicious things bubbled with vitality, and possibly (I never asked them) the fourteen young stallions were wrestling with the same problems that I had – physical, mental and emotional. Thirty pulsating young minds and bodies held great promise for the future!

But the most immediate concern was our first 'lunch'. On that first day the only thing in my new satchel was a newspaper-wrapped packet of fish-paste sandwiches – or it could have been jam or sugar. Mother used to try to vary the diet. We had been told by the school authorities to bring them, being miles from home. A hot drink would be supplied for one penny per day. At noon we all sat down in a wooden shed at long trestle-tables. The shed was actually the girls' domestic science room doubling as a dining room. Well, not so much a dining room – more a large pig trough.

Our hot drink was thick black cocoa, without milk or sugar, poured like steaming mud out of large enamel jugs.

The 'hot-dinner children' were different. They were the 'toffs'. For 8d a day they had a hot dinner, eaten with knives and forks, at a separate table from the cocoa proletariat. Thus were the plebs divided from the bourgeoisie; but at the tender age of eleven such bolshie thoughts were far from my mind. Other things enthralled, like those awe-inspiring teachers, those books, and those girls.

Our teachers were an impressive collection of specialists. Our headmaster was Mr Schofield, then a man in his fifties, already thin on top and greying. With a short, clipped moustache, and always dressed immaculately, complete with spats, he was a severe-looking man who had great dignity and authority. Nobody was ever in any doubt about who was boss. He believed in corporal punishment. And he practised what he preached. He got a lot of his practice with a long cane on my hands and backside. Invariably I deserved what I got.

Our senior mistress was Mrs Boyd, a middle-aged Scot from Glasgow who taught us English. We thought she might have lost her husband in the First World War, but that was just a guess. She was a lovely lady, jolly and warm, who obviously loved the children in her care. Physically she was generously endowed. She was like a stately galleon sailing round, spreading her charm as she let us into the treasures of the English language and its literature. Forty years later, as a Member of Parliament, I received a touching letter from Mrs Boyd's family in Glasgow informing me that she had recently died, in her eighties. They wanted me to know that she had followed my career throughout my years in Parliament. I found that very moving. Had I known, I would have been delighted to visit her, for she was truly a great teacher. She had an electrifying personality, and has to this day an influence both on me and my second wife, Margaret, who also went to the Washington school.

There could hardly have been a greater contrast than between Mrs Boyd and Miss Loudon, our French teacher. She taught us irregular verbs, or rather drove them into us, like a riveter punching rivets in a ship's plates. She had severely cut, straight, steel-coloured hair. Sturdily built, with nothing bursting out anywhere, she had eyes like pools of molten lead. I can never remember that face creasing in the faintest smile; nor was she ever seen chatting generally with any of the children. She was a great teacher. But for me it was an acquired taste – which I never acquired. She was a grey, forbidding battleship. I liked the stately galleon a lot better.

Among the men teachers, Dixie Crawford and Bill Baker were for me the most memorable. Dixie was the Laughing Cavalier of our staff. With a rolling gait like a retired sea captain, he was often decked out in tweedy plus-fours – baggy trousers tied at the knees – woolly stockings and tough brown shoes. He taught us history with an infectious enthusiasm. And on Saturday mornings he delighted the school footballers and cricketers by regular turning up to our matches, sometimes refereeing or umpiring, sometimes just cheering. He was a great guy and an exciting teacher.

It was strange how the two most impressive lady teachers, Mrs Boyd and Miss Loudon, had characters and characteristics as widely different as my two favourite men, Mr Crawford and Mr Baker. Mr Bill Baker was the slight, bespectacled Quaker who taught us physics. He presided over a laboratory with six large flat tables, each with Bunsen burner gas points in the middle. Ranged round the lab were racks of test tubes, weighing scales, magnets, electroscopes and other equipment.

For me it was a marvellous toyshop. There we played purposefully with iron filings and magnets both straight and horseshoe-shaped. Those filings formed fascinating patterns around the magnets. From those beginnings we were led on to coils of copper wire and the mysteries of electricity. Then to the fascination of heat: boiling and freezing liquids, heating metals and measuring their expansion and contraction. It was heaven to explore all these new worlds opening up before me. And all the while Mr Baker was displaying his pleasure at our delight.

It was my greatest good luck that he also happened to be the master in charge of Penshaw House. We were divided into four houses: Washington, Usworth, Boldon and Penshaw. Ours, Penshaw, was mostly made up of boys and girls from the mining villages of Shiney Row, Fatfield and Penshaw. I liked the fact that our house colour was red. I was soon to become the Captain of the House, and captain of both the football and cricket teams. I had an addiction to sport. Perhaps that was the reason I never became an academic high-flyer. That's my excuse, anyway. At primary school, I excelled. At secondary level, I was sometimes below average, seldom much above, and rarely out of trouble. I disliked homework. Facilities for doing it were non-existent – no privacy, no peace or quiet. And anyway, I liked to get out to play, or to get down to the local YMCA where there were billiard and snooker tables, chess, draughts and other table games – as well as a good reading room and a small library.

I also liked to help Mr Albert Taylor, the local farmer. With his big horse and cart, he used to empty our dry netties every week. Each netty had an opening on to our back street, like a small sliding shutter. From there I shovelled all the weekly deposits of ashes and excreta and hurled it onto the open cart. The housewives wisely closed their back doors if there was a strong wind blowing – or even if there wasn't. Being hygienic, there was a bucket containing a pink disinfectant concoction slung under the cart, and after the shovelling was finished I sprinkled that powder like confetti round each shutter. We then took the cartload up to Albert's field. Ploughed in, it produced fine crops of potatoes and turnips. It was a great community service, and I was happy to be part of it. I got no pay, except for a few free turnips and a can or two of fresh warm milk straight from Albert's cows. In those days the milk was not tested for disease of any kind.

On dark evenings, my mates and I used to raid those netties and collect the newspapers which were used for wiping. We took the papers to the local fish and chip shop where we got a free packet of fish and chips for them. We all believed in helping each other. It was a good bargain for everybody, except perhaps for those whose fish and chips were wrapped up in the papers.

In the summer months the routine was different. Cricket and tennis took over. Philadelphia Cricket Club had a lovely ground only 300 yards from the Dolly Pit. The field was the property of the coal company and the groundsman was Tommy Thomson, a full-time worker with the company. He had been a soldier in the First World War and had caught malaria at Gallipoli. He chewed twist tobacco and was the most skilled spitter I have ever known. He could squirt his tobacco-laden saliva through the eye of a needle at five paces. In the summer holidays I used to love to help him tend the cricket field. At the beginning of a new season a few of us would whitewash all the railings around the ground. The fence was six feet high, and there must have been a quarter of a mile of it. It was donkey-work, and we did it happily, for love. We helped with the rolling of 'the square', that sacred bit of the turf where the actual match pitches were prepared by Tommy. We oiled the bats with linseed oil, kept the pavilion nice and tidy, and put up the practice nets. As a schoolboy, my Cricket Club subscription was 2/6 for the season, or five shillings for Tom and me. It was a good investment. It got us both out of the house for every summer evening except Sundays. The Club provided all the gear – bats, balls, pads, gloves and stumps. Everything except the spiked boots and the white flannels and shirts.

That cricket ground was my Mecca every summer. Every minute there was pure heaven. Nothing could keep me away, neither homework nor choir practice – nothing. I would only leave the ground when it was too dark to see a cricket ball any more.

Just over the ground's fence stood a granary, where the pit ponies' fodder was stored. There were also stables where the wild untrained ponies were brought to be 'broken in'. On those warm sultry summer days we used to stand on the seats to watch the ponies being 'broken'. Mr Pow was the horseman who did this job. I suppose it was essential, if it was necessary to send the animals down the pits. But it looked very cruel to me. First the pony would be led out to what looked like an open-air circus ring. The pony had never been used to any kind of tethering. It was wild, and now very frightened. The first stage of the breaking in was to get the animal to run round the ring at the end of a rope. The next stage was to get some kind of collar around the beast's neck, then to get it into the shafts of a pit tub. That always produced the most terrific struggle. The pony would kick and snort furiously. How Mr Pow escaped serious injury I never knew. But he was a master of his craft, and he literally had the whip hand. After harnessing, and a cooling-off period, the pony was 'persuaded' to trot round the ring with its load behind it. The pit tub was at that point empty. When the animal appeared settled and no longer lashing out, a chunk of wood like a pit prop was stuck in the tub's spokes to simulate a loaded tub, which meant that the pony had to pull a lot harder. The whole ordeal could take at least half an hour for each animal, by which time it was lathered in sweat and apparently subdued. I was never certain how long it was before the poor things went down below. They were always very small, and I'm told they were well looked after by the miners down there. But they went down for years on end, denied God's daylight and fresh air in the most brutal way.

Much later, when my younger brother Arthur chose to go into the mines rather than the Army, he was put in charge of one of those ponies. It kicked, tried to run away and to bite. Arthur used to cry about 'his pony'. We never knew whether he was crying out of fury against the pony, or sympathy with it. But one day he came home and told us a gruesome story. It was about a pony which that day had been caught in some cutting machinery and, before his eyes, had been cut to ribbons. It had all been over in a few seconds. And the work had gone on as if nothing much had happened.

Yet the miners were always kind to their ponies. They had their stabling below and their constant fodder was dry hay. One day one of Arthur's mates thought he would give his pony a treat. He fed it with a couple of turnips. The little thing wasn't used to such delicacies. The result was a volley of equine farting which nearly gassed the men and blew up the pit. Turnips were off the menu, and the pit was saved.

ONWARD CHRISTIAN SOLDIERS

I can't remember when or how I became a member of St Oswald's church choir; nor how my mother joined the Mothers' Union; nor how my pa became a church warden.

For twenty years at least, Father was a funny mixture of political radical and respectable regular churchgoer. He must have liked dressing up every Sunday in his bowler hat and navy blue Sunday suit. It made a change from the stinking pit clothes and heavy boots. Mother stayed at home to cook the Sunday dinner. That was the big family meal of the week and consisted of brisket, boiled potatoes, leeks or carrots, followed by rice pudding. Always rice pudding, and nearly always cheap brisket. In the summer, Auntie Nellie across the road made and sold ginger beer, at 2d a bottle, and we would buy a couple of bottles as a Sunday treat. It was gassy stuff, so by the time the six of us had had our fill, the atmosphere was similar to that in the pit after the pony had eaten its turnips!

St Oswald's Church at Shiney Row was small and with no architectural merit. Its parsons were of similar worth. St Oswald's was a dumping ground for clapped-out clerics – one after the other. How an intelligent man like my father put up with it for so long I never could understand. And we were made to go along with it. Thrice every Sunday we were called on to endure the agony: Sunday-morning service, afternoon Sunday school, then evensong. With regular choir practice every Tuesday evening. But we were bribed. The bribe was one ha'penny for each service, and another for choir practice. It came to about a shilling and sixpence each three months. I missed out on many of the choir practices, especially in the summer, when I made my own choice of Phili cricket ground. Not for the last time, that led me into conflict with the Church Establishment, and with my parents.

Yet, when I became a teenager and my voice broke, I conformed by joining the Young Men's Bible Class. It was run by a miner, who tried valiantly to put the Bible stories into a modern context.

As soon as possible I threw off the shackles of regular churchgoing and toyed with the idea of joining the Quakers. Their pacifism had an emotional attraction, as did their total lack of any connection with what I now know as the 'Establishment'. Nothing came of that attraction. I still profess to a vaguely Christian faith based on socialist principles. Durham was a solidly mining county with a profound belief in socialism and the brotherhood of man, but those beliefs were always buttressed by Methodism rather than Marxism, on respectable radicalism rather than revolutionary communism.

SCHOOL PROGRESS

Right from the start, I always seemed to be struggling. It was a great relief when at sixteen I finally matriculated and, under pressure from my parents, was persuaded to stay on into the Sixth Form. There had, meanwhile, been a few distractions. One was called Peggy McKay. She was the first young lady I ever dared go out with, and we were both still at school. We went to the local cinemas, secretly, on several occasions. For me it was exciting calf-love. It didn't last long. Peggy got fed up with me. She left school at sixteen and branched out on a nursing career, leaving home at that tender age to go to St Helens in Lancashire to be a slave – *on £26 a year*. Peggy was a bright young girl. If she had been pushed or guided she would have made a very successful university undergraduate.

She was one of a multitude of working-class children whose talents were never stretched. Still, in the late 1980s, the nation is suffering from that neglect.

From the time Peggy left school she went out of my life, and that seemed to be that. Not quite. It's a delightful story. But it can wait.

SIXTH FORM

Suddenly I discovered some freedom of choice at school which had never been there before. I was free to choose the subjects in which I would like to specialise for the purpose of Advance level exams (now called A levels). I opted for history and English at the higher level, and maths and French at the less demanding Ordinary level.

For the next two years our Sixth Form totalled about twelve boys and girls, which meant much smaller classes and therefore much more personal tuition. We also had fewer formal lessons, which left us with more free time in which to engage in personal study and reading, demanding a greater degree of self-discipline and initiative. I didn't appreciate it at the time, but that was to be an initiation into the kind of academic regime which I was to enjoy – or abuse – at university.

To cut the story short, I managed to get some slightly above average examination results, sufficient to get me accepted as an undergraduate at Sheffield University. In great excitement and trepidation, I left Shiney Row in October of 1936.

5

University, Conscientious Objection and War

I enjoyed that summer of 1936 as I'd never enjoyed any summer before. I felt on top of the world. My parents and brothers were as proud as peacocks. I was the first member of all the families of Hamiltons and Chickens ever to have made the grade to university.

I played my cricket at Phili with all the fierce enthusiasm of the young man on the way up. So I thought.

I first had to get money. Grants, loans, awards, anything from anybody. We couldn't afford to be fussy. I got an Intending Teacher Award from the Government. The condition of the award was that after qualification I would teach for at least five years in a local council school. Then there was a Student Grant Scheme, financed jointly by the Durham Miners' Union and the local Coal Owners' Association to help miners' children through university.

My father fixed up an interview for me with Will Lawther, then a top official with the Miners' Union. The interview was at the HQ of the Miners' at their Redhill offices in the city of Durham. Will Lawther was a blunt Geordie, with a mind as sharp as a razor. He loathed the mineowners and the money-grabbing system which they stood for. He told me there was an application form to fill in before I could get any grant. 'Now it is our money you are after,' he said. 'Your father has made it. So you want to get as much as you can. So, Will, when you fill in that form, tell as many bloddy lees [lies] as you can get away with.' The rich Geordie accent is lost in the written word.

I left that interview with a song in my heart. I filled in the form. I didn't tell fibs. And I got some cash. I also got some help from the local council, thanks to the grafting of my father. He walked miles, 'tapping' this councillor and that local official. He never seemed to tire. I remember at that time he was also organising to try and get a district nurse into our area. With no such thing as a National Health Service, and few local health services of any kind, a lot was missing, especially in the maternity field. Giving birth to a baby was just a little less primitive than that birth in a manger nearly 2,000 years before.

My father and the friendly local Methodist minister, a Mr John Coulson, got together. The Reverend Coulson was an angel of a man, brimful of energy, and an incurable optimist. A meeting was called in the local YMCA. The Dolly miners sent their officials, and they agreed that the miners would each pay 1d a week for the district nurse. They also agreed to hold a Flag Day, to be called the Queen Alexandra Rose Day. All these efforts took time and energy. I remember Mr Coulson calling unexpectedly at our house to talk about it all. He caught my father bathing in front of the coal fire, on his knees, washing his hair and torso. The whole household was humming. Mr Coulson wasn't the slightest bit embarrassed. He put us all at ease by getting down on his knees and washing my father's back. When my mother seemed to protest, our genial minister said: 'The Bible story tells us how certain ladies washed the feet of Jesus. So there's nothing wrong if I wash Joe Hamilton's back.' He was a saintly man. The right man in the right place at the right time. We got our district nurse. And we bought her a bike and a little black bag. From that day, every baby born in Shiney Row was safely delivered by our new goddess.

I had never been further from my own village than Sunderland. We were painfully parochial, unable or unwilling to move very far from hearth or home. To go to Roker Park to watch the First Division football team of Sunderland was a rare luxury. We thought nothing of walking the five miles each way, then standing on the terraces for the game. Sometimes we went to the local cinema to watch a silent film.

To get on a long-distance coach to the mighty city of Sheffield was a nerve-racking ordeal. I don't know what Columbus felt in 1492, but in 1936 Willie Hamilton was terrified.

I didn't have much luggage. My wardrobe was that of a man of the road. Rarely two of anything. But my parents had bought me a pair of new football boots.

I had been advised that I would be accommodated in the brand-new students' hall of residence at Crewe Hall, Clarkehouse Road, Sheffield 10. I was to report to the Hall Warden, a Dr Arthur Chapman, at his magnificent house within the Hall grounds.

Doc Chapman was a chemistry man, in his late forties. He had a pleasant, rubicund face, on which was perched a pair of rimless spectacles. He eyed me with a civilised, welcoming smile. I had never been inside such a mansion. The study was palatial – a million miles from my bug-ridden hovel in Durham.

'First,' said the Doctor, 'I would like your full name and home address.' As he explained, he was now to be '*in loco parentis*'. I guessed that meant he was to be my father and mother. But first the address. I spelt it out: 7 Barrack Row, Shiney Row, Philadelphia, County Durham. As if in disbelief, the gentle man leaned forward and gazed glassily over his spectacles. It seemed as if I might be something from outer space. And in a sense I was. Probably neither before or since has anybody from Shiney Row set foot in Sheffield University.

My address had surely made me a marked man, a rare species. My fears were groundless. Dr Chapman proved to be a dear friend and adviser, not only to me but to the other eighty or so students fortunate enough to find themselves in that sparkling new Hall.

Not all were undergraduates. Some already had their degrees; some were in their second or third years. They were representative of all the faculties: Arts, Sciences, Engineering, Medicine. And quite a few were from foreign lands like Egypt and Burma. All were male.

Just over the boundary wall, within smelling distance, there was a similar hall of residence for women students. And therein lay the future seeds of trouble. Not in the halls, but in the wall. Walls are made to climb over. However high, no wall can contain randy students if there is forbidden fruit on the other side. More especially is this true if there is little or no parental control.

Blinkered authority thought to thwart the sexual appetites on both sides of that wall. No Crewe Hall student could invite any girl into his monastic den. At weekends, though, the rule was relaxed. We had a small hospitality room where we could entertain, on tea and buns, but under supervision, and only in daylight hours. All parties had to be over by 6 p.m. Hall gates were locked at 10 p.m. Virginity was assured by lock, bolt, and a middle-aged chemist.

It was like trying to put out a forest fire by peeing on it. Each of us had his own separate bedroom-study. Each was at the height of his sexual prowess. And no doubt the young ladies over that wall had similar urges. The rest needs no imagination. Autobiographies never tell all, or even half the truth. And this one is no exception. Private lives are not for public eyes. So no stories will be told by me of what went on between those two halls of residence. There were exciting moments!

Nineteen thirty-six was a momentous year in our history. Our King Edward abdicated to marry a divorced American lady, a Mrs Simpson. The upset to the constitution caused a great furore which shook the British Establishment. It bitterly divided the royal family itself, and top politicians, including Baldwin, then Prime Minister, and Churchill, as well as the Church of England, wallowed round in dangerous and uncharted waters. But as I recall, there was scarcely a flicker of interest in the affair among students. In the event their judgement was probably sound. After the original turmoil the abdicating king and his gold-digging bride took themselves off on a long life of idleness and sloth.

Of vastly greater moment was the Spanish Civil War and the threatening clouds of war as Hitler and Mussolini flexed their muscles in military adventures in Europe and Africa. The Spanish Civil War was to be the curtain-raiser for the 1939–45 conflict, and one of my first forays into politics was to join the Labour Club at university and go on protest marches against the Franco dictatorship. At home my father had already made me an individual member of the Labour Party. So my political course was set. It has remained consistent ever since. More or less.

At the university I tried unsuccessfully to get on to an honours degree course, first in modern history, then in economics. Eventually I had to settle for a general degree in three subjects: modern history, economics and geography. Had I worked hard enough I think I could have managed a good honours degree. I owed it to my whole family to work hard, and to those who helped me financially to get my opportunity. But circumstances worked against me.

At the end of my third year, the second world war in my generation broke out. I had graduated in July, and on 3 September, while I was at home on vacation, war was declared on Germany. And almost overnight, under the Defence of the Realm Act, Parliament rushed through legislation which literally gave the Government control over everybody's lives and property. It was effectively dictatorship by Parliamentary edict.

As university students, we were permitted to complete our studies. But many of my friends at Sheffield volunteered immediately for military service, and several of them opted to enter training for what was then known as the Fleet Air Arm. I suppose it sounded romantic and daredevil. But in what seemed like weeks some of them were killed, perhaps while in training.

After discussing my own situation with my parents, my father persuaded me to register as a conscientious objector, on both religious and political grounds. I was allowed under law to do that, and procedures were laid down. In due course I received a form on which I had to give a reasoned case for my objection. I was called to a Conscientious Objectors Tribunal in Leeds, and was subject to a cross-examination by a tribunal of a few middle-aged men. It was not a pleasant experience.

The cross-examination was brief and acrimonious. I made the tactical error of being impertinent to my elders and betters. When Judge Stewart asked me if I had listened to the broadcast made the previous evening by Dr Hugh Dalton MP, I replied I had not. 'Do you know,' replied the Judge, 'that Dr Dalton is a leading Labour member of the Coalition Government, and that he said in his broadcast that we were fighting for our freedom and democracy? Do you believe that, Mr Hamilton?'

'Well,' I replied, 'we all know that in war the first casualty is truth.' A silly answer in the circumstances. Typically Willie Hamilton, the bull in the china shop. My answer was like a red rag to a bull.

Judge Stewart: 'You aren't here to tell us what we all know. How dare you!'

'All right,' I replied, 'it is a well-known saying that in war the first casualty is truth, and I don't know whether Dr Dalton was telling the truth or not.'

Judge: 'Are you a member of any political party?'

Self: 'I fail to see the relevance of that question.'

Judge: 'You are not here to tell us what is relevant and what is not. Now answer the question.'

Self: 'All right. I am a member of the Labour Party.'

The usual questions were asked:

'What would you do if you saw a German raping your wife or daughter?'

'Are you against all forms of killing?'

'How often do you go to church?'

As COs, we got standard replies to these questions from the Quakers and other interested organisations. But I did not like such help, though it was given with the best of intentions. I preferred to put my foot in it in my own way – and I did that, no mistake.

It was easy for the Judge to make his decision.

'We find this applicant defiant, repellent and rude, and he shows little sign of a genuine conscientious objection. His case is unanimously rejected.'

And that was that.

But it wasn't. I had the right to appeal. The Reverend Coulson supported my appeal by a letter which said that he thought I was sincere enough to refuse to put on any military uniform. The appeal was heard at Thames House, a few hundred yards along the Thames Embankment from the Houses of Parliament. It was my first trip to the big city, and I was terrified. I was overwhelmed by the noise, the smell, the traffic and the bustle. It was like a monstrous anthill, with millions of people all in a hurry. And that was fifty years ago. It is infinitely worse now. After only a few minutes I was given conditional exemption from military service. The condition was that I should do some kind of non-military service. I opted for forestry work, and within weeks of leaving university in late July 1940, with a poor degree and an Education Diploma, I was ordered to report to Minehead in Somerset for my forestry assignment. Very apprehensive, I travelled alone on the long train journey from Newcastle, all through the night. When I arrived, I discovered that about thirty other lads from the North East had also done the trip. Like me, they were all conscientious objectors and going to do forestry work. They were a mixed bunch, as I discovered – librarians, teachers, local council workers – all under twenty-five, and most of them with some religious convictions. One of them was Len Jones, from the Newcastle area. He was a librarian with a keen interest in art. A rough diamond, with a smile as wide as a farm gate. I was to meet him again much later in the war, when both of us were in Army uniform in what was then Palestine.

At Minehead we were herded onto a lorry and driven to a pretty village called Brendon in Devon, by the side of a swift-flowing river which sang its way to the coast at Lynmouth. At Brendon we were packed into a disused youth hostel. It was rough, and a far cry from the luxury I had enjoyed at Crewe Hall. But we were all from the North-East, and that was a great comfort in what we all knew would be a hostile world.

Straight from that lorry journey we were taken to a forest in the beautiful Doone Valley, of *Lorna Doone* fame. A delightful setting. We were each given a heavy axe, and told to get cracking and fell the trees. Just like that. We had all been pen-pushers. None of us had lifted anything heavier than a library book. The axes looked like very dangerous instruments. There we were, in a big forest by the side of a river, on a slope, and directed by our forester boss to 'get cracking'. So we did. We had no supervision, no training, no safety equipment of any kind. It was chaos. The trees, mostly larch, began to fall in all directions. Many fell over and into the river. I think the biggest trees were little more than six or seven inches in diameter.

In our hostel that first night the place looked like a hospital casualty ward, and smelt like the local gasworks. Many of us had blisters the size of golf balls. Every muscle seemed to ache. And enough gas was exploded to light a small town. An atmosphere was built up of friendship in adversity, and farts. The reek drove Len Jones and me across a footbridge over the river to the local pub, where we soaked ourselves with heavenly Devon cider at 3d a glass. The locals must have thought they were being invaded by foreigners. Only our pockets kept us from getting drunk. So began our stint as foresters. With experience, we soon learned the tricks of the trade, and we began to enjoy the work.

But there were problems. Living in cramped conditions can create all kinds of nasty habits. One or two bad apples with quirky preferences can be upsetting. So three of us decided to look for other digs. We found a farmhouse on the edge of Exmoor, and the farmer was glad to put us up for £1 a week each, for bed, breakfast and an evening meal. The place was up a steep valley from Brendon. We were in clover. The farmer's daughter, Ivy, was lovely. In her mid-twenties, with raven-black hair, petite and sparkling, like the stream outside, she loved our company and our accents. She cooked our hot evening meal, which was usually rabbit pie and vegetables. It hardly ever changed. Rabbits breed fast, and Exmoor was lush with them. Ivy's brother Ted was a skilled ferreter. We went rabbiting on the moors with Ted one Sunday. He had with him his ferrets in a bag, and his nets. The lad could tell just which burrows were occupied. He set his nets over each outlet, and let his ferret down among the rabbits. With our ears to the ground, we could hear within seconds the scuffles between the ferret and rabbits. Then out would fly the furry furies, straight into the entangling nets. Swift as an eagle, Ted pounced, and with a deft twist of the wrist bunny was ready for the pot. Two hours of skilled ferreting yielded a large bag of rabbits. With that kind of skill in the countryside, the war rationing of meat presented no problems. Not only were there rabbits in abundance, but deer, too. The smartly clad hunters who rode straight through us in the forest, contemptuously flicking their whips as they chased their quarry – deer or fox – didn't know there was a war on. For them rationing was a joke.

High up on Exmoor, we watched from across the Bristol Channel the bombing of South Wales by the Germans. From that safe distance it was like a spectacular fireworks display. The ugly truth was that innocent folk were being killed or maimed, their homes destroyed, and their villages and towns smashed to the ground. In that context, those huntsmen made me sick with anger.

We had little to do at weekends or in the evenings except chat and read. So my father thought it would be a good idea if I did some political studies under the guidance of the National Council of Labour Colleges – the NCLC. The NCLC was a radical organisation which believed in independent working-class education. It was a voluntary body, financed by contributions from the trade unions, co-operative societies and individuals. The NCLC had no time for the orthodox State system of education. It was biased in favour of the status quo; existing social and economic systems were accepted without question.

Originally, the NCLC was Marxist-orientated. It believed that within our capitalist society all labour was exploited for profit by the ruling class. This had to be challenged and overthrown not by violence, but by education and persuasion. The NCLC sought to put a human face on the Marxist philosophy.

With its headquarters in Tillicoultry in Scotland, the NCLC organised correspondence courses in Economics, World Geography, Basic English, Public Speaking, Working-class History, Labour Party History, Trade Unions, the Co-operative Movement, and many others. Weekend and summer schools were arranged in which prominent left-wing politicians annd scholars lectured and debated.

My father persuaded me to have a go at some correspondence courses. He sent me books and pamphlets, and I got to work. My written work was sent to Tillicoultry, marked and returned. I won an NCLC essay competition by writing on 'The Importance of Working-class Education'. My prize was a week at an NCLC summer school, which was held at University College in Bangor in North Wales.

It was the summer of 1941. And it was at that summer school that I first met some miners from Fife. I was living in the same digs in Bangor as Adam Hunter, one of the miners, who later became the Member of Parliament for Dunfermline. Another was John Wood, who went on to leave the Labour Party and become the Communist General Secretary of the Scottish Miners' Union. His was the first bed I slept in in Fife. Yet another was Willie Mill, with his gentle wife Mary. Willie was to become the West Fife Labour Party's Treasurer for many years, and a prominent member of the Fife County Council.

For the whole of that glorious week we debated, cracked jokes, danced, played tennis with folk from all over the land – all working for the socialist Utopia that in our bones we felt to be within our grasp. Willie and Adam were marvellous raconteurs; and friendships were made which still survive fifty years on. It was a truly memorable week for me.

Back at my forestry work, it wasn't long before I was in trouble. Our digs were crude, although good. But we had no drying facilities for our clothing. And it was very wet in North Devon. We often got soaked in the forest. When we got back to our farmhouse we had few other clothes to change into, so we were going to our work very wet and uncomfortable. I led the way to our 'boss', and asked if we could have some waterproof gear. We got short shrift. 'You're lucky not to be in the bloody Army,' he said; he in a safe, reserved occupation. So I led my first walk-out. When the rains came, the lads sought shelter and built a big fire. Our boss was as mad as a hatter. 'This will get you all into uniform!' he bellowed. 'And you, Hamilton, had better collect your cards at my office, tonight.' I was shocked, and just a bit frightened. I would now be in one hell of a pickle. I had no money. I would have no job. I would have no roof over my head. And I was far from home. I had visions of ending up in Dartmoor Prison.

I duly got my cards, and early next morning I walked the few miles to the nearest Labour Exchange in the Linton–Lynmouth area. Luckily God was on my side. The manager of that office was a sympathetic pacifist. He listened to my tale, gave me a rail ticket to Newcastle, and advised me to go to the nearest Labour Exchange there, and explain what had happened.

The journey back to Newcastle was a terrible ordeal. The train was delayed for hours because of bombing by the Germans. It was completely blacked out, as were all the railway stations. It was packed with military personnel: soldiers, sailors and airmen, and women in uniform too. There was nothing to eat or drink, and during the night it was freezing cold. The journey took over twenty-four hours. Always I was afraid that somebody would ask me how I was still not in uniform. I stood out like a sore thumb. I thought of possible answers, like I was in a reserved occupation, or I was doing secret work, or that I was a secret service agent. Luckily, nobody asked the question.

When I got home, hungry, ragged and filthy, my mother nearly had a fit. She was petrified. I could be shot. I could be put in prison for life, and she could be punished for harbouring me. 'Get out,' she said. 'Tell the authorities whatever you have done.'

I did. And I was sent to another forestry job, this time in the Yorkshire Dales, in a feudal village called East Witton.

I had to find digs, and a Mrs Dinsdale took me in. She was a kind old lady, so poor that she needed any little money I could offer. Within a few days I was again felling trees, on piecework, alongside a few Danish seamen who had been stranded in a British port when war had broken out. It must have been a lot safer felling trees than being on the high seas.

At weekends I got home by bus. I used to take eggs bought from the surrounding farms with me, packed in sawdust. My father would take a few to Mr and Mrs Bainbridge, an old Labour Party couple who were family friends. Like most folk, they were having to feed themselves on the meagre rations we then got. The old lady had thought she would try stewing some of her lovely lawn cuttings. 'They looked so fresh and tender,' she said. But they didn't go down too well. She was glad of the eggs.

I was soon in trouble yet again. In mid-1941 the Soviet Union joined the war. Immediately, my father advised me that the character of the conflict had now changed, and I should, therefore, apply for military service. I did so, and put in for flying duties with the Royal Air Force. I was duly called to Edinburgh for physical and mental tests. That meant taking a day off my forestry work in East Witton. I went without telling my boss, so when I arrived back I got the sack – again – for indiscipline. So I had to get another job. I was sent up to a God-forsaken hole somewhere south of Jedburgh, this time planting trees.

Meanwhile, I was informed that I had passed the intelligence tests but failed the medical on the grounds that I was colour-blind, and therefore disqualified from flying. But I could opt for training as a radio mechanic, and I accepted that.

While I waited for my call-up papers, still near Jedburgh, I had to plant some trees. First I had to find somewhere to stay. In a rural desert, that was not easy. Eventually my unsympathetic boss suggested I kip down in an old shepherd's shelter. It hadn't been used for years. I doubt if anybody had ever slept or lived in it. There was no lighting, no heating, no water and nothing but an earthen floor to sleep on. There was an open fireplace.

I had no choice but to make the best of it. I slept on that bare floor on a sack full of straw given to me by the farmer. I bought candles and food, and ordered a bag of coal from a local merchant. I had to fetch my water from a tap in a cemetery just over the road, opposite my hut. It was a nightmare.

During the day I must have planted thousands of young fir trees. Thankfully, in the early evening after work, I could spend a few hours with three other lads, who were also conscientious objectors. They belonged to some funny religion, all came from Birtley near Newcastle, and had got themselves an old bus which they had converted into some kind of habitation. They were very kind to me at a time when I seemed not to have a friend in the world.

Thankfully, just a few weeks before Christmas 1941, my papers arrived telling me to report to the Air Force base at Cardington, in Bedfordshire. I was glad to give my notice in to the boss who had put me in that hovel. He appealed to me to give him another week or two of my work. Once again, I took great pleasure in being 'defiant, repellent and rude'.

6

Armed Service. For King and Country

I was now the possession of His Majesty's Armed Forces. I no longer had the right to think for myself. No longer could I go where I liked, live where I liked, or say what I liked. My days of being defiant, repellent and rude were over. From now on, I was to be an obedient servant, carrying out every order given to me, without reason, without argument. I was somebody else's property.

Cardington was much like any other military base. The barking of sergeant-majors, corporals and other petty tyrants, the banging of marching feet on concrete drill squares, and the stench of greasy food, were all to be repeated with excruciating boredom over the next four years of my life.

But first, kitting out in ill-fitting uniforms, the allocation of beds in the barrack room and, as important, the compulsory shearing of the head. All were warnings of things to come.

Bedding consisted of three 'biscuits', a couple of coarse blankets, and a straw-filled bag for a pillow. Those biscuits were square mattresses of similar size to a paving stone, and just about as comfortable to lie on. The blankets were designed to rub the rough edges off you. It was all part of the plan to toughen up those muscles that had got soft in civilian life, and, above all, to dull the brain and create a feeling of complete subservience.

To that latter end we were very quickly at drill on the freezing sea front at Skegness, after an initial period of similar torture on the Parade Square at Cardington.

At Skegness we did rifle drill in brass-monkey weather. Already I was praying that somebody – anybody – would end this war soon. And I was only *beginning* my training.

The polishing of every button on that uniform, the blancoing of every square inch of the 'webbing' kit, the daily shining of the heavy boots, and the morning laying out of blankets, biscuits and pillow, with socks and spare boots in military order on the bed, all combined to fill in the senseless days. Out of our pay we had to buy our own bullshitting material, the polish, the Duraglit, everything.

When you are 'joined' in His Majesty's Forces, you are told you will be fighting 'For King and Country'. And that is the biggest bit of baloney of all. We were conscripts. We were forced labour, with no right to bargain about our pay, living or working conditions, or anything else. For the most part, we believed we were fighting a just cause, and got on with it. But for King and Country? Balls. Who was the King, anyway? How did he get his job? Was he conscripted? And what were his qualifications?

Our squad of new recruits was a very mixed bag of British youth. One little lad from Durham caught the eye, especially when he got on to the drill square. As timid as a mouse, Fred – that isn't his real name – was terrified by the dog-like barking of the drill sergeant. But when that moron saw how Fred marched, he became apoplectic. Fred was unique. When he marched, his left leg and left arm came forward together. So, of course, did his right arm and leg. It's a difficult skill. Just try it yourself. But the lad's unorthodoxy went unrewarded. The war couldn't be won with skills of that kind. So Fred was put on to intensive private tuition, and we didn't stay together long enough for me to see the end result.

I don't know what hidden hand directed my military postings after training. I was shuttled up, down and across the country with bewildering regularity. Down to Gosport for a course at the School of Electric Lighting, where one weekend evening my mate and I were accosted in the street by some Bible-thumper and offered a free supper if we would to agree to be 'saved by Jesus'. The supper was the bribe, and we got a free wee Bible as well. We felt a lot better after that, physically if not spiritually. Man does not live by bread alone, but, by Heavens, in the forces in 1941 we were near to it. We would have sold our souls for a fish and chip supper.

Another of my RAF postings was to a huge base at Watton in Norfolk, near the market towns of East Dereham and Thetford. There, three or four of us were assigned to a job near the village of Swaffham. We were to be in charge of a dummy airfield. By a combination of dummy runway lights, operated from a little lookout, we were to simulate the take-off and landing of aircraft as they bumped along a non-existent runway. To put it bluntly, as soon as the air-raid warning sounded, we had to get to work to attract the German bombs onto our heads. The measure of our success would be the size of our funerals and the award of some posthumous medals. We were proud to be making the sacrifice for King and Country. A few bombs did fall on Swaffham. But no medals came our way – and no funerals. We had a vested interest in being inefficient. Still, we did our duty.

One of my other postings lives in my memory. We were sent on a course on radio and electrical communications at Birmingham Technical College. We were billeted on local people. My pal Jack, who was from Leeds, and I, were sent to some grubby folk in a side-street. From the outset it was clear to us that they were out to make a bit of easy cash out of the war. No nonsense about King and Country from them. We found ourselves sleeping in a double bed, with no light in the room, one double blanket which had been crudely cut in half, and no sheets. To keep warm, we wore our RAF gloves and socks. In the morning, for breakfast we were given only a slice of fried bread and a cup of tea each.

After two nights, we had had enough. We reported the facts to our CO, a Squadron Leader Castle. He fell on that couple like a thunderbolt, and we were out before the day was over. But not before a heap of abuse was hurled at us by the vampires.

Soon we were transferred to the Army, to form the nucleus of a new regiment called the Royal Electrical and Mechanical Engineers, REME for short. And in that capacity, now in Army khaki, I went on another electrical and radio course at Huddersfield Technical College. I cannot now recall the exact date, but the posting was a lucky one. I was allocated lovely civilian 'digs' with a very kind family in the respectable suburb of Birkby. The Brier family lived very comfortably, and treated their two soldier lodgers like gentlemen. The elderly Mr Brier had made his money by hard work and was the owner of a number of rented properties, a lot of them quite old.

Subsequent postings took me to a hutted camp near Nuneaton, to Bury in Lancashire, and to Huddersfield, though the chronology is now hazy in my mind. At Nuneaton, living conditions were crude. The rumour that it had been turned down as a German POW camp because of its inadequacies was credible. Our toilet facilities consisted of buckets placed in stalls, each about the size of a telephone kiosk. Periodically a lorry would come round to empty the buckets. That was our initial training in gas warfare. When that 'honey wagon' came round, you were asking for trouble if you struck a match or smoked a cigarette.

Transfer from Nuneaton to Bury in Lancashire might have been a scented blessing, but our barracks there were barely out of smelling distance of a glue factory which apparently melted bones to make that stinking product. There was nothing to choose between the Nuneaton pong and the Bury reek. The Bury factory seemed to be in the middle of the town. How the natives put up with it, I don't know.

It was while I was playing soccer with an Army team at Bury that an injury to my knee necessitated a cartilage operation at the Davyhulme Hospital in Manchester. After the operation I had a period of convalescence in the pleasant leafy suburb of Didsbury. A former Methodist Training College had been taken over by the armed forces as a military convalescent home, dealing mainly with men who broke limbs while doing their parachute training at the neighbouring Ringway airfield.

The convalescent home was set in its own pleasant gardens. We had beautiful young nurses to look after us, so it soon became the main purpose of every wounded soldier to stay there as long as possible. The visiting Army doctor came round every week, and the night before his visit the boys made frantic efforts to worsen the look of their broken limbs, or to bring on a relapse of whatever malady they were suffering from – the better to convince the doctor that they needed another week or two of nursing bliss. These battles of wits were fought in earnest, but the doctor usually won.

I chiefly remember that home because it was there I met my first wife, Joan. She was one of those nurses. She used to help in my physiotherapy. She also helped by playing table tennis with me. Before too long we were going to the local cinema together, and occasionally going into Manchester for a cheap meal at the local museum. I was dressed in the well-known royal blue hospital suit with white shirt and red tie. That uniform was familiar on the crowded buses down to Manchester. I was deeply touched when passengers offered their seats to 'that poor wounded soldier'. I hadn't the heart to disillusion them. I just took the seat!

Within a few weeks of my discharge from hospital, I had proposed to nurse Joan Callow, and shortly afterwards I was posted to Dalry in the west of Scotland, while Joan was transferred to a hospital in Lincoln. And it was from there that she wrote a letter which I have never forgotten. It was a tear-jerking confession that she was an illegitimate child and had adopted her grandparents' name. They had brought her up, although her parents subsequently married. She resented the stigma, and had left home to train as a nurse at the age of sixteen. 'Now that you know that,' she wrote, 'I would understand if you decided to end it all between us.' That possibility never crossed my mind. I could hardly wait to reply. I assured Joan that there was no such thing as an illegitimate child, that she had nothing to be ashamed of, and that my feelings were unchanged. We married on 3 March 1944 in Cleator Moor Parish Church in Cumberland. We had three days' honeymoon at the Anglers Inn by the shores of Lake Ennerdale; then I had to report back to Dalry.

Years later, as an MP, I was to raise in Parliament the whole question of the law on illegitimacy. The Labour Government of the day had set in train an inquiry into the complex problem, and as a result some progress has been made towards a more liberal approach and the removal of the stigma.

Shortly after our honeymoon, I was sent on an Officers' Training Course in Wrotham in rural Kent. I am hazy as to how I got there. I must have been one of the most inefficient soldiers in the British Army, yet there I was, chosen to be 'A Gentleman and an Officer' in that very outfit.

That training was a kind of civilised brutality, a hectoring savagery. The NCOs elected to put us through it seemed to be sadists. Assault courses would involve wading waist-deep in freezing streams, in full kit, rifle held dry overhead, to be followed immediately by sitting on soaking wet grass for about an hour discussing the exercise.

On one occasion we were weighed down like packhorses, with packs on our backs, pouches containing two hand-grenades, plus a rifle over the shoulder. On that assault course we had to climb walls, crawl through narrow pipes and under barbed wire, swing like monkeys over muddy, stagnant water into which we were bound to fall – and then, covered with slime and sweat, we were urged on by those monsters with their three stripes to *run* up the chalk escarpment. When I gasped back to base, I discovered that one of my hand-grenades was missing! All hell broke loose. But I was only given a rollicking, and put back a week on the course. That story was recalled many years later in a piece in the *New Statesman* by one of my colleagues who witnessed the incident. He swore the grenades were live. But I doubt that, otherwise I would have been court-martialled.

We were taught to ride a motorbike, and to drive all kinds of Army trucks. The three-ton-truck was a nightmare. Double-declutching was a hell of an operation. It wasn't enough just to depress the clutch once while changing gear. It had to be done twice, very quickly. I never knew why. There must have been some good mechanical reason. But it was hair-raising when you were climbing a steep hill. Failure to engage gear could mean disaster if your truck started to go downhill.

Once we had got used to driving, our corporal instructors thought we might be more profitably employed gathering fruit from the Kent orchards. It was there by the roadside ready for the picking. We happily made pigs of ourselves. To hell with King and Country.

One of my instructors had other ideas. He directed me to drive into one of the hop fields, where Cockneys from the East End used to spend their family holidays picking hops. The whole family, from Granny to the nappy-clad baby, camped out for weeks in the picking season. My instructor said he knew one particular family. And he obviously did. He went off to pick with a luscious young lady. He was away for well over an hour, but I don't think he was picking hops. The rest of the family kept me well fed with buns and tea, so everybody was satisfied.

A motorbike rider is a potential killer, of either himself or of anybody who can't move out of the way fast enough. I think the motive for putting budding young officers onto such machines was to weed out the accident-prone. So, after initial training on the roads, we were quickly initiated into the suicidal art of cross-country riding. Riding the bucking monsters over streams, rocks, ploughed fields and through bogs was like signing your own death-warrant. At best you could probably expect a few broken ribs or a cracked skull. We managed to get by with a few bruises and one broken ankle.

One other bit of knowledge which I gained as I trained and which would be of no use at all later in my life, was how to strip and reassemble a Bren gun. The Bren gun was a cheap, mass-produced portable machine-gun which could be broken down into hundreds of bits and pieces, little springs and bolts and nuts, each beautifully machined and oiled to fit like a glove into its allotted place. It was essential to be able to break it down and put it together again in a matter of seconds. Your life could depend on your efficiency. For days, we stripped and assembled, tore apart and put together again, until we could do it blindfolded. It seemed futile at the time. But in battle situation the skill could have been decisive. Luckily, I was never put to that test.

And so my officer training came to an end. Certainly I was fitter and stronger. I had a lot more knowledge of battle tactics and of weapons, and I felt I was quite smart at square-bashing – the drill to numbers, then the same drill without shouting out the numbers. We were all well trained in the military arts. Hitler didn't know what he was in for.

THE UPPER CLASSES. OFFICERS AND – GENTLEMEN?

Now an officer, I ruminated with some amusement, and not a little worry, on the fact that I had started the war as a conscientious objector and was now an Army officer with 'The King's Commission'. It may have been a worthy entry in the *Guinness Book of Records*.

To begin with, however, I had to be fitted for my smart officer's uniform. And for the first time in my life I had to open a bank account. Ordinary soldiers could be paid weekly in cash, but officers had to be paid monthly, and into a bank account. There was no choice in the matter.

So, at the age of twenty-seven, I had several 'firsts'. I had my first fitted suit, my first chequebook, my first step up the military ladder. And for the first time in my life men began to salute me. In a few days I got my first posting as a second lieutenant, complete with a shining 'pip' on each epaulette, and an officer's cane.

A cold fear came over me. A fear that I was betraying my father and my class, and also a fear that I had got where I now was by false pretences.

I appeared to be, now, one of the 'ruling class'. I never asked my father about my promotion. I never learned whether he was proud, ashamed, or disappointed. When we were children at home, he would never allow us to join even the boy scouts. The putting on of any kind of uniform was, for him, the first step towards indoctrination by the military-minded ruling classes.

I sweated over my new-found status and authority. I was perturbed that I would be as inefficient as an officer as I had been as an ordinary soldier. I had never thought of myself as a 'gentleman'. And I had always bridled against any kind of discipline imposed by anyone, even my own father. To be blunt, I was an anarchist at heart, with an unreasoning hostility towards all kinds of authority.

Yet here I was about to play the part of one in authority. Was I a traitor to my class? Should I have blushed with embarrassment every time a private saluted me, even though I had been told the salute was not for me personally but for 'The King's Commission'? Perhaps I should have felt like telling them to cut out all the bullshit. But it was too late now. Truth to tell, I felt none of those things. I detested the bullshit, the polishing of endless brass buttons, the blancoing and mindless square-bashing as we were marched for endless hours, counting out loud as each movement of arm, foot, or body was made, the better to co-ordinate the efforts of a squad of harassed men. How those hours dragged when you loathed every second. But now I was at the other end of all that. And I began to *like* having my boots polished by somebody else. I soon began to *like* having my morning cup of tea brought to me. I *liked* the privilege of eating my meals in the Officers' Mess, and wearing a clean suit that fitted, even if it was khaki. In short, I was learning the lesson that it is easier to preach about the injustice of privilege when others have it, but it's quite a different matter when you have a bit yourself. As Lord Acton said, 'Power tends to corrupt and absolute power corrupts absolutely.' To which may be added, 'And a little power can corrupt quite a bit.'

THE HAMILTONS' WAR

One of the costs of war that can't be measured is the cost of separation. Husbands separated from wives, sons and daughters from Mums and Dads and from each other. The heartache of leaving home and family, not knowing when you will see them again – if at all. These things are a searing misery which defies description. In that respect we had a lucky war.

My elder brother Tom was the unluckiest. He drew the short straw. As an early conscript, he was drafted into the Scottish Black Watch, an infantry regiment with a record of toughness and bravery unsurpassed in the British Army. Before you could say 'Scotch whisky', those lads were sent to Iceland. The purpose of occupying that forbidding land was to deny its possible use by German submarines as a base from which to attack our vital shipping routes in the North Atlantic.

From the outset, the soldiers were billeted in tents. In some of the most ferocious weather in the Northern hemisphere, those tents were often blown away in the middle of the freezing night. The bad weather cut them off from supplies of all kinds, food, letters and other comforts. When letters did get through, Tom begged his mother to send him some food. 'Even if it was soaked in sea water, or stale', he would eat it. That was the message. He described how on route marches it was not uncommon for soldiers to be literally blown into the sea by the force of the gales.

Tom's health suffered. When he got home, he was a broken man. He contracted tuberculosis and a heart condition. How much of that was due to his experiences in Iceland nobody will ever know. But Tom died prematurely in 1962 at the age of forty-seven. He was a gentle man, kind and generous. We all missed him greatly.

My younger brother Jack was probably the ablest of the four of us. He was a practical man, good with his hands, and powerfully built. In his youth he was a tough footballer who played happily as an amateur in Durham, mixing it rough with teams of coalminers fed on iron girders. By sheer hard work and guts, he did a seven-year apprenticeship as a carpenter, or a 'joiner'. The last three or four years of that apprenticeship were a form of cheap skilled labour for the benefit of the boss.

When the war started, Jack was classified as being in a reserved occupation. He went down to Cirencester to work in the aircraft-frame industry as a pattern-maker, but after 1945, he returned to Durham, ending up as the Head of the Building Department at the City of Durham Technical College. Later, Jack's son Peter was a brilliant scholar who got a First Class Honours degree in physics. I suggested to him that he should try to get to Cambridge University, and I remember his reply: 'No, Uncle Willie, my accent is not right for that.'

My youngest brother Arthur opted to work in the coal pits rather than join the armed forces. At least it would allow him to stay at home, but very soon he wished he had put on a uniform. Nevertheless, he stayed in the pits until the end of the war, and subsequently became a full-time trade union official for the shop workers in Newcastle.

As a coalminer, our father was also in a reserved occupation. During the war years he did air-raid warden duties, I think on a voluntary basis. The north-east coast was an important industrial target for the German bombers, but it escaped relatively lightly, compared with the devastation of cities like London and Coventry.

Our mother was in command of the Hamiltons' kitchen throughout the war years. She was in charge of the ration books. She had to do all the queueing for the weekly ounces of meat, butter, sugar, cheese and the one or two eggs. Everything was rationed except the air we breathed, even clothes and furniture. Mother had to concoct meals from things like dried eggs, dried milk, a mysterious meat called Spam, something called Woolton pie, and whale meat.

Women like my mother who 'manned' the front line in the home made as great a contribution to the war effort as anybody in the armed forces. They kept the home fires burning and the families' bellies full.

For my part, I was glad in a sad sort of way to be away from home. The tension that existed between our parents often became unbearable, so that I was seldom happy when I got home on leave. I suspect the trouble was rooted in financial problems. As a youngster, I used to collect my father's pay at the pit office. It was seldom much above £1 a week, yet when he finally left the pits after the war to become a hospital porter, the last coal seam he had worked in was seventeen inches high. Imagine, if you can, any human being digging coal with a pick and shovel for eight hours a day in a filthy dark place where you had to work on your belly. Such conditions were not fit for a dog. Having made a rough calculation of my father's total life earnings over about forty years, the figure would have been much less than £4,000. Looking back now, it is unbelievable.

So the Hamiltons came through the war years relatively unscathed. We all escaped the worst horrors. We were never bombed. None of us except Tom did any service overseas. None of us fired a shot in anger, and none of us was wounded or killed. God was good to us. We counted our blessings. One of those blessings was that within a few months a new Labour Government was elected with a thumping Parliamentary majority. Ours was a land of great promise.

7

1945 and All That

Right up to 1944 I had never seriously thought of a career in national politics.

My father had always been ambitious for his family and he worked tirelessly to make sure we got the best educational opportunities then available. He himself was immersed in local politics, but never had any aspirations at national level. The inferiority complex was deeply ingrained throughout working-class communities. The highest aspiration of most men and women was to join the teaching profession. Job security was the main objective. That, the wearing of a white collar and a clean shirt every day, and a decent living wage, was the most they expected.

None of my brothers had shown any interest in active politics. Nor did my mother. I think they got a bit fed up with my father's obsession. It was meat and drink to him. He hoarded newspaper cuttings. He collected piles of *Plebs*, the monthly magazine of the NCLC. We didn't have the space to stack these accumulations, so they were stuffed in drawers, under beds, anywhere that could accommodate more paper. In me he saw scope for more political ambition. Having got to the grammar school, my father thought I might be an election agent. That would be a useful career, either full time or as a supplement to teaching.

But immediately before the General Election of 1945, more exciting prospects loomed up – in West Fife.

It had been agreed by the political parties that all servicemen and women selected as Parliamentary candidates should be released from their service for something like six weeks unpaid leave: three weeks for the actual Election campaign, and three weeks afterwards to allow the ballot papers to be collected from all over the world and be counted in the UK.

The thought of escaping from the Army for six weeks made an irresistible appeal to me.

THE 1945 ELECTION BATTLE

It was only after I was selected as a candidate for West Fife that the miner friends I had made in Bangor, and who had suggested me as a candidate, told me that I had been Hobson's choice. The local Communists tried to infer that I had been inflicted on the local Party by the English-based Labour Party hierarchy, but there was not a grain of truth in it.

My personal problems were terrifying. I had no money. I would be without any income for six weeks, and had no savings to fall back on. I had nowhere to sleep in Fife. My wife Joan was living with her parents in Cleator Moor, near Whitehaven in Cumberland, and expecting our first baby in July. I had no clothes. I was an Englishman in a foreign land, with no political experience of any kind. The local Labour Party had been in abeyance during the war, and had neither money nor organisation. Finally, I was up against one of the best-known MPs in the UK, who was also very popular, certainly in Scotland.

The omens were not good – or so it seemed. It is hard to measure the worth of enthusiasm, and conviction, and voluntary effort. West Fife had never been Communist. Willie Gallacher and his Communist allies in the Scottish Miners' Union had exploited the miners' legitimate grievances in the mid-1930s for their own political ends. Willie Adamson, the then ageing sitting Labour MP for the constituency, paid the price for his own moderation, as well as for his age and lack of charisma.

When Gallacher won the seat in 1935, it was with the support of miners who were not Communist (in the political sense), but who were disillusioned with the apparent lack of militant leadership from both their trade union and the Labour Party. With the coming of the war in 1939, Gallacher got a clear run in Parliament, remaining ten years without a challenge. Being the only Communist in the House of Commons he could, as a 'minority group of one', participate in every debate on every subject, with maximum coverage of his speeches in the *Daily Worker*, then the only Communist paper in the land. He was an eloquent and witty speaker. He had already made a name for himself among the group of radical MPs and independent Labour Party workers in Red Clydeside in the twenties and thirties, so he was not without friends inside the Labour Party.

One way and another, my job in Fife in 1945 was not a very promising one.

Almost all of my active supporters were miners and their wives and families. Willie Mill and his wife Mary gladly gave me a bedroom of my own in their upstairs flat in the village of Kelty, and I could have had no better treatment in a five-star hotel. Throughout the campaign I got royal hospitality. In every mining community – and there were about a hundred – I got the warmest friendship and kindness. Often as poor as church mice, there was always a cup of tea, or something stronger, a meal, and even a bed.

My election agent was a young coalminer called Willie Marshall. He was the youngest Labour councillor on the then Tory-controlled Fife County Council. Willie was just recovering from a serious back injury sustained in the pits. He looked on the Election campaign as a part of his convalescence. He was an intelligent, astute and articulate organiser. He planned that campaign in meticulous detail. Within the first forty-eight hours he had prepared my schedule of public meetings for the full three weeks. It was a punishing programme, involving at least three meetings every night, and four each Sunday, Sunday being the really big day for meetings in mining villages. And in my spare time – usually Saturdays – I went to neighbouring constituencies in Perth and East Fife, to support the Labour candidates there. In those days the TV screen was not sovereign. No home had one. There were no TV confrontations with Party Leaders. The public meeting, the big rallies in town halls, radio programmes, these were the tools we worked with. My public meetings were a huge success. Packed Miners' Institutes, crowded school classrooms. It was exciting, and frightening. I learned my public speaking the hard way. The National Council of Labour Colleges, the NCLC, with which I was associated, had had a correspondence course on public speaking. I had always thought that was a useless exercise. You can only be a good public speaker by speaking as often as possible in public, but it means meticulous preparation and practice beforehand. When I first started on my public career, I wrote out word for word what I was going to say, and then read it aloud to my long-suffering wife. When I was younger I had a photographic memory, and could remember what I had written. Sometimes, however, the mind went completely blank, and that created embarrassing silences. Fortunately most of my audiences in Fife were sympathetic and helpful, and I am conceited enough to believe that I was a quick learner. There is no substitute for constant practice, and I got plenty of that in the red-hot politics of Fife in those first few years. My agent helped enormously, by careful selection of my chairmen, who were eloquent and physically powerful men, miners or, occasionally, schoolteachers, good supporting speakers. Nothing was left to chance.

With tight schedules, getting to each meeting on time demanded a lot of discipline. Local Communists would try to disrupt our plans by asking a lot of questions at each meeting, and would try to leave the impression that I was afraid if we left for the next meeting before they thought we should.

My transport was in the hands of a Robbie Burns romantic. John Lister was an insurance agent who travelled round in an old Ford 'banger'. It had no heating, it leaked, and it couldn't go very fast. But John knew every side-road and short cut in Fife. He and his canny wife lived in that buzzing village of Kelty. Mrs Lister used to make the most delicious treacle scones especially for me, and late in the campaign, when my wife came up for a few days, the Listers put us up.

That was the whole spirit of our campaign. Wonderful, exhilarating, nerve-tingling. The local Labour Party was overflowing with practical working men and women, longing for the new socialist Utopia which they saw within their grasp, and willing to slog their guts out to get it.

At first we had no money. But soon it began to roll in. We took a collection at every meeting. Every village had its own way of collecting money, such as going round doors with collecting tins, or standing outside cinema queues with tins, or organising local raffles. The local trade union branches chipped in, so did the local co-operative societies. By the time the Election was over, we had made a small profit!

The Communists hated us. For them, Willie Gallacher was King, and, like any other hereditary title-holder, they believed he should not be opposed. A violent campaign of character assassination was begun at a very early stage in the fight. I was 'an unknown young Englishman', and an Army officer. But I had also been a conchie, so I was a turncoat too. I claimed to be the son of a well-known Durham miner. But Joe Hamilton was unknown in political circles down there. And so it went on. With no experience in these tactics, I was hurt and embarrassed, and not a little worried.

The Communist HQ in the constituency was a village called Lumphinnans, the birthplace of the Moffat brothers, the notorious Communist leaders of the Scottish Miners' Union. Lumphinnans was full of miners' rows, depressing slums owned by the Fife Coal Company – a real hotbed for the breeding of extremist politicians and agitators. They 'dared' me to go in there and hold a public meeting. They boasted it was a 'no-go' area for the Labour candidate. But they had reckoned without the guts and courage of the likes of Willie Mill of Kelty, and the Bevin Boys who lodged near him. They were tough young lads from Glasgow who, like my own brother Arthur, had opted to work in the coalmines rather than do military service. They would be my bodyguard in Lumphinnans. And in we marched. We held our first public meeting on the concrete top of an air-raid shelter. As I said my piece, my Bevin Boy supporters in the village dangled their legs over the side of the shelter. It was an exciting display of 'physical democracy'. The local and vocal Communists tried to rush us off the shelter, but the boys, six feet above where they stood, crushed the Commies' hands with their feet. At which point our women supporters in the village showed their hand. I had never before seen such boxing skills. Well, it was more like all-in wrestling. Those brave women laid into those Communists with the kind of upper cuts and blows in the groin of which only soldiers trained in the art of unarmed combat are expert. It was inspiring. We held subsequent meetings in Lumphinnans, and they were never without some display of physical intimidation. But our Women's Labour Section, now organised and very tough, relished the combat. They were great. Their spirit was humbling.

It wasn't all roses. A chronic shortage of money meant we had to improvise in all sorts of ways. North Queensferry is a wee community nestling beneath the northside towers of the Forth rail bridge. It looked like a God-forsaken village, but there was a population of about a thousand, and we felt they had a right to a public meeting.

We arranged one, but we couldn't afford to advertise it. So with two supporters, I went to the local school, borrowed a big handbell, and went round the streets ringing out the details of our meeting that evening. That had the great advantage of enabling the local folk to *see* their Labour candidate advertising his poverty and showing his enthusiasm, as well as ensuring a good collection at the meeting!

The climax of our campaign was reached on the eve of the poll, with a meeting in the Lochore Miners' Institute. Lochore was a tough place, with a strong local Communist Party. We had set up a local Labour Party, but it was inexperienced and a bit overawed by the noise of the Communists. The hall held about 500 people. It was packed that night. Folk were sitting on the window-sills and standing wherever they could. Our platform was crowded with Labour councillors from all over the county, sympathetic trade union officials, as well as Willie Marshall, my agent, who lived in Lochore. The Chairman was a tough local miner called Bob Harrower. Built like a bull, and with a roar to match, Bob loathed the Commies. He knew them all by Christian name.

They kept the meeting going for a couple of hours until I arrived from my previous meetings. I had been hard at it all day. It was 11 p.m. when I arrived. But the sight of that packed hall was unforgettable. Bob was in full flow. The Communists were howling like a pack of wolves. When I rose to speak, the noise was deafening – cheers, boos, catcalls and clapping.

As soon as I began, the Communists started to rush the platform, which was raised about three feet from the body of the hall. They were out to break up our meeting. Too late, they realised the strength of our supporters. Especially the women. They were terrific. They laid into the Commies with fists, legs and tongues. A Miners' Union leader on the platform belted the Communists with his cap, and lost it forever.

In fifteen minutes the fracas was over. By law the meeting had to finish by midnight, and Bob saw that it did. Our supporters were elated. We adjourned to another room in the hall where those same women fighters had prepared tea and sandwiches. I was their hero, the man they'd been waiting for for fifteen years. And for the next forty years I was to be the most hated politician in the British Communist book.

NATIONAL VICTORY, LOCAL DEFEAT

The landslide victory of the Labour Party in 1945 was like a shining beacon after the grim darkness of the war years. Our democracy, and the maturity of the British people, were displayed in all their glorious unpredictability.

Winston Churchill had addressed huge crowds wherever he went. He had been *our* leader, had he not, in the war? It was a foregone conclusion that the people would show their gratitude by giving him a thumping vote of confidence in the Election. He made great miscalculations. Not least were his intemperate attacks on those Labour MPs who had been prominent members of the wartime Coalition Government. Overnight, they became 'the enemy within', who would impose a Gestapo on Britain.

Churchill couldn't have misjudged the British people more. They remembered the grim days of the pre-war years, the dole queues, the grinding poverty, the injustices and inequalities. They held pre-war Tory Governments responsible for all that, and had not forgotten the Tory appeasement of Hitler which had led to the war.

So, for the first time in the history of the UK, a Labour Government was elected with an overwhelming mandate to carry out the most radical reform of our society that had ever been attempted. And it was to be led by a diminutive figure, Clem Attlee, a middle-aged, ex-Army major with no great oratorical gifts. That man of few words was to change the face of Britain over the next five years.

I was not to enjoy the privilege of being in that memorable Parliament. We lost the battle, but we were to win the war. Our voting figures were:

> W. Gallacher (Com): 17,635 (42.1%)
> W. W. Hamilton (Lab): 15,580 (37.3%)
> Dr R. S. Stevenson (Con): 8,597 (20.6%)

A young, unknown Englishman had challenged the well-known and established Communist MP and given him a good run. We had proved that West Fife was not a Communist constituency. With no money and with sketchy organisation, we had come within an ace of victory. The writing was already on the wall.

Now, however, I had to pick up the pieces and restart my life where I had left it. I was penniless, but still in the Army.

The day before the Election result was announced I had received a telegram to say that Joan had given birth to our first child, a daughter, at her parents' home at Cleator Moor. It was vital that I should get there as quickly as possible, but I didn't have the money to pay my train fare down to Whitehaven. My predicament was well understood by the local Labour Party. They had emptied their pockets to pay for the Election, but at our post-Election social and dance they had a whipround, and collected enough to pay that fare, with a little bit to spare! It was gestures like that which made the Labour Party the greatest workers' political movement in the world. Over the next thirty-five years and more, I saw no reason to change that view.

I got to Cleator Moor and saw Joan and our daughter in good health and in the kindly care of my in-laws. They were ordinary working-class folk living in a council house, but their help to us was unstinting. Nevertheless, I wanted our own independence and in that regard both the Army and the Brier family in Huddersfield came to our rescue.

Within a week of the Election declaration, I got a direction from the Army to report to an address in Highgate in North London, prior to shipment to Palestine – now Israel. I immediately wrote to the Briers who had been my landlords during my Army days in Huddersfield. They owned a number of houses, so I asked them if they could possibly help us with our housing problem. They kindly offered us one of their properties, a back-to-back slum in Fartown, which was the best they could do. It had a cellar, an outside toilet, no bathroom, no hot water, and no heating except an open coal fire. But it had a roof, also a living room and one bedroom. As beggars we couldn't be choosers. We were grateful to the Briers for their help.

Joan had never met any of them. Nor had she ever been to Huddersfield in her life. She had to go, alone, with our weeks' old baby, to meet strange people in a strange town, to live in a house which she had never seen. She had to travel alone on a long train journey from Whitehaven to Huddersfield. How she managed I do not know. The Army thought they needed me more than Joan did, so off I went south, and within a few weeks I was despatched to the Middle East, from Newhaven to Dieppe, by train to Marseilles, and then by boat to Alexandria.

We stayed for a few days in a transit camp on the Nile delta, near the Suez Canal. We were in tents in the desert. While sleeping one night, some animal ate a hole the size of my fist in my army greatcoat. It was enjoying its meal within a foot of me. It could have been my private parts.

Our latrine at the camp was an enormously deep shaft, sunk into the sands by our hygienically-minded engineers. The hole had a surface diameter of about ten feet, over which were cleverly designed wooden planks. The shaft was so deep that your job was almost completed before you could hear the dull plonk of your offering at its final resting place.

My ultimate destination was to be above the port of Haifa, on the top of Mount Carmel, with a breathtaking view overlooking Haifa Bay. Mount Carmel was a fascinating contrast of cultures. Halfway up the mountain was the Arab quarter, with its great noise and clamour, its cafés and bars, and its flies. Further up the hill were the prosperous Jewish quarters, with their elegant houses and gardens, and at a lower level, nearer the sea, was the Carmelite monastery. Pervading it all was the British Army presence.

In those troubled times of 1945–6, our Labour Government was trying to keep *out* of Palestine all the Jews then trying to get *in*, fleeing from Europe and the memories of the Holocaust. They yearned to have their own country, and every day shiploads of them were trying to enter what they regarded as their rightful homeland. A struggle between the British authorities and the Jews was inevitable. It was ruthless, brutal and bloody. We called it terrorism. The Jews called it their struggle for a permanent homeland. I watched from the top of Mount Carmel the blowing up of great oil storage tanks down in Haifa Bay. I carried, permanently, a loaded revolver at my waist. I was lucky; I never had to use it. Menachim Begin, later to become Israeli Prime Minister, was then a leading 'terrorist', so establishing a pattern in which so many 'terrorists' in British colonial days became respectable and honourable prime ministers and presidents.

My main job, however, was not to keep Jews out, nor to shoot anybody. It was much more interesting and humane than that. I was to be a lecturer at what was quaintly called the Army Formation College. Our purpose was to give lectures to servicemen and women shortly before they were due for demobilisation into civilian life. Lectures were given in economics, history, philosophy, and many other kindred subjects. It was a kind of sophisticated Butlins holiday camp. Morning lectures were followed by visits to places of historical interest like Nazareth, Jerusalem, the Dead Sea, Jaffa and Jericho, all of which were rough rides in Army trucks. Occasionally some of us went on more risky expeditions. I got friendly with one of the Jewish women on the admin side of the college. She escorted me to see some of the early Jewish kibbutzim. There everything was communally owned. All the work was shared. So was all the property and wealth.

At that time it was all tented accommodation. But the Jews felt that they had at last come home and seemed very happy, and very determined that they were there to stay.

It was known to the British authorities that arms caches were hidden at those settlements – for the blowing up of British property and personnel. If the Army authorities had known that I, a commissioned officer, was visiting these places as a sympathetic friend, I would have been court-martialled, and probably dismissed from the service in disgrace.

But to balance things out, or to make matters worse, according to your point of view, I also visited the Arab leaders in Haifa, along with an Army major who, I learned, was a Communist. We got a kick out of thumbing our noses at the British authorities. We were not in sympathy with what the Government – *my* Government – was then doing to the Jews, and looking back now, I think we were right.

One of my fellow lecturers in Haifa was Huw Wheldon, then a major with an impressive military record behind him. He was a superb raconteur and companion. We enjoyed a marvellous leave together, skiing in the mountains above Damascus. It was a unique experience to stand in the snow up there and look down on the shimmering heat of the city.

Huw was to become a celebrity on TV and a much-loved figure of the Establishment. I met him several times later, notably as one of the leading lights in the Festival of Britain in 1951, when I was a young MP and he had his foot firmly on the promotion ladder of BBC culture. A far cry from the killing fields of Palestine.

By a strange coincidence, my old friend Len Jones came on to a course of lectures at our Haifa college. I had met him as a conscientious objector in Devon in 1940. Subsequently he, too, had decided to put on a military uniform, for non-combatant duties in the Medical Corps. In Haifa, Len got hooked up with a Jewish girl who was also serving in the British Army. He took her back to the UK, where they married, had a family and settled in mid Wales. I think they became Roman Catholics. War can produce some strange liaisons.

My economics and history lectures, and the trips to the Christian shrines, reached a climax at the Christmas of 1945. A trip to Jerusalem and Bethlehem was organised for Christmas Eve and thousands of British servicemen and women converged on those holy shrines. On the truck that took us to Bethlehem were many Irish soldiers, and when they burst into their rendering of 'Silent Night', the emotion was overwhelming. The war in Europe had ended. Peace was on its way. That hymn was the most wonderful sound I had heard for many a long day.

At Bethlehem, the sharp Arab traders were doing a roaring trade selling Christian emblems. I bought a Bible with a mother-of-pearl cover, probably printed in Hong Kong and sold at a great profit to a mug from England. But it made me feel good, and that Bible is still treasured by my daughter. On show were half a dozen stables where Jesus was born, and at Nazareth as many carpenters' shops. God and Mammon lived happily side by side. Nobody seemed to mind.

By the middle of 1946 I was on my way home, with the rank of captain. Travelling by land and sea, I had time to ponder over what the future might have in store. But first I had to be fitted with my demob suit, a hat and coat. I forget what other 'goodies' we got. I say 'fitted'. By that I mean it fitted where it touched. I was allowed to keep my officer's gear, some of which I still have, like my canvas camp-bed, my canvas chair and my tin trunk. It was a merciful relief to throw off that uniform for the last time. Life in the armed forces may be fine for some. They say it builds character, that it is good for discipline, that the friendship is splendid. Not much of that ever convinced me then, and nor does it now.

It was late August when I finally arrived in Huddersfield. Joan thought it would be a good idea if we had a holiday together at the seaside. And heaven knows, she needed it. But we had no money. My Army gratuity would be some time coming. So I had to get work, quickly, and when I applied to the Huddersfield Education Authority, they made it clear that I had to start teaching at the beginning of the September term.

So poor Joan got no holiday. And that was the start of an increasingly strained relationship. She'd had a rough time ever since we married. Separation, pregnancy, then setting up home in a strange town with no friends and a weeks' old baby. Joan found it hard to cope. That dreadful house in Huddersfield became almost overrun with rats. All alone at night, she heard them gnawing at the floorboards. Terrified, she got the local council workmen to inspect. After digging round and tearing up the floorboards, they discovered a broken drain, through which the rodents were marching. The problem was resolved, but it left Joan in a state of deep depression – all alone. I heard that story only after I had got home. We had to get out of that house – but how?

The winter of 1946–7 was one of the worst for years. The snow lay several feet deep and lasted for weeks, so there was a great shortage of fuel. I used to get out of my bed at 5 a.m., walk the mile to the Huddersfield Coke Works, queue for a half-hundredweight of coke, walk the mile back home, have some breakfast, and get off to school.

Our life together could not have got off to a worse start. So when my Army gratuity of £150 arrived, we put it down immediately as our deposit on a semi-detached house. The total price of the house was £1,000, the first we had ever owned, and we felt as proud as if we'd bought Buckingham Palace. We had back and front gardens, a bathroom, hot and cold water, and a separate little kitchen. I felt like a financial tycoon – except that I was again penniless. I had an £800 mortgage round my neck. We couldn't afford a pair of shears to cut the grass! We bought a woodworm-eaten, second-hand sewing machine so that Joan could make dresses for our baby, Sheila. I sold as many Army vests, socks and shirts as I could, and got a few shillings for them. I took on evening classes to supplement my teacher's salary. In the evenings the school ran a youth club, and I was glad to be offered the job of paid supervisor. I also took on paid part-time work with the NCLC as a tutor marking the work of correspondence-course students. In addition, I became a paid lecturer for the Workers' Education Association. This was fascinating evening work, and together with the weekend schools was very demanding but very satisfying.

All this meant I was working almost round the clock for five days a week, and often at weekends as well. My family life suffered greatly, as it was to do for the next forty years. I regret to confess that I was never a good husband or father. I was far too selfish and introverted.

Things didn't get any easier when our second child, a boy, was born on 5 July 1949. Whoever said money is the root of all evil had never been poor. Folk with money can never begin to understand the evils of poverty: and when that poverty is accompanied by young children – the one often goes with the other – the situation becomes even more unbearable. It's easy for the well-off to lecture to the poor about their fecklessness in having children they can't afford. The poor get sick and tired of haranguing from the likes of Mrs Thatcher.

My four years of schoolteaching convinced me that I was not cut out for the job. It has always been a hard-working profession. I found it demanding, physically and mentally. It's a silly notion that teachers have cushy jobs and long holidays. In the mid-1940s, Huddersfield had a Liberal-controlled council that was more reactionary than many right-wing Tory councils. When at some local elections I spoke publicly about their awful record in education, they tried to sack me, and after a while I left of my own accord and went to teach at the Batley Technical College. I was glad to get the job at Batley, although it meant a longish bus journey each day. I was immediately happier. The staff were more mature, and my students were in their later teens and anxious to make something of their lives. I taught them modern history and elementary economics. I stayed there until the 1950 Election, having organised an exciting mock election in the college before I left. It was no surprise that the Labour candidate won.

In those years 1945–50, the local Labour Party in West Fife began their preparations for the next battle. They soon decided that I must have another go at Gallacher, so for those five years I travelled up to Fife every few weeks. It was always at weekends, when train services were at their worst. It also meant additional strains on our marriage. My wife had never been political, her health had always been poor, and she was finding my way of life almost intolerable.

My appetite for politics had been whetted by my 1945 experience. The new Labour Government had enormous problems. Churchill himself had said that the country would be bankrupt after the war. And so we were. The war had been financed by 'tick'. Fight now and pay later was the guideline. There was, therefore, a limit to what any Government could do. Nevertheless, that Labour Government's record was one of which working-class people had a right to be proud. It had taken the coalmines into public ownership, as well as the railways, gas and electricity. It had created the NHS, and laid the foundations of a comprehensive system of National Insurance.

I was privileged to be one of the first people to go down one of *our* pits. The day the National Coal Board flag went up, I went down a pit in Kelty. It was my first visit underground. It was frightening. All Tory MPs should go down a coalmine and crawl along a two- or three-foot seam. Not to work, but just to endure the dank darkness, the creaking movement of the hundreds of feet of rock above and around you, to sense the danger and the claustrophobia. I cannot recollect that Mrs Thatcher ever *visited* a coalmine, let alone went down one.

Coalminers deserve princely wages, just for going down there, even if they just sit on their backsides. I long to see the day when every pit in Britain is closed; when our energy needs can be supplied by safer and more humane ways. That will not happen in my lifetime. But increased research into the potential of wave and wind power and solar energy, the construction of barriers across the Wash, Severn and Humber estuaries, together with an imaginative investment programme on energy conservation, could well speed up that timetable. God speed the day.

8

The 1950 Election: Victory and Defeat

The day of reckoning was to be 23 February. A winter Election in Fife was to be a freezing affair. But the West Fife Party was in fine fettle. We scented victory from the word go. We had cash, we had workers and we had the Labour Government's record to boast about.

It was all bad news for our Communist opponents. In those last five years, Communist-controlled dictatorships had been thrust down the throats of all folk in the grip of the Soviet Union – in Poland, Hungary, Czechoslovakia, Rumania, Bulgaria, East Germany, Latvia, Lithuania and Estonia. The Iron Curtain of totalitarianism had snapped down between the democratic West and the Communist East.

Willie Gallacher was with the totalitarian East. I was on the other side.

Our Election campaign was even dirtier and more violent than that of 1945 – and I loved every minute. Gallacher was getting old, and looked it. I was a strapping young man of thirty-one. The difference spoke for itself. But we made no mention of it – not in public, anyway.

The Communists threw everything at us. The painting of every village street with slogans; the fly-posting of every available hoarding; the bussing of supporters from every part of the land, and especially from Durham – all designed to con the voters into believing there was massive national support for their candidate. At weekends, Communist canvassers seemed to be active in every village. Two of them knocked on Willie Mill's door in Kelty, where I was staying. Willie went to the door. The two were from Durham. They didn't know I was the lodger there. The language which poured from Willie's mouth was like molten lead. He never let on he was my host. He laughed like a hyena when he left them. I loved that demonstration of democracy. It could never have happened in the kind of society which those two lads from Durham seemed to support.

Later in the campaign Willie was at it again. One of the few active Communists in Kelty was a John Fernie. As fast as John painted the local streets with white paint, Willie followed up with black. As fast as John stuck up his posters, Willie tore them down. One day John had gone too far, so Willie thought another democratic weapon had to be used – a mouthful of bare knuckles. John didn't retaliate. No assault charges were made. They both knew the score. One evening, while racing against the clock on our meetings schedule, somebody put sand in our petrol tank. We never found out who did it.

The Women's Section in the Labour Party in Lumphinnans was as aggressive as ever. In that village more than anywhere else, the campaign was physical. Violence was almost expected, and through all the Elections until 1964 or '66, we matched force with force. If military medals could have been awarded I would have to put up the names of Mary McKay and Mrs Quinn. Mrs Quinn was the Catholic mother of a large family, a woman of great courage and conviction who saw to it that her family were of like mind.

The Roman Catholic Church was bitterly anti-Communist. So, because I was the most likely man to defeat Gallacher, they supported me. Instructions went out to the flock, and I was invited to pay a visit to the RC Father's home, in the village of Lochore. I went, secretly, under the cover of darkness as I also had strong Protestant Orange Lodges in the constituency. The great religious divide was never as strong in the east of Scotland as it was in Glasgow. There, RC schools could be divided from the Protestant schools by barbed-wire fences. When the Nationalist Party was at its peak the unspoken fear was that if ever Scotland got back its own Parliament, it might be dominated by a Catholic Glasgow – and that the city might become another Belfast.

The Miners' Union had long been controlled in Scotland by Communists. Their power was always out of all proportion to their actual numbers. Half a dozen Communist activists could and did get and hold control of Union branches with 1,000 members or more. At Elections, those Communists in control of the Union HQ in Edinburgh often created difficulties for us in the Labour Party in matters of finance. Our local Party was entitled to payments of quite substantial amounts from the political levy paid by the miners, and the CP leaders hated the idea of handing over that cash to those who were fighting their man Gallacher. They had to do it, but it was like pulling teeth.

In that 1950 Election, the eve of poll rally in the Lochore Miners' Institute was like a replay of the 1945 scenario. The beery bellowing of the Commies was designed to intimidate. But my household cavalry was there in force: our women armed with rude tongues, sharp teeth and nails, fists and feet. I think they were disappointed not to be called on. We sensed victory, and the result confirmed our opinions, except that the winning margin was much greater than we had thought possible.

> W. W. Hamilton (Lab): 23,576 (54.8%)
> P. W. N. Fraser (Con): 10,131 (23.6%)
> W. Gallacher (Comm): 9,301 (21.6%)

The Communist vote had plummeted from over 17,000 to just over 9,000, and their percentage of the total poll was slashed to almost exactly half. The Labour vote increased by about 9,000. In effect, there had been an apparent switch of 9,000 votes from Communist to Labour since the 1945 Election.

That result put the final nail in the coffin of the CP in West Fife. They had never been much more than a noisy rabble with little popular support. When Gallacher went, everything went. Though he had the reputation of being a witty speaker and a jovial character, I fought him in two Elections, and we never exchanged a single word with one another. Nor did we ever shake hands. We were both fierce fighters. No quarter was asked, and none was given. And when that Election count was declared, Gallacher walked alone from the hall, a broken man. His death a few years later may have been hastened by that crushing defeat. Politics is a cruel business. Perhaps the only one where it is accepted that you can kick a man when he is down. My compassion for that lonely old man was, frankly, short-lived. I was too busy enjoying my own success. Yet politics can be heart-warming, too. Some of those tough women were crying with joy, and even the bull-like miners had damp eyes. They had fought hard and long for this great day, and they savoured it like a good Scotch whisky.

At our victory social in Kelty, I was 'King Willie'. Although I had never danced a step in my life, I was hauled to the floor to lead off in the 'Dashing White Sergeant' with the dear wife of our CLP Chairman, Councillor John Sneddon. Only a crowded and deliriously happy floor could hide my clodhopping. Dancing is a social grace which has never ceased to terrify me.

Our joy in Fife, however, was soured by the overall national result. A Parliamentary majority of 146 had been slashed to less than ten. The pendulum seemed to have swung 'slightly' against us, despite the impressive record of that postwar Labour Government.

9

New Member at the Palace of Westminster

I was now the Honnourable Member of Parliament for West Fife. No, that was not quite accurate. I was described as the Honourable *and Gallant* Member for West Fife. For, by convention, any MP who had put on a military uniform as an officer was entitled to be called 'Gallant' – and 'Captain'. All that sounded daft to me, so I strangled it at birth.

More pressing problems were with me straight away. I knew that my pay would be £1,000 a year, but I didn't know when or how it would be paid, and I was in desperate need. I also didn't know where I would stay in London.

The first time I entered that great Palace of Westminster it reminded me of my first visit to Durham Cathedral. It was more like a religious place, a monastery perhaps, or a medieval castle, or a large museum and picture gallery. Nobody took any notice. Nobody gave me any information about where to eat, or have a pee, or where the Debating Chamber was. Nothing, except a packet of papers from the Fees Office about money, salaries and tax matters.

For a month I had been without any income, and I had a wife and two young children to keep. Desperate, I put my problem to my CLP, and they generously lent me £40 to tide me over until I got some pay at the end of the month. I had to watch every penny. I didn't know how many new MPs were in the same plight. But I was a pauper at Westminster. With minimal savings, far exceeded by my commitments, my family and I were once again 'financially embarrassed'. So it was like manna from heaven when a Cabinet Minister's Parliamentary Private Secretary invited me to dinner to meet his boss. A date was fixed, and I was thrilled by the prospect of meeting, so soon, one of our leaders, and more importantly, getting a free dinner! I refrain from identifying the characters, except to say that the other new MP who was a guest at that dinner was Horace King, who subsequently became Speaker of the House of Commons.

I enjoyed the dinner in the posh Members' Dining Room. The silver cutlery, the stiffly starched white tablecloths, the large white linen napkins, the beautiful thick carpets and the wall tapestries, all made the perfect upper-class setting for my first foray into such an expensive-looking restaurant.

After the meal was over and the last drop of wine had crossed my lips – calamity! We were asked to pay our own bills separately. I didn't know then that I could put it on the slate, to be paid later. That dinner was going to make a big hole in my £40. It was a long time before I went back to the Members' Dining Room, and I never forgot my first meeting with a Cabinet Minister.

The £1,000 salary had to cover everything. We got no free postage, except when writing to a Government office or to a nationalised industry. There was no free telephone service except within the London area. There was no such facility as an individual telephone, still less an individual private office or desk. When a Member used one of the bank of telephones available, an attendant was waiting outside the booth with a little cash-book, and the Member paid on the spot, in cash. There was no secretarial allowance, no mileage allowance for cars. The latter didn't worry most Labour MPs; they didn't have cars! All meals had to be paid for out of that £1,000, as well as any hotel bills. The only 'perk' was unlimited free travel by rail or by air between Westminster and home, Westminster and constituency, and homee and constituency. Oh! There werre free pens and ink in the Library, and free stationery andd paper clips. There was also a cheap barber, and one or two bathrooms and showers.

But our salaries compared very favourably with the average wages that my miner constituents were earning at that time. Our 'poverty' was non-existent compared to theirs. On the other hand, I was having to keep two homes going. My wife and two young children were still in Huddersfield, and sometimes I didn't see them for two or three weeks at a time. My Fife Party were keen that I should go up there every weekend. They knew that another Election was bound to come soon, so we were all anxious to consolidate our position.

Nobody can quantify the damage that can be done to the fabric of family life in circumstances such as those I now had to face, or, more importantly, the effects on my wife and children. I was having an exciting new adventure, meeting new faces, enjoying social contacts and having new experiences every day. My wife was alone with the two children in a strange town, coping with all the chores of being a housewife and mother. Looking back, I feel ashamed of my own selfishness, and my complete failure to appreciate the harm being done to our family life.

The Palace of Westminster is a maze of rooms and carpeted corridors. Miles and miles of corridors. Hundreds of rooms, large and small. A billiard room and a blacksmith's shop. A shooting gallery, TV rooms, cafeterias and tearooms, a smoking room, and a chess room, countless bars and drinking dens, press galleries and Strangers' rooms, toilets for Members Only, and not too many for others, or specifically for ladies. The Commons is still a gentlemen's club. Statues, busts, paintings, tapestries and policemen are all around you – hundreds of them, staring at you from every corner.

Though much of the Palace was burnt down in 1834, there is every-where an aura of reverence for the old, the decaying and anything that can be called 'traditional'. You learn to love the place like you love an old friend. New Members start off as revolutionaries – especially new *Labour* Members. They want to take new brooms to everything they see; but very quickly they are caught in the cobwebs. They begin to enjoy their status, with those prestigious letters 'MP' after their names. They become good members of 'The Club', as they begin to realise how hard it is to change things – *anything*.

Meanwhile, where to live or lodge was my immediate problem. The kindness of Tom Fraser, the Labour MP for one of the Lanarkshire seats, got me a bed at his digs at Kennington, only a mile's walk across Lambeth Bridge from Westminster. Tom was very helpful. He didn't know me, but he sought me out, took me across to his landlady, and that was that. Tom was a miner before he got to Westminster, and one of the finest men you could wish to know.

But I left that place when I found ants in the sugar bowl at breakfast. I then joined a few Labour MPs shacking up at a bed and breakfast place near Russell Square for 10/6 a night. I wasn't long there before Joan and I decided we must live in London. At least that would mean I could see the family every day.

Eventually, after much searching, I settled for a semi-detached house at Hillingdon in Middlesex. The price was £2,000. It was not a good choice. I didn't know anything about the geography of London; nor did I understand the absurd hours of work at the House of Commons, or much about travelling on the London tube trains.

My family moved down in the middle of 1950, just a few months after I had been elected. We made a little on the sale of our Huddersfield house – enough to put down a small deposit on the Hillingdon place, though we were now saddled with a much bigger mortgage.

I was soon taking packed lunches to the House of Commons. It took me about two hours to get there, by bus and tube, and two hours back at night. And our new house was some distance from the tube station.

Our daughter Sheila started school in Hillingdon in the autumn of 1950, and that gave a little relief to Joan. But life in a London suburb can be very lonely. My hours at Westminster were unconscionably long. Often I got home in the early hours of the morning, and sometimes not at all. Most of my weekends were spent in Scotland. Holidays were out of the question. So too were evenings out with my family. Mine was a life of interest, excitement and hard slog. Joan's was one of drudgery, worry and loneliness. And hanging over us was the threat of another early Election, with all the uncertainty and cost that that would involve.

Parliament was, originally, a place for amateurs. It was never meant for full-time workers. It was built, and run, by the wealthy gentry for the well-heeled club men. It was never meant to be a serious workplace. If it were a factory, it would be condemned as unsafe and insanitary. As a workplace, it is a slum. It *looks* magnificent. The tourists gawp at it, both inside and out. It would make an attractive museum, with lots of strange figures moving round wearing funny clothes, men in wigs and silk stockings, lawyers in gowns and shiny black shoes, all making fortunes out of the incomprehensible laws made by lawyers. The Houses of Parliament have always been choked with lawyers. They are the most powerful, greedy and conservative trade union in the whole world. They know better than anyone else how to feather their nests. Parliament works on a part-time basis, and at ridiculous hours, primarily to fit in with the more lucrative work of its lawyer Members at the law courts in the mornings. No miner, no farmworker, no manual worker, could be a part-timer. Lawyers and journalists are the folk who can most easily combine their work with that of a Member of Parliament.

When I first arrived at the House of Commons in 1950 I was allocated a locker about the same size as the one I had at my school in Washington. That was all. I had my own separate desk at Washington, but none at Westminster. No desk, no telephone, no secretary, no equipment of any kind except glue and ink in the Library – and thousands of books and pamphlets.

So this was the Mother of Parliaments? It was more like a creaking old geriatric. Here lay the power in Britain? Codswallop! The idea that Parliament is sovereign is the most monstrous confidence trick ever perpetrated on the British people. The average MP is little more than a glorified clerk, a welfare officer, and above all, a public relations operator.

When MPs are elected, they need have no qualifications for the job. The job itself is incapable of definition. And once they can say they are MPs, they are their own boss. They have no other. They can work as hard as they like, or not at all. If they want to take a day off, or a week, or a month, they can do so – and many do. The pay still goes on. There is no clocking in or out. Your MP is his or her own master, answerable to nobody except his or her own conscience – and electorate, whenever it has to be faced at an Election. And this is where the MP's skill as a public relations operator comes in. By deft use of the House of Commons Order Paper and skilled manipulation of his local papers, the Press Association, and other media avenues, it is the easiest thing in the world to convince the electors what a great MP they have got. And the MP need never go near the House of Commons for weeks, months, or even years. There's no record of attendance.

The Member is elected to Parliament to exercise his or her judgement on a variety of subjects, from taxation to defence, from abortion to foreign affairs, from pensions to prisons and nuclear bombs. Members

cannot represent *all* their electors on *all* these matters *all* the time. To
please them all is an impossibility. Day after day, the year round, they are
bombarded with leaflets, circulars, pamphlets and books from pressure
groups and vested interests of an infinite variety. Their purpose is to
persuade, bully, cajole, frighten, threaten or blackmail Members into
accepting a point of view. Much of this cascade of paper is merely
informative. Seldom is it sinister or malevolent. Members quickly begin
to sort the corn from the chaff. The massive wastepaper baskets in
the House are one of the most indispensable pieces of furniture in
the building.

On arrival at the House in the morning, the MP's first port of call is
the Members' Post Office, to collect the mail. It is all neatly bundled
up and tied with elastic bands or string. These days, that is the daily
chore of the Member's secretary. Great care must be taken to ensure
that letters from the Member's constituency are dealt with as speedily
as possible; they can literally be matters of life and death. And the MP's
re-election could depend on a few votes won or lost in the handling of
the post. Constituency letters were always my priority.

That made me all the more angry when I saw one Member handle his
post in the most brutal and insensitive way imaginable. He had obviously
been absent for some time. It was equally clear that he had made no
prior arrangements for the collection of his mail. When the mail arrived
on the Post Office desk, it was enormous. Piles of it. Letters, magazines,
circulars, the lot. I began to feel sorry for him. All that backlog of work.
What a slog. Not so. The MP – his first name was John, and he was a
Scottish Member – took one look at it. Then, without a word, he got
one of the biggest wastepaper baskets, and with a sweep of his arm the
whole lot ended up in that receptacle. Unopened, unread. I never again
saw a repetition of such irresponsibility. But the story demonstrates what
power a Member can have over the lives of ordinary citizens. In that
pile of letters there could have been vital documents. Whenever an MP
neglects his constituents, he is weakening the democratic process.

I never forget the information and guidance offered to me by an old
miner colleague from Durham. 'Willie,' he said, 'the poorer the writing,
and the worse the spelling, the more care you should give the letter. The
person who wrote it must have made a great effort to write it at all.'
That was some of the best advice I ever got.

One of the most agreeable characteristics of British Parliamentary
democracy is the close link between an MP and his electors. The relatively
short distances between even the most remote parts of the country and
Westminster, and the reasonable means of communication by road, rail,
air and telephone, ensure that any good MP can keep in very intimate
contact with those who have elected him.

And yet, to the ordinary citizen, Government and decision-making can
still appear remote, cold, incomprehensible and inhumanly bureaucratic.

We now, in the 1990s, have the most centralised system of government in the Western world. There is urgent need for the dispersal of power to the periphery, to the Scots, the Welsh, to the North-East and the South-West, and even for the moving of Parliament itself to a more central region of the United Kingdom.

In those early months as a Member of Parliament, the slummy nature of my workplace did not strike me as forcibly as it did over succeeding years. For the moment I felt threatened and overwhelmed on all sides. Threatened in Fife, by my bank, and by my marriage. All the time choked with paper, letters from everywhere about everything, notices to attend meetings, appeals for money. I was never a fast reader, or writer, and as I had neither typewriter nor secretary, all my letters had to be written by hand. It was a painful process.

Attendance in the House of Commons Chamber itself was urged on new Members by our Party Whips to get the atmosphere, to understand the quaint modes of address and not least, to try to comprehend the procedure.

The Houses of Parliament had been bombed by Hitler and the old House of Commons smashed to the ground. So the Commons began to use the old House of Lords as their Debating Chamber – and that is where I made my Maiden Speech. So I have already spoken in the House of Lords. Our newly rebuilt House of Commons was reopened in November 1950. By common assent it is small. It can seat only about half its total membership of 650. When there is a big debate, the benches are packed. Standing-room only creates an electric atmosphere. Other debates can be conducted in a more intimate and conversational manner, with no need to raise voices. That is the theory, anyway. It sometimes doesn't work that way. The Chamber is a place of many moods. It can be intensely boring or wildly exciting. In seconds, there can be a flare-up, or it can be empty for hours. The complete unpredictability of the place was for me one of its fascinations. No two days, no two minutes, were the same.

I never cease to marvel at how the democratic process of one man, one vote, unscientific and haphazard as it may seem to be, has the uncanny knack of producing 650 men and women of such infinite variety of talent, experience and character.

I only heard Winston Churchill when he was long past his prime. He was, therefore, much less scintillating than Nye Bevan. Bevan was the lion from the Welsh valleys. Churchill was the ageing bulldog who had had his day. In an acute way, those two symbolised the differences between the two main Parties. Bevan, the self-educated miner from South Wales, and Churchill the aristocrat born with a silver spoon in his mouth.

That first Parliament in which I served was not noteworthy, except that it produced for the Tory Party many of its future leaders, such as Ted Heath, Iain Macleod, Enoch Powell and Reg Maudling. Over the years, their fortunes fluctuated wildly. All were to reach Cabinet rank. Heath became Prime Minister, and Powell Minister of Health. Maudling was to become Chancellor of the Exchequer, and Iain Macleod Minister of Health and, later, a liberal Commonwealth Secretary.

As for the Parliamentary Labour Party, it was in turmoil. Personality and policy clashes were as regular as the chimes of Big Ben. Nye Bevan and his supporters vehemently opposed the introduction of NHS prescription charges. I was one of them. I always opposed the imposition of such charges.

There was fierce opposition, too, against the formation of the North Atlantic Treaty Organisation, NATO, initiated by the Labour Foreign Secretary in 1949 as a counter to the Soviet threats to Eastern Europe. The Parliamentary Labour Party had more Foreign Secretaries than any other political party in the world. Everybody seemed to be an expert.

On the other hand, ever since their crushing defeat in 1945, the Tories had set about reconstructing their image. It had to be a 'caring' one, more compassionate, more liberal, more humane. The old wolf had to put on sheep's clothing. This delicate job was put in the hands of R. A. Butler, a smooth manipulator of minds who had a sensitive nose which smelled the need for radical change in his Party. Rab, as he was popularly known, had been responsible for the 1944 Coalition Government's Education Act, designed to widen opportunities for all. Liberal and revolutionary in its concept, it never lived up to the hopes it inspired, and forty years on, our education system is probably the worst in the Western world.

By 1951 the Labour Party had sown the seeds of its own defeat. The leaders of that inspiring 1945 Government were worn out. Some had died or were in poor health. Meetings of the PLP were often like dog fights. The targets for attack were defence spending, the stationing of American troops in the UK, and NHS charges. A new and young Chancellor of the Exchequer, Mr Hugh Gaitskell, was the *bête noire* of the Left. In his 1951 Budget, when he sought to raise £38 million by means of NHS charges, all hell broke loose. Bevan resigned from the Government. He was followed by Harold Wilson and John Freeman, then a Junior Minister.

These seemed to be the death throes of a Government which had lost its way. So, as it turned out, it had.

When 25 October was announced as the date of the 1951 Election, I viewed the prospect with some trepidation. For a start, it meant three weeks without pay. I couldn't even draw unemployment benefit, since I was classed as self-employed. If the worst came to the worst, I could be without a job altogether if I lost the Election. And the thought of being separated from my wife and children for three weeks depressed us all.

10

The 1951 Election

After his humiliating defeat in 1950, Willie Gallacher lost his taste for the fight. He decided to quit – on the grounds of ill health. He was shattered – a broken man. It would be churlish of me not to admit that he had won a lot of friends and admirers in Fife.

From the early 1900s, Gallacher had been in the forefront of 'extremist' left-wing politics in Glasgow. His name was linked with stalwarts like Jimmy Maxton, Manny Shinwell, John Wheatley, Tom Johnston, John Maclean, Davie Kirkwood, Pat Dollan, Keir Hardie, and many others.

Looking back now, I feel it was a great pity that he and I never talked to one another. For whatever differences we may have had, I am convinced we had a lot in common. Like me, he was from a working-class home and loathed the poverty and deprivation that went with it. We both wanted to change the capitalist society that produced these injustices. I believe he also had a religious streak in his make-up, though he never publicly admitted it. Party conflict is too often painted in stark black and white. Far oftener the truth is a dirty shade of grey.

The tattered Communist flag in West Fife was now to be carried by a Mr William Lauchlan, an unknown official in his Party's hierarchy. Meanwhile, the Tories dredged up yet another new candidate, Mr J. P. Fyfe, who disguised his political credentials by posing as a Liberal Unionist.

For my part, I now had sixteen months' experience as a Member of Parliament. I had listened avidly to the top debaters of the day: Churchill, Attlee, Bevan and Bevin, Sir Stafford Cripps, Quintin Hogg and Harold Macmillan, Iain Macleod, and fiery back-bench MPs like Leslie Hale (the fastest speaker at Westminster), and Dick Crossman, who had such a brilliant intellect that he could argue both sides of a case with equal conviction and fluency. There were also firebrands like Bessie Braddock, the big bonnie Labour fighter from Liverpool. I learned a lot of the tricks of my trade by watching and listening to experts like these. I was fast becoming hooked on politics, as incurably as any drug addict.

Whatever the overall national Election result might be, I was confident that we would have a big victory in West Fife. By now our local

Party had built up a magnificent fighting machine. We also had a few hundred pounds in the kitty. More importantly, we had an army of voluntary workers: miners, of course, and their wives and families; a lot of headmasters and schoolteachers; and a number of Church of Scotland ministers, all as radical as Jesus. With such a team, and with morale sky-high, it promised to be a walk-over.

Public meetings were still very much in favour, and for the three weeks I seldom spoke at fewer than three a night. We could afford to have a little fun at our public meeting in the pretty seaside resort of Aberdour, on the north shore of the Firth of Forth. Aberdour was about the only Tory community in the whole of West Fife. So we gave them a treat. We put on our platform a Church of Scotland minister, a headmaster, and myself. We got a packed hall and took a very good collection. We also got a lot of good-humoured heckling. I was fast becoming a cocky platform performer.

The loud-mouthed Mr Lauchlan still felt his Party had a hereditary claim to the West Fife constituency. More especially, the Party felt that Labour having put an Englishman up against their champion, Willie Gallacher, had added insult to injury. The Communists' most eloquent advocate was not Mr Lauchlan but Lawrence Daly, a young coalminer not yet twenty-five. He was a fluent public speaker and was well versed in Scottish culture, especially in the songs and poetry of the national bard, Robbie Burns. He was a good singer, too, and loved his drink. Though a fierce opponent in 1951, he left the Communist Party and became General Secretary of the National Union of Mineworkers, and a good friend of mine. If the local Communist Party had adopted Daly as their candidate in 1951, he would not have won, but he would have put up a much better fight than Lauchlan did.

As things turned out, Lauchlan came a very poor third when the votes were counted. The result was:

> W. W. Hamilton (Lab): 29,195
> J. P. Fyfe (Lib Unionist): 11,038
> W. Lauchlan (Comm):   4,728

That Labour majority of over 18,000 was the biggest in Scotland. It looked as if there had been a straight switch of another 5,000 votes from Gallacher to Hamilton. It should have been crystal clear to the Communists that without the personality of Gallacher they were like a ship without a rudder; and the ship was leaking badly as well.

The overall national result showed how unfair our electoral system is. The Labour Party nationally polled about 700,000 more votes than in 1950, and 230,000 more than the Tories. Yet in the new House of Commons, the Tories had twenty-six more Members, and that was enough to keep them in power for another five years.

The only comfort I got from that result was the fact that for four or more years, I could relax in the knowledge that I had a secure job, and that in that time I could establish myself more securely, both in Fife and at Westminster.

Joan always breathed a sigh of relief when an Election campaign was over. She was always gentle and supportive, but she was never politically-minded and was content to be a good mother and wife.

FOOTNOTE

In the Dartford constituency of South London, a certain Miss M. Roberts was the Conservative candidate. She lost to Labour by over 12,000. We were to hear more of her later.

11

The Long Haul

The Labour Party's strong instincts for hara-kiri continued after 1951 as if nothing had happened. We had more than our share of flat-earthers and self-righteous chest-thumpers. The Tory Party, too, had an ample supply of cavemen and Ancient Britons.

The great difference between the two was that the Labour Party believed in, and practised with great gusto, open bleeding, blood on the carpet, whereas the Tories practised quiet, internal haemorrhage. Tories preferred the stiletto, the gag and the poisoned dart. Labour's weapons were the axe, the fist and the boot.

While the new Tory Government set about massaging its image, and the rules of the House of Commons, the Parliamentary Labour Party was frenetically organising its own bloody civil war. Scapegoats had to be found for that Election defeat. Old scores had to be settled and old wounds reopened. New leaders had to be found, and bodies torn apart. The scent of blood was strong in the air.

Meetings of the PLP were our weekly blood-letting sessions. From 10.30 a.m. until 1 p.m. every Wednesday, tongues lashed, heads were broken and shins kicked – all safe in the knowledge that, officially, the meetings were private and confidential. No minutes were taken and no records kept. The press was excluded, officially. And the PLP had its own unwritten Official Secrets Act.

None of it worked. We were a vast jungle of unrestrained private enterprise. Every man and woman for him or herself. Each one of us had a career to make, a constituency to be nursed or hoodwinked, or both. At all costs an image had to be created. It is a grisly, ugly game, made tolerable by the emergence from time to time of veins of humour, warm streaks of humanity and kindness, often from the most surprising quarters. But the stench of hypocrisy is never far from the Parliamentary scene.

Information from those PLP meetings was freely available to any curious journalist. 'Incorruptible' Labour MPs would leak it without even asking the price of a glass of beer. One time, the meeting was still in progress when the ticker-tape news machine began tapping out the words of wisdom that had been uttered by Mrs Barbara Castle.

The fact was that at that meeting Mrs Castle wasn't even called to speak.

On another occasion, Harold Davies, the voluble little MP for Leek, was letting off steam about atomic bombs. Harold had a heart of gold, and a silver tongue. For an hour, it seemed, he sprayed his captive audience with Doomsday rhetoric. 'The world will be reduced to a heap of ashes. There will be no winners. We have to do something.' All very true. Clem Attlee sat patiently through it all, wreathed in his own pipe tobacco. A man of few words, he rose to the occasion. 'It's a serious business. We'll have to watch it.' End of meeting. Our A-bomb was safe in the little man's hands. I liked and respected Attlee. But it was hard to love him.

The Soviet Union had lost twenty million lives in the 1939–45 war. They were resolved not to let it happen again. Germany was seen by all as the main murderer, and all were determined to keep that nation divided and weak. Military blocs were built up around her, the Warsaw Pact to the East, NATO in the West. NATO meant a continuous military presence of American forces in Europe, including Britain. And American submarines, armed with nuclear weapons, were to be established in British ports, notably in Scotland.

The Labour Party had to have a policy on these matters. The 'Left' was showing off its virility by making threatening anti-American noises. And people like me, with pacifist tendencies, felt very unhappy with all the rearmament going on so soon after a major war.

So what were we to do? Well, we would hold some PLP meetings. Motions would be put and debated. Something would be done. The evening before one of those meetings, I was in the Members' Cafeteria having my fish and chips with Cyril Bence. Cyril was an engineer, a Soft Left Member for a west of Scotland constituency. A benign Member, not easily diverted from the path of righteousness. Suddenly we saw Mrs Castle approaching. She knew her man. In my presence she put a piece of paper in front of Cyril, saying it was a Motion she was putting before the PLP the next morning which she hoped would unite the Party. 'Read it, Cyril, and if you agree with it I hope you can add your name.' Cyril read and signed. I was ignored. She knew me too.

Now I know that politics is often the art of compromise – sensible so long as the end product is credible. I asked Cyril if he would let me into the secret Castle magic. He agreed. The idea was simple. Those American nuclear submarines in Scottish waters would have American captains. We were to insist that the majority of the crew in each case should be British, and that it could outvote the captain if he threatened to press the nuclear button. I swear by Almighty God that this is the truth, and near enough the whole truth.

Perhaps when she drafted that motion Barbara was thinking of the block votes at Labour Party Conferences. Anyway, it was hooted down with derision at the meeting. But Barbara's image as a left-wing intellectual was preserved. She went from strength to strength. Her facility with words never left her. For my part, I was more interested in domestic bread-and-butter matters. Especially with the workings of the NHS. I was getting constant requests from constituents asking for help with the free supply of things like dentures and spectacles, and one weekend I visited an old man who wanted a new pair of glasses. When I saw what he was wearing, I said I would get him a pair, on condition that he would give me the pair he already had.

I have still got those glasses. They are a reminder of what *was*. Let me try and describe them. The rims are cheap metal. The lenses are plain glass, and one of them is cracked in two places. One of the arms consists of a safety pin and bits of string. The other consists of two safety pins, a length of what looks like fuse wire, and string. The glasses worn by that old man are still kept in the same little box in which he handed them over to me. I got far more satisfaction out of dealing with human problems like that than with getting all worked up about German rearmament or NATO's defences.

There were lighter sides to proceedings in the House of Commons itself.

Mrs Bessie Braddock was a heavyweight, physically and politically, with arms and legs like tree trunks. Bessie was merciless with the Tories and a darling to her working folk. She sat on the Front Bench below the gangway, which was as near as she could get to the Tory Front Bench. In the 1950 Parliament that meant she was within three yards of an old Tory gentleman called Lord Winterton (I think it was an Irish title). His Lordship never said much, but he felt threatened by the 'Bolshie' Labour Government. He was very tall, at least six feet six, and as thin as a beanpole. He had a rubicund complexion and a severely clipped grey military moustache. When His Lordship erupted, he muttered in an almost demented manner, and began to cross and recross his matchstick legs like some human windmill out of control.

Bessie was within spitting distance. 'Sit still, you old bugger,' was her muttered repartee – muttered so that Mr Speaker couldn't hear, but loud enough to reach Winterton. I enjoyed that immensely. Over the years I realised that incidents like that kept you from going insane.

My domestic problems were getting no easier. Our expenses in London rapidly increased. I had to supplement my Parliamentary salary. My only way of doing so was to seek part-time teaching, and that I did – for several years. In 1954 we were able to buy a much better house – in leafy Beckenham – for £3,000. It was a *Tory* area, however, and my children had to go to *their* schools. When my daughter Sheila failed the eleven-plus, she had to go to a school where no opportunity was given to take O levels. I had a row with the local education authority about that, and after some acerbic correspondence I asked the then Tory Minister for Education, Edward Boyle, to intervene on my behalf. The upshot of it was that Sheila got to an LCC comprehensive school just down the road, and eventually got academic qualifications good enough for University Medical School, though she ended up training to be a nurse at Guy's Teaching Hospital. Sheila was just another example of a child dubbed a failure at eleven by that damnable system of selection.

COMMITTEE WORK AT THE HOUSE OF COMMONS

In 1951 there were few select, that is, all-Party *investigative* committees which could probe in depth and at length the spending of Government Departments.

The Public Accounts Committee was the oldest and the most powerful. Some authorities said it was greatly feared by Government Accounting Officers. They certainly respected it, and so, I think, did all other senior civil servants who were called before it for cross-examination. By convention, the PAC Chairman is a senior MP from the Opposition benches, usually a former Minister with Treasury experience who knows his way about Whitehall. The PAC is assisted by an independent official called, in my day, the Comptroller and Auditor General. He had a large staff of experts, though few were actually accountants. Their job was to audit the expenditure of all Government Departments, and if they found irregularities to report them to the PAC for further examination. As a result the PAC produces, still, very powerful and well-informed reports which are presented to the Commons for debate. Unfortunately, the House itself is too often uninterested, and the PAC is lucky if it gets more than one day each year for such debates, and even then the attendance is seldom more than that of the Committee members themselves.

THE ESTIMATES COMMITTEE

The EC was much larger that the PAC, but less prestigious, much less feared and much less respected, primarily because it had no expert advice comparable to the Comptroller and Auditor General. Though I sat on the EC for a number of years, and in 1964 became the Chairman, the work was not very effective. All it could do was to examine the estimated expenditure of each Government Department, from Agriculture to the Foreign Office to Defence. It was farcical. Total Government expenditure is thousands of millions of pounds. On defence alone it was over £8,000 million in 1980. By 1985 it was over £17,000 million. Nobody could control such vast sums. In the late 1940s, Mr Attlee could spend over £100 million on developing our own atomic bomb, and nobody ever noticed.

It remains a constant problem for all Governments. To try to control

such astronomical sums spent by so many different bodies is like trying
to drain the North Sea with a teaspoon.

In the 1980s there was a burgeoning growth of select committees,
roughly one for each Government Department. It is perhaps too early
to judge their effectiveness, though there is little doubt that with the
introduction of the TV cameras, plus the greater staff given to the
committees, much more notice is taken of their reports – by the media
and by the House. To that extent, the experiment must be judged a
success, though whether it has resulted in more effective control of total
public expenditure is debatable.

The extension of select committee activities has meant a significant
increase in the workload of those MPs who choose to serve on them. It
also means there is a greater problem of actual physical accommodation.
The buildings were not meant to accommodate such full-time workers.
Over the last thirty or forty years, regular extensions have been tacked
on. Looking at the Houses of Parliament from the outside, nothing
seems to have changed. But on the inside, MPs and their staff have
been treated little better than battery hens. As long as they are prepared
to tolerate such conditions, and as long as the Government of the day
is determined to impose them, or do too little to improve them, control
over the Government by Parliament will become less and less efficient.
The Houses of Parliament as a workplace are no more than a workers'
slum, and a disgrace to any modern democracy.

12

Two More Elections,
Two More Labour Defeats

Any Prime Minister has the potential power of a dictator. Even with an overall majority in the House of Commons of little more than a handful, he or she can exercise frightening powers of patronage which reach into every corner of public life.

Not the least of the PM's powers is that of deciding the date of the next Election – within the five-year maximum life of any Parliament.

A few weeks after taking over from Winston Churchill, Sir Anthony Eden decided to have his first Election as Prime Minister on 26 May 1955. So, I was to fight my fourth Election in ten years. I was getting to be an old hand. Quite frankly, I feared the worst for the country as a whole. I was getting a wee bit smug about West Fife, but it was not typical.

Members of the Commons had received a pay increase of £250 in May 1954, and I had recorded in my diary on Tuesday, 1 September of that year that my bank balance was £21. Whatever else was happening regarding my membership of London's best club, it wasn't making me rich.

In West Fife, I was glad to see that my Communist opponent was to be Mr W. Lauchlan. The roaring lamb yet again to the slaughter, I thought. The Tory candidate was to be Norman Wylie, a barrister from Edinburgh. Yet another lamb for the chop, though Mr Wylie was to become a Scottish Tory MP, to be followed as surely as night follows day by elevation to an eminent Tory judgeship. My diary records that from May 9th to 26th I spoke at fifty-five public meetings, in addition to attending other functions, such as the inauguration of Councillor John Sneddon as the very first Labour Convenor of Fife County Council. John had been a coalminer all his life. A passionate teetotaller and a man of complete integrity, he had become one of my staunchest friends.

When I had first become a Member of Parliament, I was under some pressure to live in Fife. My wife and I were not entirely hostile to the idea. Since we were then living in Huddersfield, it was plain that the triangular circuit of Westminster, Fife and Huddersfield was, from everybody's point of view, inconvenient. John Sneddon was at that time Chairman of the County Housing Committee, and most of the houses in the county were either owned by the Coal Board and occupied by miners, or owned and rented by the county council. There were long waiting lists for these houses, and John Sneddon made it very plain to us that we could not expect any favoured treatment as far as our housing problem was concerned. 'You will have to try and buy one,' he said.

We looked around, but we had no money to buy. Over 95 per cent of all the houses in Fife were NCB or county council property. We got no help from Councillor Sneddon – and I admired him for that. He was incorruptible. He carried it to absurd lengths. Some years later, he was appointed Vice-Chairman of the Glenrothes New Town Corporation by virtue of his county council position. The appointment carried a salary. John refused it. I argued with him about that, on the grounds that he made it difficult for a possible successor who might be just as sincere but who would need the salary on account of family commitments. John was not persuaded. On another occasion he carried his teetotal principles to laughable lengths. Prince Philip was visiting the county and a lunch was laid on by the county council. John Sneddon decreed that the drink would be – *water*! I had a belly laugh at that.

For the rest of my life, I dearly loved and respected John Sneddon and all his family.

Our own result in that Election was almost as predicted:

> W. W. Hamilton: 26,849
> N. Wylie: 10,638
> W. Lauchlan: 5,389

Joan spent the last two days of the campaign with me in Fife. She didn't mind watching the votes being counted, because she knew that by then all the shouting and abuse of her husband would be over – and she enjoyed being on the winning side!

Overall, the Labour vote fell by about 1.5 million, and the Tory majority in the Commons grew to fifty-nine, enough for another five years of Conservative Government.

But it was clear that as soon as the new Parliament met, the PLP would begin where it had left off. We had another four to five years to get our act together.

I was never one of the extreme Left. In fact, I have always deplored the classification of MPs as 'Left', 'Right', 'Middle', 'Centre Left' or 'Centre Right'. No man of independence should allow himself to be wrapped up like a parcel and pigeon-holed. Alas, there are some who think, still, that it is a sign of virility to be 'Hard Left', or 'Real' Socialist, or some other mark of the genuine article. My father used to drum into me the vital importance of unity and loyalty to the Party. In the pits he never ceased to preach that the bosses were always seeking ways of dividing the men. It's the same with the media and the Tory Party today. By creating or exploiting splits in the enemy's ranks, your own position is strengthened by default. That was largely the source of Mrs Thatcher's good fortune in the 1980s.

POST-1955

Once more, the Labour Party began its post-Election inquest, under the eagle eye of Harold Wilson and a small committee.

Their report revealed a 'penny-farthing machine' inappropriate for the twentieth century. But the Party didn't seem to be interested in organisational problems and nothing much happened. Policies and personalities were more interesting. On 7 December 1955, Clem Attlee resigned as Party Leader. The decision had been expected. To be Leader of the Labour Party is one of the toughest jobs in politics.

Attlee had been Leader throughout the war years, and a prominent member of the Coalition Government. From 1945 he had been Leader of the most radical Government of the twentieth century. I was only able to observe him in his declining years. It was an unnerving experience. To watch him poring over the county cricket scores in the Members' Tea Room over a cup of tea, or to spy him scurrying for a London tube train late in the evening, it was hard for anyone to know that the modest little man with the briefcase had been a major force in British history for so many years. He had led the Labour Party to the pinnacle of its power and achievements. His leadership was a watershed in its fortunes. I was glad I was there, if only to watch the closing chapters.

There wasn't an obvious Crown prince, though there were many pretenders from among a wealth of talent and ambitions. Nye Bevan, Herbert Morrison and Hugh Gaitskell seemed to be the front runners. All had a lot to commend them. In terms of self-confidence, there was nothing to choose between them. Being a young man myself I felt we needed a younger man. I consulted with my local Party, but they never tried to instruct me on who to vote for. As the leadership decision was then left entirely in the hands of MPs, local Party members were content to air their views to me without taking a vote. They trusted me to make a judgement in the interests of the Party as a whole. They felt instinctively that since the Leader must be a Member of Parliament, what could be more sensible than to leave the matter to the MPs, themselves elected by the people. Twenty-five years later that process was claimed to be a kind of Parliamentary élitism.

Just a few days before Christmas 1955, the PLP chose its new Leader. The vote was more decisive than most of us had predicted, with Gaitskell getting 157 votes, Bevan seventy, and Morrison a derisive forty. When the result was declared, Morrison got up and left the meeting. He resigned as Deputy Leader, and from the Party's National Executive Committee. It was the end of a truly remarkable record of service to the Labour Party. In my younger days, Herbert Morrison had been one of my father's heroes. In the London County Council, Morrison did more good for the people of London than almost anybody has ever done before or since. And yet there he was, thrown out by his Parliamentary colleagues like a pair of old socks. My heart ached for him. Party politics can be ruthless and cruel.

The ageing former Welsh miner, Jim Griffiths, became Deputy Leader. He was a loveable gentleman. He would have made a great bishop, if only he had been English. As it was, with Gaitskell and Griffiths in charge, and fiery Bevan not in the best of health, the Party seemed to be embarked on smoother waters.

Our Labour Leader had been elected by democratic processes. Anthony Eden had emerged as the successor to Churchill by means of what Iain Macleod later bitterly called the 'Magic Circle'. He had seemed tailor-made for the succession. Middle-aged, handsome and a foreign affairs 'expert', Eden appeared destined for an illustrious Premiership. Within twenty-four months, he was out and broken, out of the House of Commons and in the House of Lords as Lord Avon. So do the mighty fall. Books have been written on the Suez Canal fiasco. It was Britain's last attempt to behave as if we were a colonial power to be reckoned with.

In a nutshell, President Nasser had nationalised the Suez Canal. Eden put in British troops to teach Nasser a lesson, and the House of Commons was in a turmoil. Gaitskell at first made an ill-considered speech supporting Eden and comparing Nasser to Mussolini. Within a few days he had made a smart about-turn. In my own Party in Fife, the Suez affair revealed more than a streak of jingoism, and a few thought those 'wogs' ought to be taught a lesson. Not for the first, or last, time, the intervention of the United States proved decisive. Their opposition to our adventure, plus the divisions within the Tory Government itself and the threat to our currency, compelled an ignominious withdrawal of troops. It also took a deadly toll on Eden's health, and on 9 January 1957, he resigned.

On this occasion, there was no obvious heir apparent. We in the Labour Party watched the Tory 'Magic Circle' in operation with some amusement, although it seemed more like a rather high-class secret society. Anyway, Harold Macmillan emerged as the victor over R. A. Butler. I was almost glad I wasn't involved in that kind of skulduggery. I was still a humble back-bench Member of Parliament who had the horrible feeling of impotence; unable to influence in any way the flow of events on the world scene, or to make any worthwhile contribution to the solution of problems nearer home. At Westminster I was a cypher, however important I might feel in Fife.

The most I could claim in those early days was that I had a ringside seat at the national political theatre. There were some brilliant actors there who could excite, amuse, deceive, convince and educate. There were just as many who could empty the Chamber faster than a bomb scare.

I could not claim that I had yet made a memorable speech on any of the great issues of the day. For a start, it was very difficult to take part in those big debates. There always seemed to be a horde of self-styled experts on every subject. It has long been the practice for Members to write little notes to the Speaker well before a debate, staking a claim to speak, often on the grounds of special knowledge. Or, alternatively, to approach the Speaker while he is in the Chair during the debate and make threatening noises. The myth that Members play a game of chance over 'catching the Speaker's eye', either in debate or even during Question Time, is just that, a myth. Not only that, but in all the big debates there are favourite Members who receive preferential treatment. It is assumed that all ex-Ministers, however junior, have more knowledge than the wisest other Member. Likewise, it is assumed that all Privy Counsellors, however thick, must be given priority at Question Time or in debate over all other Members. To add insult to injury, spokesmen for minority Parties, like the Ulster Unionists, the Scottish Nationalists, their Welsh counterparts, the Liberals, and latterly the Social Democrats, all claim privileges in debate not available to the ordinary foot soldiers. And that is why I looked for other ways of making my presence felt. One of those avenues was the daily Question Hour. Another was the daily half-hour Adjournment debate, which was balloted for. And then there were the select committees.

I threw myself into all three activities. In the 1950s I asked a large number of questions at a time when there were almost no restrictions on the number any Member could ask. It has always been good fun, but never very productive. Question Time in the House of Commons is a charade, a kind of *Children's Hour*. It does little good or harm to anybody. Like the monarchy, it survives on myths. The claim that Question Time calls the Government to account is just a joke in bad taste. I think I could go to the Commons next week, arm myself with any Minister's Civil Service brief, go into the Chamber, and field his questions with no bother at all. And anybody with an average IQ could do the same.

Similar cynical observations could then have been made about the work of our Select Committee on Estimates. I worked on it for many years, and we did dig out a lot of useful information. But so far as controlling anything or anybody was concerned, it was about as useful as attacking a battleship with a few leaking rowing boats. It was hard work, but utterly futile; nobody took much notice of what you were doing.

AN OVERSEAS JAUNT

One of the most valued perks of being a Member of Parliament is the chance of seeing the world.

Prior to 1950, I had been to foreign lands only by courtesy of HM

Armed Forces. With those magical letters, 'MP' after my name, the world was wide open, although I didn't realise it at the outset. As with so many things in Parliament, I was as innocent as a child. Within the Palace of Westminster there are many doors to be opened. Two of them are the ones marked 'CPA' and 'IPU'. 'CPA' stands for the Commonwealth Parliamentary Association, 'IPU' for the Inter-Parliamentary Union. The one provides tours within the Commonwealth, the other for the rest of the world. Members are not forced to join, but most do. For a nominal annual subscription, a Member is entitled to apply for any of the trips, whenever they are publicised, which is almost every week.

My trip to West Africa began on 22 February 1956, and ended on 29 March. Looking back on it now, I am deeply ashamed of what I did. For five weeks I deserted Joan and our two young children. I left them in a strange South-East London suburb, hundreds of miles away from any of their friends. Joan was left to cope alone with the children and all the household chores, and without a car. Worse, I had arranged for all my Parliamentary correspondence to be forwarded to my home. Without any secretarial assistance, not even a typewriter, and with no home help, Joan was on her own. She never complained. But it should never have happened.

These overseas visits are a mixture of jaunting, education, and hard work. In our five weeks in West Africa we visited Nigeria, the Gold Coast (now Ghana), Sierra Leone and the Gambia.

Local politicians and British officials were anxious that we should see as much as possible, so timetables were crammed. We were often out of bed by 5 a.m. and buzzing around until after midnight. In the tropical heat, with no air-conditioning and few bathrooms, I often longed for some Scottish weather and hospitality.

After five weeks of buffeting in stifling conditions, travelling on dusty tracks and meeting hundreds of tribal chiefs, Governor-Generals, local functionaries, of visiting timber mills, banana plantations, schools, a leper colony, palm-oil mills and projects like new river dams, bridges and ports, as well as a coalmine in eastern Nigeria, I felt utterly exhausted.

The coalmine was a drift one – a tunnel driven into a hillside. The native Nigerian miners walked to work in their bare feet and were almost naked. The humidity was a killing 100 per cent. We sweated even as we just sat there. How men can work in such a hell is a mystery. And the wages were £6 a month. 'Very expensive labour,' said the Scottish manager. 'You see,' he explained, 'these men will work one, perhaps two, shifts a week. The rest of the time they want to be out in the glorious sunshine, hunting, fishing and farming.' Very wise miners, I thought. And they probably didn't think they were poor.

I learned a lot about the mind-boggling problems of the developing world. I also began to grasp the meaning of real poverty.

I had the feeling that there was some arrogance and stupidity in the way we were attempting to impose *our* methods of government, *our* definitions of democracy, *our* ideas of economic development, even *our* standards of behaviour, on people with their own culture, their own history, their own tribal divisions. There are better civilisations than those based on urban squalor and overcrowded, evil-smelling cities with large pockets of homelessness and deprivation. The old folk in any African village are looked after far better than they are in 'rich' Britain, or in the wealthy USA. Nor is the quality of life best measured by the size of a nation's gross domestic product.

After the African trip, it was depressing to find that back at Westminster the Parliamentary Labour Party was still as fractious as ever. 'We are a broad church' was too often the excuse given for our constant bickering. Hugh Gaitskell, dubbed as 'a dessicated calculating machine' by Nye Bevan, tried for years up to the 1959 Election to paper over the cracks and to give the Party some semblance of unity. I warmly supported Gaitskell's efforts, but the unity was never more than skin-deep.

And meanwhile, Harold Macmillan, as slippery an operator as ever occupied 10 Downing Street, was busily erasing from our memories the tragedy of Suez. I disliked his polished humbug and hypocrisy. In the House of Commons and in the country he behaved like a smooth second-hand car salesman selling clapped-out Fords as if they were Rolls-Royces. But one of his shrewdest appointments was the promotion of Iain Macleod to the Cabinet as Minister of Labour. As a debater, Macleod was one of the best. His first job, as Minister of Health in 1952, had been his reward for one of the most devastating speeches I have ever heard in the House of Commons. It was on 27 March, on an NHS Bill, and we in the Labour Party regarded the NHS as our most beautiful baby. In Tory eyes, the carving up of Nye Bevan was one of the greatest demolition jobs they could have hoped to witness. For me it was sickening, yet awe-inspiring. If Macleod had not been dogged by ill health, he would probably have become Leader of the Tory Party, though his middle-class background might have robbed him of the top prize.

FAMILY BEREAVEMENT

On 7 August 1957, I had an urgent call to go to Sunderland Royal Infirmary, where my mother was dangerously ill. She barely recognised me when I got there. My brothers were keeping an all-night vigil. Mother was obviously being heavily sedated and slept almost continuously. One brief waking moment she whispered to me, 'Nae wonder Nye Bevan went mad.' They were her last words to me – a reference to Nye Bevan's fight to preserve his beloved Health Service. It was a fitting epitaph. Mother died peacefully on 11 August. I wondered if this might have been an act of well-intentioned euthanasia. We never asked the doctors. Cancer is a fearful disease. We knew that those wonderful doctors and nurses treated our mother with the usual diligence and humanity that we all expect. If that is euthanasia, I would be happy to leave it at that.

One day I hope that someone will write a book about women like my mother. She was a saintly slave. I doubt whether in all her relatively short life she enjoyed more than a few days of complete happiness and security. Morning, afternoon and night, seven days a week, she administered to her husband and family like a full-time guardian angel. Cooking, washing, cleaning, shopping, baking every loaf of bread we ate, washing and ironing every shirt we wore, toiling endlessly on a shoestring budget of less than £2 a week. In the summer her weekly pleasure was to walk to the Philadelphia cricket ground on Saturday afternoon, to watch one or other of her sons play cricket, though her sight was so poor she could hardly see anything that was going on.

Looking back now, I often feel that I did not sufficiently repay my parents for all they did for me. For the first eighteen years of my life I had lived in the family home, and in our rough-and-ready way we had been a closely knit family. Whether we liked it or not, physically we had never been far away from one another. We had all been slaves to our scruffy environment. As a 'deputy' at the local pit or pits, my father had had three topics of conversation: his family, the pit, and politics. My mother had always been very thin, plagued by poor health and even poorer eyesight.

But from 1936 onwards, I never lived in the family home. In the early 1940s my father was left a small sum of money by an old aunt and with that he decided to buy his own little house, which actually had its own grotty little bathroom. Over the course of the next twenty years, I visited that house only intermittently.

To be quite honest, the tensions within our family, as well as the squalor of the environment, were in such stark contrast to my lifestyle at university, as an Army officer, and later as a Member of Parliament, that I became more and more alienated. Yet I knew that all my family were very proud of the progress that I had made; and whilst I was in Sheffield, most of them made trips to share the pleasures of my new lifestyle.

When I became a Member of Parliament, my family's joy and pride were unbounded, although only rarely could they afford to visit me at Westminster. When my mother died, I felt she had savoured the full joy of seeing her family prosper in ways she had never thought possible.

Such women find no place in the history books. God rest her soul.

A few months later, just a few days before Christmas, there was another disaster, this time at the Lindsay colliery in Kelty in my constituency. Nine men were killed and eleven injured. I went there as quickly as I could and visited the bereaved.

But life went on.

1957 had been for me a traumatic year, full of drama and a lot of unhappiness.

1958

1958 saw the Parliamentary Labour Party at its fiercest. The nuclear defence debate sizzled. The Campaign for Nuclear Disarmament had been launched in February and there was an upsurge of moral support for the unilateral renunciation of our manufacture and possible use of nuclear bombs. The PLP split into at least three factions: the pros, the cons, and the don't knows. There was nothing to be ashamed of about that situation. Most people are perplexed and puzzled by the arguments on nuclear weapons, and I had a contempt for anybody who thought it was a simple case of yes or no. Having been a pacifist and conscientious objector in the early part of the war, I had been glad after I joined the forces that I was never called on to a fire a gun in anger. I have always had the greatest suspicions of the motives of the defence industry lobby, yet I could never join the unilateralists. Successive Election results seemed to confirm that the British electorate did not like the idea of Britain throwing away her bombs unilaterally, so I have consistently been on the side of the multilateral disarmers.

However, I took no active part in this campaign because early in the year a strange and painful illness kept me away from the House of Commons for ten weeks. Large red blotches appeared on my legs below the knee and had the effect of completely immobilising me. It was like permanent pins and needles, and I was unable to stand on my feet, much less walk. My own doctor was unable to diagnose just what it was, so he got me into Lewisham Hospital in South-East London. There I was told the only cure was complete rest. I still don't know what it was or how it went, but it kept me out of Parliament until mid-April. I informed the local press in Fife of the situation, and assured my constituents that my good wife would attend to all their letters.

THE 1959 ELECTION

Politics have taught me how not to cry. And how never to be surprised. Human nature is as unpredictable as our weather. So it proved in the Election of 1959.

Harold Macmillan called for an Election in October, at a time when both major Parties had some fragile semblance of unity and when the memory of Suez was beginning to fade. Mac's timing was uncannily astute. He gauged the innate jingoism of the electorate much more accurately than we in the Labour Party did.

As a Party we had nothing to fear in Fife. The Tories had a young, pink-faced farmer as their candidate, a Mr Alex Buchanan-Smith. The Communists again put up Willie Lauchlan, no doubt because they could not think of anybody else. And there was a newcomer – Lawrence Daly, whom I had first met during the 1951 Election. Daly described himself as a member, probably the only member, of the Fife Socialist League. In his youth, he had been the rising star of the Communist Party. He deserted them, I think, when the Soviet Union sent its 'people's' tanks to invade Hungary while we were invading Egypt in 1956. Daly was to appear on my platform in the 1964 Election – but for the moment he was parading the streets of Fife, dressed in his pit gear, complete with pit lamp. That caused much rude comment among the miners who supported me. 'We get out of that bloody gear as soon as we can,' they said. But Lawrence thought his gimmick was a good one. At any rate, when the votes were counted he got more than Lauchlan, and saved his £150 deposit. I savoured my result.

> W. W. Hamilton (Lab):　25,554
> A. Buchanan-Smith (Con):　11,257
> L. Daly (Fife Soc League):　4,886
> W. Lauchlan (Com):　　　3,826

My share of the vote was, at 56.2 per cent, down on the 1951 and 1955 percentages, but we in Fife were well satisfied, not least because of the annihilation of the Communist Party as an electoral threat. From the 21.6 per cent Gallacher had got in 1950, there had been a drop to 8.4 per cent in 1959. And even that was not the bottom of the barrel. In the 1970 Election, the Communist candidate was to get a minuscule 1.7 per cent of all the votes cast.

But when I heard that the Tories had gained an overall majority of almost 100, I found myself almost weeping with rage. I had thought that after eight years of Tory Government, and with the Suez fiasco to account for, we would win comfortably. It was a bitter lesson. The headline in *The Scotsman* on Saturday, 10 October 1959 was to become a familiar one over the next thirty years: 'Tories must take action on unemployment situation'. They didn't, and they still haven't.

Meanwhile, I had the personal consolation, such as it was, of knowing that I had another five years' lease. My family was growing up, and getting more expensive to keep. My salary, at £1,750, including £750 expenses, was a little better than the £1,000 I had got in 1950. With a mortgage to pay, and four hungry mouths to feed, I still had to keep on with my part-time teaching in London schools and colleges. Nevertheless, we decided to buy our first car – on hire purchase. It was big enough to transport the four of us down to the South Coast at weekends – to Brighton, Hastings, Worthing and Eastbourne – as well as to the many picturesque little villages and towns in Kent, Surrey and Sussex. It was trips like these which brought home to me how much we were divided as a nation. Culturally, commercially, socially and politically, my constituency in Fife was as different from the smug gentility and relative prosperity of Kent and Sussex as a Scottish coalminer is from a wealthy gent in the Surrey stockbroker belt.

As a family we had other problems thrust upon us. Living in a semi-detached house can be good. We had been quite happy for five years – until we got new neighbours. They were a young couple, with two very young children. They soon showed us how quickly a quiet, peaceful heaven can be turned into a noisy hi-fi hell. The aural assault went on non-stop every weekend. My attempts at reasoning were met with verbal abuse. I took legal advice from a kindly Labour solicitor. 'The price of living in the London sardine tin,' he said, 'is that you might not get on with the sardines next to you. To try to seek a remedy through the courts is costly and risky. It would be far cheaper for one of you to move.' So we moved – to a more expensive house near the pretty village of Dulwich, about six miles from the centre of London. It was a four-bedroomed detached house for which we were to pay £6,000. It was a heavy millstone to put round our necks. But over the years it proved to be a sound investment. How lucky those folk are who can afford their own house, and to keep up their payments to the moneylenders. I have been fortunate in both respects, though it might be said that by these activities – buying a car and then buying my own house in London rather than in Fife – I was isolating myself more and more from my electors by becoming a part of that alien culture in the South of the kingdom of which I have just been complaining. I accept that that danger was there, and had been since I first decided in 1950 that the family home must be in London, where my work was from Monday to Friday, and not in Fife, where I would be spending most of my weekends. For Members of Parliament representing constituencies in or near London, these decisions about family abode are easy to take. For provincial Members it is much harder. Whatever decision a Scottish Member takes about whether to make his home in London or north of the border, he faces long periods of separation from his wife and family. The price of being an MP is paid by his wife and children. It can be very high. Sometimes I have wondered whether it was worthwhile.

13

A Trip to the USSR

In July 1960 I was on the first ever IPU delegation to the USSR.

We arrived in Moscow on 16 July. Our hotel was huge, but almost deserted. My room, too, was large. I had no bathroom plug. It was explained that any letters written had to be handed in, unsealed, to the desk. It was an unhygienic habit in the West to seal letters by licking.

The very first morning after our arrival I was leaving my bedroom for breakfast when I bumped into Willie Lauchlan with his wife and family – the self-same Mr Lauchlan who had been my Communist opponent in the previous three elections in Fife. Few words were spoken. Mr Lauchlan was probably there for his brainwashing and indoctrination course!

We, too, were quickly subjected to the absurd propaganda treatment. Within twenty-four hours we had visited the USSR Exhibition of Economic Achievement, a permanent display of the Soviet 'miracle'. We went to have a look at the Kremlin, where we were offered fifty roubles for £1. (We had got a 'favourable' rate of twenty-eight.) We had been assigned a vivacious female interpreter, whom we were asked to call Elizabeth. She was a dedicated Communist who spoke perfect English, and she was to trail us everywhere. Immediately, I had the uncanny feeling of being an enemy.

It was a funny but depressing experience to have to listen continuously to the incessant drip of the Party propaganda from Elizabeth, an obviously intelligent and well-educated young woman. One story illustrates the point.

We were taken to a big soccer match in the magnificent Lenin Stadium in Moscow. It was bigger than Wembley, and most of the enormous crowd were seated. It was obviously a needle game between two Army teams, the home side Moscow, the visitors from Kiev. Norman Pentland, a bluff Durham miner, and I sat either side of Elizabeth. Very soon the atmosphere was electric – like a Celtic–Rangers match in Glasgow. The visitors from Kiev were getting the upper hand, and a few of the crowd invaded the pitch to attack the referee. They were beaten off by what looked like armed policemen. After about half an hour, Kiev were awarded a penalty, and scored. The crowd went berserk. The pitch was invaded. The referee disappeared among thousands of

Moscow supporters. After some minutes it was announced over the loudspeakers that the game had been abandoned. Elizabeth was very embarrassed, and when Norman Pentland innocently asked, 'Why did that happen?', the faithful little Commie replied, 'Well, Mr Pentland, it just goes to show that the people's justice must prevail.' Elizabeth didn't understand why we roared with laughter.

On 19 July we flew to Georgia, en route to Armenia in the South. The Georgians love their wine and vodka, and they plied us with it from the minute we arrived. At our dinner that same evening, after an hour of almost compulsory wine-drinking, we found ourselves at dinner with glasses already full of neat vodka. Each member of the delegation was asked to drink a toast to someone or something, and each time the whole glass of vodka had to be emptied. 'Bottoms up,' was the call. I was never a drinker, ever since that first wartime experience of Devonshire cider, and I felt cornered. I had drunk two vodkas and already felt unwell. It was my turn to toast. The Soviet leaders in Moscow were trying to run an anti-drink campaign, so I tried to follow their example by proposing we should drink a toast in soda water. There was a roar of consternation and disapproval. Elizabeth, sitting next to me, said it was an insult to my hosts, and I must not do it. So I yielded. It was vodka again. I was ill. I was led out to a verandah. Soon I was joined by Norman. Norman liked his beer, but was not used to vodka-swilling. Before I passed out I just heard him say, 'They've got me, too, Bill.'

I must have been blind drunk, and I must have been violently sick. I can't remember getting on to a plane to Yerevan in Armenia. I can't remember who put me to bed. I only know that I had the most awful hangover the next morning, when my suit was returned to me, beautifully cleaned and pressed. A Tory member of the delegation had suffered too. It was something about which I was deeply ashamed, and angry. Someone at our British Embassy at Moscow later told me that this was a practice often used on visitors by the Georgians. I never told my wife, or anyone else, about this incident. I had never been drunk in my life before – and never since.

We had a delightful weekend at Sochi, one of the beautiful holiday resorts on the Black Sea. We were advised (not by the Communists) that all the holiday-makers were chosen from 'good workers' (and good Party members) and favoured military personnel. Everything was planned for us. Even when sunbathing on the beach, there were attendants *ordering* folk into the shade if they seemed to be overdoing their exposure to the sun. And when we went shopping Elizabeth insisted on coming too, staying with us every minute. Not that there was much to buy, except for very good, and very cheap, gramophone records of classical and ballet music.

In Armenia we were taken to a collective farm – a 'show-piece'. We had a look into the workers' canteen at lunch-time. It was astounding.

The place was full of millions of flies. The atmosphere was black with them – but nobody seemed to mind. When we went to an office to talk to the bosses, it was so hot that they tried to close the shutters on the windows. One fell off.

One evening we were taken to a wonderfully entertaining puppet show. Highly professional. At the interval I wanted to go to the toilet and couldn't understand when Elizabeth did her best to discourage me. But such calls cannot respond to Communist ideology. When I went, I understood Elizabeth's anxiety to stop me, for, suddenly, out of a beautiful theatre and a professional show, I found myself in almost total darkness, standing ankle-deep in urine-laden mud alongside scores of weak-bladdered Bolsheviks.

These striking contrasts constantly impressed themselves on me. Driving in from Moscow airport to the city centre, we could catch glimpses of the slums and shacks that the people were living in, but in the city centre vast blocks of modern flats were to be seen everywhere. The underground trains and stations were artistic marvels of marble architecture and cleanliness. And the fares were flat rate and cheaper than the London tube trains.

In Leningrad we were taken to the State Hermitage Museum to see one of the world's most wonderful collections of art, jewellery and other treasures from Russian history.

Near the end of our visit, we had a very long and unprofitable meeting with Mr Brezhnev, which lasted well over two hours. We also had a long meeting with the Supreme Soviet, and had to listen to a bitter speech of open hostility against the West, where, we were told, 'There are many, even workers, who don't want peace'.

It would be dishonest and ungrateful not to admit that we received the best of hospitality and kindness from our hosts. I believe the Russians craved peace. In Leningrad we were told how during the German siege in the war, they were almost starved to death and were eating their cats, dogs and even rats. They greatly feared a resurgence of Germany, and they suspected the intentions of America. As a result, a very high proportion of the gross domestic product was being diverted to military expenditure, to the detriment of more useful investment.

Like my West African visit of 1956, the fortnight in the Soviet Union was an invaluable experience. It was in no sense a 'jaunt'. It helped me to make a more informed assessment of the problems of that great country, and, not least, to see their problems from their side of the Iron Curtain.

It was to take nearly thirty years before the whole edifice of totalitarianism, with its accompanying terror and tyranny, was to collapse in chaos. The whole history of the Soviet Union after 1917 will have to be rewritten. And one courageous man, Mr Gorbachev, will surely be seen as an infinitely more positive catalyst for peace, goodwill and freedom than Lenin or Stalin ever were.

14

Sixty Days in the USA

Nineteen sixty-two was an 'off' year in the United States. That is, it was a year when there was no Presidential Election. Instead, there were elections for their Senate and Congress, as well as for Governorships in the various States.

The US Government invited a delegation of British MPs to observe those elections for three weeks, and then, for another five weeks, to visit any part of their country – with all expenses generously paid. I was lucky to be selected as a member of that delegation. We had friends from Fife living in New Jersey, and my daughter Sheila had a pen-pal in Ohio, and it was that kind of personal contact that our hosts were particularly keen to encourage.

We had extensive briefing and planning sessions before we left London, both at the British Foreign Office and the US Embassy.

The overall plan was for the whole delegation to stay together for the first three weeks, observing the elections. Then, for the next five weeks, to go our separate ways on individually devised intineraries. The visit was to last from 20 October to 11 December – sixty days.

We left London on 19 October and arrived at Washington, DC that same evening. On the evening of 22 October, at the British Embassy, we listened to that dramatic broadcast by President Kennedy on the critical and dangerous situation in Cuba, where the Soviet Union was secretly building an atomic-bomb capability which threatened the security of the USA. The world looked as if it could be on the brink of war. Kennedy wanted the USSR to back off, and laid down his ultimatum to Khrushchev. I was frightened, but full of admiration for the young President's boldness. His bluff came off and nuclear war was averted, but the incident showed how very dangerous and tense international relations were, especially between the USA and the USSR.

The first week of our election-watching was spent in Massachusetts observing the Senatorial campaign between Ted Kennedy and George Lodge. Both candidates were from wealthy families, and more money would be spent on that one election than I had spent on five campaigns in West Fife. Money talks in American elections even more than in our own. We attended one of Lodge's public meetings at Harvard University.

He was a fine speaker. He chided Kennedy for not having a meeting at Harvard himself. Was that because as a student there he had been caught cheating in his exams? (By impersonation, I think.) We never got an answer to that.

We also watched and talked to Kennedy. It was the first time he had ever fought *any* election. The Senate is the most prestigious of all US elections apart from the Presidential. When we asked an Irish taxi-driver how this could be justified, he replied jauntily, 'Well sir, you've got to start somewhere!' It was right for a Kennedy to *start* at the top. We each got a wee brass tie-pin from Ted. He gave away thousands. They alone must have cost as much as all my elections. George Lodge freely admitted to us that rich though he was, he couldn't beat a Kennedy. So it proved.

Off we went to Minneapolis via Chicago, to watch a struggle in the elections to Congress – comparable to our own House of Commons. There the Democratic candidate was young Don Fraser whilst the Republican was Congressman Judd. We listened in horror to a frightening anti-Communist speech from him at a delightful Lutheran college. The place oozed prosperity, wealth, political backwardness and ignorance. We were having lots of talks and interviews with journalists, university professors and local TV and radio. I don't know what effect we were all having on one another, but our hosts must have thought it was all worthwhile.

In every sizeable community there were always families ready and anxious to give us meals and to take us sightseeing, including to American football matches. We were driven up to the north of Minneapolis to see an Indian Reserve. It was a sad experience. The Indian minority problem is a legacy from the days when the white man fought the natives for dominance. Brute force won – as it did in Canada, in Australia, in New Zealand, and in South Africa. The problems of minorities exist the world over.

On 31 October we left Minneapolis for San Francisco. In California Richard Nixon was fighting Pat Brown for the Governorship of the State. California is bigger than the whole of Great Britain. Its wealth is enormous and the climate ideal. In early November the temperature was in the upper 70s °F. We were overwhelmed by the hospitality and fascinated by the international flavour of the San Francisco scene. Some New Zealand ladies invited us to the 'Grand National' – a rodeo-cum-Horse of the Year show, held in the enormous Cow Palace. We visited Chinatown, the Italian quarter, Fisherman's Wharf, and watched Nixon and Pat Brown in a TV election confrontation. It was clear that the campaign was a very dirty one, and 'Tricky Dicky' was in his element. We attended one of his rallies at a huge shopping centre. He knew we were there and welcomed us publicly, saying over his loudspeaker that the whole world was watching *his* election. It was a raucous cacophony, and quite frightening in its infantilism.

November 6th was Polling Day. There was a polling station in our hotel. It was an automatic machine – just like one of those gambling machines seen in amusement arcades. The ballot paper showed that there were sixty-one votes to be cast. The paper itself was about eighteen inches long and twelve inches wide. If you wanted to vote the straight Democratic or Republican 'ticket', you pulled one of two levers – just like on those fruit machines. The sixty-one votes were on all kinds of local issues and for all kinds of local officials. It was democracy gone mad.

By the evening the results showed a clear victory for the Democrats and for Governor Brown over Nixon. I was glad of that. We had spent a day in Nixon's luxuriously appointed campaign coach. He was busy handing out his yellow ballpoint pens and other trinkets. It was all very sleazy. We seemed to be associating too much with wealthy Republicans. It made me feel uncomfortable. I knew little then about Nixon, but what I did know, and what I saw and heard, I didn't like one little bit. It was immediately after that defeat in California that at a press conference he snarled, 'You will not have Richard Nixon to kick around any more.' But some years later, after Nixon had become President, investigative journalists were to play a decisive role in removing him from office in shame and dishonour. He was lucky to escape jail.

My first three weeks of American-style electioneering were an exhilarating experience. It made me realise how flexible the concept and practice of democracy is. The razzmatazz, toy trumpets, paper hats and other gimmicks were a million miles away from our sedate and sober British elections, much more costly, and, I felt, far more corrupt. I greatly regret that we have now copied the worst features of the American showbiz approach to politics.

The next five weeks were to be much more social and educative. Joan and the children had helped to plan my itinerary. Sheila had already visited her pen-pal, Linda, in Ohio, and she was keen that I should meet her, too. I was eager to look up our Fife friends in New Jersey, near New York. At the end of it all, I had a programme. I would start in the Deep South and end in New York.

After savouring Los Angeles – a quick visit to the monster funfair of Disneyland and the vulgar wealth of Hollywood and Beverley Hills – I headed for the arid Arizona region, then to brash and brassy Dallas in Texas – the city where very soon John Kennedy was to be assassinated.

My whistle-stop tour, from New Orleans in the hot Deep South up to the freezing cold of New York, could only leave superficial impressions of the enormous variety of races, scenery, politics, of the gaping disparities between rich and poor, between south and north.

Everything seemed to be on a grand scale and everything seemed to be changing, to be on the move. In the UK we cherish cobwebs. We preserve buildings and institutions that have outlived their usefulness. We love tradition. We adore antique shops. We are one big antique supermarket. In the USA there is little sense of history. There are few buildings more than a hundred years old. Atlanta was like a gigantic building site, and New York a monstrous concrete jungle. A very dangerous place in which to walk alone. However, in the midst of the exciting variety, there were some common factors. The hospitality everywhere was generous to the point of embarrassment. Royalty could hardly have been treated better. Americans are desperately anxious to be loved. Extremely rich in natural resources, danger may lie in the belief that friendship can be bought with dollars rather than earned by respect and trust. The wealthy bully has few genuine friends and doesn't deserve any. A littlle humility wouldn't come amiss.

President Roosevelt's New Deal of the 1930s was one of the most inspiring programmes of public investment ever launched anywhere in the world. It demonstrated how the States' wealth and know-how could be used for the national good, for *all* the people. The Tennessee Valley Authority was a vital part of the New Deal, designed to give work and hope to millions of despairing Americans. It was a splendid example of practical socialism. When I put that view to TVA officials they smiled, but warned me never to use that word! It was the kiss of death. To the American Establishment 'socialism' was 'communism' – just as in the last Presidential Election in 1988, Mr Bush made 'Liberal' a dirty word. Then it was sufficient condemnation to label his opponents as Liberals. We in the UK often suffer from the same deception. Mrs Thatcher often used the word 'socialism' to define the economic system that collapsed so comprehensively in the Soviet Union and Eastern Europe. It was an abuse of the English language, born out of malice and ignorance.

Almost from the day we arrived in America we had to listen to the daily drip of criticism of our National Health Service. The wealthier they were, the more virulent the venom. The doctors we met were particularly opposed to the idea. Naturally. They got a luxurious living in the land of the Almighty Dollar. They catered for the well-heeled. If you are rich in the States you can buy the best health care in the world. But God help you if you are poor. The medical profession is one of the most powerful vested interests on the American scene. The politicians are afraid of it. Most of the personal debt in America is caused by medical charges. Our 'socialised medicine' is still among the best in the world. No political Party here dares to express open hostility to the basic principles of our NHS. By contrast, American health care is based on profit, greed and social immorality.

Private investment and *private* profit were automatically *good*. No argument about it. *Public* investment in *anything* was bound to be *bad* – by definition. That was the dogma we heard incessantly.

One of the guiding principles that disfigured Mrs Thatcher's disastrous decade of power in the UK was her unquestioned acceptance of this simplistic and absolutist doctrine. Her sudden and swift demise in 1990 was a national blessing which we enjoyed, appropriately enough, on Thanksgiving Day. But she left a legacy of neglect, that will take decades to repair. And just as Mrs Thatcher's 'miracle' is going to be a mirage, so the American dream is turning into a nightmare. Everywhere in 1962 I saw squalor, poverty and degradation in the midst of opulence and privilege. Today, the USA is the largest debtor country in the world. Over the years yet another powerful lobby, the armaments industry, has maintained a vested interest in nurturing the concept of 'the Communist menace', the better to protect its own enormous profits.

Day in and day out, I had to listen to horrific rhetoric about 'the Communist menace', everywhere, by everybody – or almost everybody. The brainwashing was almost as complete as it was in the Soviet Union. In that respect, my visits to these countries were two sides of the same coin. The USSR preached about the menace of Western capitalism, which meant American capitalism. The Americans ranted on about the menace of communism. So that they could justify their erroneous and unsustainable defence expenditure, both needed an enemy. There was some element of truth on both sides. The Soviet Union had a real dread of war. They feared a German resurgence, incited by the Americans. I believe it was a genuine fear. So they rearmed. In their turn, the Americans felt the Soviet threat was real. It was a vicious circle. The arms race became self-perpetuating.

In the USA one of the consequences had already been the anti-Communist witch-hunts of the coarse Senator Joseph McCarthy. McCarthy saw Communists everywhere – in the armed forces, in Hollywood, inside the Government, under the bed and in the bed. This thug's investigations were conducted on television. It was one of the most disgraceful episodes in American politics. I saw with my own eyes, and heard with my own ears, nice families being torn apart by the canker of McCarthyism. I found it terrifying. McCarthyism exposed the fallacy that Americans enjoy free speech. It is free only within very strict limits.

I am a very moderate, even right-wing socialist. If I had been in America when McCarthy was conducting his inquisition, I would have been a condemned man. Any trace of unorthodoxy was ridiculed or victimised. Nor was the McCarthy approach very much different from the general attitude to trade unions. Organised labour has always been disliked by capitalist employers and the Republican Party Establishment.

In 1962 the UK hadn't yet joined the Common Market and I was invited by several academic organisations to lecture about the British attitude to membership. As a pro-Marketeer, I got sympathetic hearings, though for different reasons. Many Americans saw the Common Market as an anti-Communist bloc. That seemed to be sufficient justification for its existence. My own case was based on the fact that in my lifetime we had endured two world wars, largely caused by the mutual fears and suspicions of France and Germany. The Common Market sought to interlock *all* the West European economies and so diminish the danger of war engendered by narrow nationalism. In particular, the integration of the German and French steel and coal industries made a war initiated by either a practical impossibility. In my view, no price is too high to pay for the avoidance of a third world war. Those two world wars may have put an end to American isolationism. I made several efforts to put these thoughts before audiences in places as far apart as Atlanta, Detroit, Philadelphia and New York.

By the time I got to New York, I felt worn out. Though I had been in regular correspondence with my family, I was homesick. I had little inclination to explore that great city on my own, so I spent most of my stay there visiting my Fife friends in New Jersey.

I have been forever grateful to the American Government for affording me the opportunity to see so much of their exciting country and to meet so many of their kind people. Such exchanges can only improve international understanding and co-operation.

Between 1956 and 1962, I had visited Africa, Russia and North America. They all had their own distinctive histories, cultures, languages, peoples and forms of government. Each was trying to improve the lot of its own people in its own way. In both the Soviet Union and the USA I found a very boring, dogmatic and myopic view of society, although the extreme Right was far from being as repulsive as the fanatical Left. Neither saw any merit in the other. Both were unmitigated evils. Both demanded orthodoxy and conformity with the prevailing doctrine. However, the American obsession was much less objectionable than that of the USSR. The Soviet Union in 1962 was a closed society, repressive, stifling and dull, with no genuine personal freedoms and a ruthless stamping out of any form of dissidence. Most of the people were obviously intimidated and poor. It was a police state. The USA on the other hand was composed of a rainbow of peoples on the move, bubbling with a variety of cultures and ideas, some more crazy than others. In rich cities like Dallas I watched people queuing for food parcels alongside three-car mansions. I saw neglect of the old and the sick, and no thought for the homeless. In Atlanta I admired those people, black and white, who were fighting nobly against racial discrimination and segregation. And I met trade unionists prepared to fight against the Establishment for the rights and dignity of working people.

I made some lifelong friends in the United States; yet I found the African scene more congenial. The economic and social problems were mind-boggling. By our standards, the poverty and the disease were indescribable and yet the people were cheerful. The tropical climate perhaps inclined them to laziness and sloth but their very primitiveness was more attractive than the sophisticated cunning and corruption of both the USA and the USSR. Nobody preached about the relative merits of capitalism or communism. There is a lot to be said for the simple life in an African village. Arguably, it is preferable to living fearfully in a skyscraper flat in New York, Dallas or Moscow.

15

Lord Home and Mr Wilson: Aristocrat Versus Academic

'... Show the people that our old Nobility is not noble, that its lands are stolen lands – stolen either by force or fraud; show people that the title deeds are rapine, murder, massacre, cheating, or Court harlotry; dissolve the halo of divinity that surrounds the hereditary title; let the people clearly understand that our present House of Lords is composed largely of descendants of successful pirates and rogues ...

'On his Forfarshire estates, the Earl of Home ... still extracts tribute for four weeks every year from the stalls in Kirriemuir market place ... he levied 2d on every pound of butter, and 4d on every dozen of eggs that went into market ... in the Upper Ward of Lanarkshire his tyranny is even more scandalous and unbearable.

'They [the Home family] acquired a detestable reputation for instability and treachery ... The Lord of Home ... stuck at nothing (from murder down) to fatten the revenue of his house.'

Thomas Johnston, *Our Noble Families*, 6th Edition 1916

[Our Scottish noble families] 'have grown rich by laying their hands upon property that belonged to other people and ... have increased their estates by a ruthless exploitation of smallholders and peasant owners.'

J. Ramsay MacDonald MP, Preface to *Our Noble Families*

I acquit the present Lord Home of any guilt for his ancestors' crimes of theft and treachery. He was content to be a beneficiary of the proceeds of their felonies.

He allegedly went into national politics to help the miners, the unemployed and other hard-pressed citizens. He was also a practising Christian. Like so many Conservatives, before and since, Home found no difficulty in worshipping God and Mammon simultaneously.

I knew him only briefly in the House of Commons in 1950, when he sat on the Tory Opposition benches as Lord Dunglass.

He did not stand out distinctively as a scion of one of those notorious Scottish noble families. He left us, unremarked, in July 1951, on the death of his father. He was then magically reincarnated as the 14th Earl of Home. Fate had decreed that he should join the 'living dead' in the House of Lords.

From that day, promotion was as automatic as it was meteoric. A very rich, likeable, modest and unambitious Scottish landowner had all the qualifications needed to ensure unimpeded progress to the top Tory table. Over the next twelve years the wheel of fortune spun so dizzily in his favour that by 1963 he was Prime Minister.

No heather had been set alight in those intervening years. But he emerged, unelected, as the new Tory Prime Minister. It was all seen on television, by me and millions of others. Well, not *all*. We were not allowed to see the gentlemanly skulduggery behind the scenes.

The deteriorating health of Harold Macmillan, and the rumblings against his leadership within the Tory Party's ranks, were making his resignation inevitable. Macmillan, for his part, was determined to stop Rab Butler from being his successor. It had nothing to do with us in the Labour Party, but we thought that Butler would be the man. At the time, nobody anywhere dreamed that Lord Home would make it to Number 10.

But Macmillan had other ideas. Lord Hailsham was his man. The shenanigans at the Tory Party's Annual Conference in October 1963 made fascinating television. I was especially amused and nauseated by the juvenile antics of Lord Hailsham. The sheer humbug and vanity of the clown were matched only by his all too obvious overweening ambition. There he stood, in full public view, 'meekly' avowing that he would renounce his peerage; for the greater good of the country and of his Party of course – and only incidentally of himself. The squalor of the performance was too much for even a Tory Party Conference to swallow. Hailsham had defeated himself. Nor did Rab do himself any good. I listened to, and watched, his speech at that Conference. It was weak and uninspiring, not at all the speech of a budding Prime Minister. So, by default, and in the total absence of any democratic electoral machinery within the Tory Party – this was later introduced by Home himself, and used with such deadly and deserved effect on Mrs Thatcher – the Party's 'Magic Circle' got to work on behalf of Lord Home. To the great chagrin of intellectuals like Iain Macleod, Enoch Powell and others, Macmillan put Lord Home's name as his successor to the Queen, and being of similar Scottish stock herself, she willingly acquiesced.

So we were now saddled with an unelected Prime Minister who had a seat only in the unelected House of Lords – and a General Election probable within the next twelve months. It was a scenario tailor-made for us in the Opposition.

A safe Tory seat in the House of Commons for Lord Home was speedily fixed up, and a feudal seat next to mine in Perthshire was made available. The Home peerage was discarded like an old sock, and Lord Home became Sir Alec Douglas-Home. During the course of that by-election the country was without a Prime Minister at all. Being the MP in the neighbouring constituency, I had a lot of fun. So too did Willie Rushton, the well-known TV and radio wit and comedian. He stood as an independent candidate, just to take the mickey out of the British Establishment. As I recall, his Election address was a special edition of the satirical magazine, *Private Eye.* I wish Willie could have won. Democracy deserved him.

The new MP for Kinross and West Perthshire took his seat again in the House of Commons, not as a back-bencher with the name of Lord Dunglass, but as the Prime Minister with the title of Sir Alec Douglas-Home.

Few in the Commons, certainly on the Labour side, could take him seriously. Harold Wilson, Leader of the Labour Party, foresaw easy prey, ready for eating alive. Some of us on the back-benches also thought we could have one or two cheap meals. On 16 July 1964, I had put a question to Sir Alec complaining about the way he had been avoiding answering my questions. Sir Alec got his statisticians to work. They calculated that if all MPs had as many questions answered by the Prime Minister as I had, he would have had to answer 1,400. A bullseye. Everybody laughed. The episode got full coverage in the national press. All it showed was what a frivolous place the House of Commons can be, especially if you are faced with a frivolous Prime Minister.

At best, Sir Alec was a very poor speaker. He was even worse on television. His skeletal head defied all artificial aids; and his self-confessed use of matchsticks to understand, still less solve, our national economic problems, was a constant source of merriment. Roy Jenkins referred to Sir Alec's economic consultants as 'Messrs Bryant and May'.

On the other hand, Home's very fallibility, his obvious sincerity and niceness, proved attractive to the politically uncommitted. I remember watching him on TV one evening. He was making what I thought was a complete cock-up; but my wife, who was sitting with me, had a startlingly different reaction. She was non-political, maternally protective, and compassionate. She thought Sir Alec came across as a thoroughly decent man, with no pretensions, no bombast, and none of that certainty so irritatingly claimed by other politicians.

So it was that in the 1964 Election Sir Alec lost by a whisker to Harold Wilson. There couldn't have been a greater contrast between two men. Wilson had a brilliant academic record, both at Oxford and in the civil service, before he entered Parliament in 1945. Just before that, his first book, *New Deal For Coal,* was published, in which he advocated nationalisation of the industry – at the ripe old age of twenty-eight. It was recognised as a masterpiece. When I was first introduced to him at our Party's great pre-Election Conference in 1945, he recommended his book to me. Harold then sported a clipped moustache and looked like a smart City gent. His rapid rise to the top was based entirely on academic brilliance, coupled with scheming personal ambition, a ready wit, and a complete mastery of any brief which came his way. Home, on the other hand, had no worthwhile academic record, no ambition, but enormous wealth.

From day one in Parliament, Wilson had his eyes and mind on high office. There is nothing wrong with that in any politician. Sure enough, he became a junior Minister in that Attlee-led Government, and he never looked back.

After my own 1950 Election I was able to watch Harold at close quarters. He was appointed President of the Board of Trade in 1947, and did a first-class job both inside and outside Parliament while the national economy was still suffering from the debilitating effects of the 1939–45 war. He resigned in 1951 over the proposed NHS charges.

After our 1951 Election defeat and during the next thirteen years of Opposition, Wilson proved himself to be one of the most effective debaters in the House of Commons. He had allied himself to the Left of the Parliamentary Labour Party, which was led by Nye Bevan. I was never convinced that that was an alliance of conviction, but rather one of calculated convenience. Harold, I thought, was a 'semi-detached' member of the Left. The posture served its purpose. Harold's perky brilliance in the Commons, his self-assurance, his comparative youth, and even his overt conceit, almost ensured his election as Leader of the Party on the sudden death of Hugh Gaitskell in January 1963. I voted for him. He outshone, on all counts, the other two candidates in the field, George Brown and Jim Callaghan. Moreover, I thought that of the three, he was the one most likely to unite the warring factions within the Labour Party.

In the first few months of 1964, in the course of a series of major speeches made all over the country, Wilson presented to the nation the most inspiring and imaginative picture of a Labour Britain that had ever been put forward. He spoke with a vast knowledge of national and international problems, and with a wealth of intellectual ability that made Sir Alec look like a carthorse racing against a thoroughbred.

But my own wife had sounded the alarm for me. Home may have been a clumsy and cack-handed amateur, but his very vulnerability and modesty made him attractive.

During the 1964 Election campaign, Home understandably played on the obvious splits in the Labour Party, especially on defence and foreign policy, so that Wilson was relieved to have an overall majority in the House of Commons of four.

My own victory in West Fife was a formality. I had a majority of almost 17,000 over the Tory opposition, and the Communist candidate lost his deposit.

My heart had not been in the Election at all. My wife was dying of cancer. I was also involved in the developing scandal of the CADCO affair in my constituency. So I was relieved when the fight was over, even though I knew that another Election couldn't be long delayed.

Although my family problems were of more immediate concern, I had expected to be considered for some Ministerial post in the new Government. I learned later that Willie Ross, the newly appointed Secretary of State for Scotland, had put my name forward for promotion, but to no effect. In the course of the next few years my name was again suggested for Ministerial office by Manny Shinwell when he was Chairman of the PLP, by Ted Short when he was our Chief Whip, and by George Lawson when he was our Deputy Chief Whip; all with negative results. George was a close Scottish colleague of mine who had put my name to John Silkin, then our Chief Whip. Apparently, Silkin told George that he could not put my name for consideration to Harold Wilson because of my unreliability on account of my anti-royalist views.

George conveyed the gist of that conversation to me. I was then writing a regular fortnightly column in the Scottish *Sunday Mail*, so I wrote a vitriolic piece about how a Labour MP could be victimised by his own Government for having certain views on the monarchy. Within a few days George was hauled before Silkin, who demanded to know where my information had come from. The answer was obvious, and George was sacked as Deputy Chief Whip. I felt I had let George down and told him so. But he was adamant that his sacking was nothing to do with me. It was more to do with the fact that George was at odds with Silkin on the matter of discipline within the PLP. George had a long and honourable record of hard work for the Labour Party and felt strongly that there must be loyalty and unity within the Party. He was all for a stern regime of discipline for Labour MPs, while Silkin preferred a much looser rein, and that was why George had to go.

The Party hierarchy then tried to stop me from becoming Chairman of the Estimates Committee. They had their own nominee for the job, even though I had served on the Committee for ten years. On hearing of the ploy, I stormed into our Party Whips' office. A colleague, who shall be nameless, but who now sits as a Labour peer in the House of Lords, listened to me, either frightened by my onslaught, or sympathetic. He offered to send me as a Labour delegate to the Council of Europe, or onto some other international gravy train, as a kind of consolation prize. Neither of the bribes appealed to me. I had a wife in a precarious state of health, I liked my work in the House of Commons, and in any case I have always reacted violently against the whole practice of patronage within political parties. To witness it being operated by Party Whips was stomach-turning. Most of our Whips in 1964 had come into the House of Commons *after* me, so it all stuck in my gullet.

I did get the Chairmanship of the Estimates Committee, and it kept me very busy. Its forty-three members subdivided into six subcommittees and most of them met between 4 and 5 p.m. each week. As Chairman of the full Committee, I had a duty to attend as many of the subcommittees as I could. Looking back now, it was like chasing shadows. There was no depth in any of our work, and no worthwhile end product. As an exercise in the control of public expenditure it was a monumental waste of time. So far as the Government was concerned, they probably felt that it was a convenient way of keeping troublesome back-benchers like me out of greater mischief.

THE WESTMINSTER MAZE

Immediately Parliament met after the 1964 Election, I decided to try to do something to help our new Labour MPs find their way round the place. The Palace of Westminster is a maze. It is easy for any MP to get lost *every day*. The procedures of the House of Commons, developed over hundreds of years, are part of that maze, and it is just as easy for an MP to get lost in them.

When I first went into Parliament, nobody seemed to be on hand to help. I remember wandering into the Library and asking a Mr Holland to show me round. He was obviously a senior librarian, and he kindly obliged. I recall him showing me 'the pornographic book cupboard'. It was always locked, he explained, presumably because of the tendency of some MPs to borrow those books 'on extended loan'. I suppose if you asked for the key to that cupboard you could be a marked man. I never inquired. I don't know whether that cupboard is still there, or whether it is still locked.

I discussed my ideas with our Chief Whip, and he gave me the all-clear to go ahead and arrange a few meetings with the new Members. I did that. We talked about simple things, like the drafting and tabling of oral and written questions, how to apply for Adjournment Debates, how to frame Early-Day Motions, how and where to apply for Ten-Minute Rule Bills, how to read and understand the daily Order Paper, how to use both the Commons and Lords Libraries. These were just a few of the topics we discussed. As the meetings developed, so did the scope of the subject matter. In addition to the meetings, I volunteered to conduct a few guided tours around the buildings. I had always felt that this was an important part of the job of any MP. The Palace of Westminster belongs to the people who sent us there to represent their interests. In all my years as a Member, I never once hired a professional guide to show my constituents around. They had a *right* to expect their own MP to be their guide, and I never let them down.

Most of our new Members expressed their gratitude for what I had tried to do. So, after every subsequent General Election until 1983, I continued with similar talks.

PUBLIC SPENDING

As the new Chairman of the Estimates Committee, I took part in some interesting TV and radio programmes on questions about the control of public expenditure. One of these was in early 1965, when Reggie Maudling, who had been Chancellor of the Exchequer in the previous Tory Government, and I discussed the cost of some of our defence missiles – the Bloodhound, Blue Streak and Blue Steel.

Blue Streak had cost us £300 million before it was cancelled, so that was money down the drain.

The *estimated* cost of Blue Steel was £12 million, but it soon rocketed to £60 million.

On the contract for the Bloodhound Missile, it was discovered that Ferranti's had made a profit of 63 per cent, or over £5 million. That was £4 million more than it should have been. The original estimate for the *development* of Bloodhound was about £1 million, but the *actual* cost turned out to be £32 million. For producing this missile, Ferranti's were paid £13.5 million, of which nearly £5.5 millions was profit. The Government of the day had intended the profit to be less than £1 million.

These facts were only discovered by the Comptroller and Auditor General, helped by his staff of over 500. As a financial watchdog independent of the Government, the Comptroller and Auditor General reported to the House of Commons Public Accounts Committee. The PAC made its subsequent devastating exposure, but only after all that money had been spent. Neither the PAC nor the Estimates Committee could do much about those scandals. They could only investigate after the money had been spent. They could try to lock the stable door, but only after the horse had bolted.

Today, in the 1990s, the control of public expenditure by the House of Commons is hopelessly ineffective, and control by the Government is hardly any better. Neither of them can match the wiles, skills and duplicity of huge outside private contractors and companies, many of which are international conglomerates, such as the major drug companies who make fortunes out of our National Health Service.

In the early 1980s I was a Member of the PAC investigating the profit margins of defence contractors. We were taking oral evidence from Sir Frank Cooper, then the senior civil servant dealing with these matters. I asked Sir Frank if he knew of any defence contractor who had ever gone bankrupt. 'Not to my knowledge,' he smilingly replied.

Sir Frank retired shortly afterwards and soon after was reported to have been employed in those fields which he had known so intimately and where his knowledge of the workings of Government would be invaluable.

Meanwhile, the drama of the Tory Party leadership was once again beginning to hit the headlines. Sir Alec could just about manage the job when as Prime Minister he had the help of a vast army of civil service advisers. Now, as mere Leader of the Opposition, he was like a political nudist, stripped of all visible means of support. He was probably relieved to throw in the towel in July 1965. As was said at the time, he was dispatched by his Party because his image was wrong, and because he had lost an Election. Just as Home's successor, Ted Heath, was dispatched in 1975, and Mrs Thatcher in 1990. Things don't change much in the Tory Killing Fields.

16

CADCO, or This Little Piggy Went to Market

The press can be a valuable asset to the back-bench MP with limited resources at his disposal. That was the case when I became involved in this affair.

After such a long time, I cannot be certain when I first became aware of the CADCO scandal. But I remember a bright young investigative journalist, Mr John Barry, then working for the *Sunday Times*, who came to see me at the House of Commons. We had a long talk and he supplied me with a vast amount of information which he had dug out about the principal characters: Messrs Loraine, Roe and Sanders. In addition, I was receiving letters from private firms who were owed money by CADCO, and from workers employed on the project in Glenrothes. The matter was politically sensitive because it had started when the Tories were in control, and after the 1964 Election had to be handled by a Labour Government with a small majority.

CADCO was the name of a company started by the famous film star, George Sanders, who had played the part of 'the Cad' in many of his films. The company itself had been established in Curaçao in the Dutch West Indies to be a safe haven for Sanders's film earnings.

The details of the whole story were outlined in a report published in 1966 by two inspectors appointed by the Board of Trade to investigate the affairs of three companies: CADCO Developments Ltd, Royal Victoria Sausages Ltd and Victoria Wholesale Meats Ltd.

The complexities of the CADCO web of villainy are set out in the *Observer*'s chart of 4 December 1966 (see p.211).

The flavour of that report can be savoured by reading some of the newspaper comments:

Edinburgh Evening News, 30 November 1966: 'Film actor George Sanders is accused in a sensational Government Report today of playing a big role in the frauds, falsehoods, falsifications, and gross extravagances associated with the ill-fated CADCO piggery project which crashed in bankruptcy in 1964.'

The *Observer*, 4 December 1966: 'Quite apart from the CADCO affair, fraud at present seems to be one of our growth industries. But the machinery for dealing with it still belongs to the penny-farthing era.'

Daily Record, Glasgow, 1 December 1966: 'The small men of Fife – builders, painters, blacksmiths, merchants, and a photographer – were the big losers in the CADCO crash.'

That report could still make the script for a hilarious film. It could have everything – comedy, drama, greed, corruption, deception, incompetence in high places, and women. It's all there.

The drama started with a small butcher's shop in Victoria Terrace, Hove, near Brighton. It ended in Glenrothes, a new town in my constituency. When I was first elected as an MP, Glenrothes was no more than a few houses and a pub in a farming area. The *raison d'être* of the new town was the prospective opening of a brand-new coalmine just half a mile away. Rothes colliery was to be the last word in mining techniques. It was to cost a lot of money, but would employ large numbers of miners and produce large tonnages of coal. It was opened with a great fanfare of trumpets by the Queen and Prince Philip.

Alas, 'The best laid schemes o' mice and men Gang aft a-gley'.

Not a ton of coal was dug, and millions of pounds were lost. The showpiece mine produced nothing but water. It had to be abandoned and the future of the new town seemed doomed. The local farmers pressed for it to be abandoned altogether. Instead, the Glenrothes Development Corporation, appointed by the Government, was encouraged to scour the world for other new industries. They had some success, but by the early 1960s had still not managed to catch a really big one. That was when CADCO struck.

That little butcher's shop in Hove had become the Royal Victoria Sausages Company, which had expanded still further at a place called Partridge Green. In the process, however, the owners, led by Denis Loraine, Thomas Roe and, later, George Sanders, incurred massive financial losses. Their plan was to recoup these by engaging in what proved to be one of the most wicked confidence tricks ever perpetrated in Scotland.

That RVS conspirators knew that Glenrothes was desperately anxious to land a big fish, so they prepared very attractive bait. It was set out at a well-publicised press conference in the posh North British Hotel in Edinburgh on 28 May 1963. The local and national bigwigs were there, along with the Scottish press, TV and radio. All seemed willing to believe anything that gave the promise of a lot of new jobs. The situation was ripe for a public rape, and the promises flowed like honey.

Basically, the idea was to feed young pigs in at one end of the industrial complex and produce pork pies and sausages at the other. The CADCO group of companies would build all the piggeries, feed and rear all the pigs, produce all the sausages and pies, pre-pack them, and build a new supermarket for selling them in the town centre. George Sanders promised that once the project was established – creating 2,000 new jobs – he would consider the possibility of starting a new film industry in Glenrothes. It was also suggested that other famous names connected with CADCO included Robert Mitchum, William Holden and Charlie Chaplin.

While all this 'misleading and untruthful' information was being churned out, the assembled company was being entertained to generous refreshments, in which, according to the Board of Trade report, 'RVS sausages played a prominent part'.

The Scottish media swallowed the bait without a degree of doubt or uncertainty. Tragically it was all a big lie.

The story of the piggeries told it all. CADCO Building, which was to build the piggeries, had no qualified staff of any kind, and had to get architectural help from the Development Corporation.

Rearing pigs and turning them into bacon, pies and sausages is a very tricky business. The Pig Industry Development Authority offered to give expert advice on how the piggeries should be built, but the offer was rejected. The structures eventually built were wholly unsuitable for their purposes. A pig produces a lot more effluent than the average human being. Twenty-thousand weaners – young piglets – would have produced as much waste as a town with a population of 50,000. This was to be dealt with by one nine-inch pipe, sloping gently into one storage tank, which could hold no more than the effluent produced by the piglets *in one day*. If ever those piggeries had worked at full blast, Glenrothes would have been swamped with thousands of gallons of pig urine and other more solid and disagreeable material.

I had raised the subject in an adjournment debate in the Commons on 1 December 1964. I got a lot of publicity and interested parties tried to shut me up. Shouting too loudly and critically, they said, might stop the jobs from coming to Fife. I must be *constructive*; I must think *more positively*.

I wrote to every Minister in the Government that I could think of, and I asked hundreds of questions in the House of Commons. I got shoals of letters – from the local Labour Party, trade unions, businessmen and individual constituents. All of them supported what I was doing, but I got nowhere. The whole CADCO project collapsed in November 1964. No new job ever came to Glenrothes from it. Nobody ever divulged the total loss of public money. In fact, some of the top brass concerned denied there had been any loss at all. I do not believe it. Some of the culprits escaped abroad. Loraine and Roe, for instance, were later arrested and given jail sentences for currency offences in Los Angeles and Switzerland respectively. The procedures for doling out public money were tightened up, but as far as I know, no heads rolled, and no Government Minister resigned.

I learned several lessons from this story. My view about the powerlessness of the ordinary back-bench Member of Parliament had been confirmed. No matter how diligent and tenacious, he or she will never get the whole truth about anything. Partial truths are often enough to placate. In the highest echelons of Government, there is mind-boggling incompetence. CADCO acted on the principle that if you want to take a risk, you have to do it on a grand scale. Gamble with millions of pounds and you stand a good chance of getting away with it. Hold back just a few pounds, say on tax or insurance benefit, and the authorities will hound you day and night. The notion that we are all equal before the law is balderdash.

I had some small consolation when I read a long accolade about myself in the *Weekly Scotsman* of 10 December 1964. Among the compliments was the assertion that 'the former schoolmaster with the flair for vitriolic comment is a man who is unlikely to reach or seek Ministerial office. He is too fiercely outspoken and independent.' It ended: 'There is no MP that Ministers fear more. And he is a man who will not be silenced just because his own Party happens to be in power. He is the kind of back-bencher that the Commons can ill afford to lose.'

All that was very flattering, and much exaggerated. No Minister ever feared me, and I would have liked to have become a Minister. There must have been good reasons why that did not happen.

FAMILY PROBLEMS

Throughout the CADCO affair, I was greatly worried by the state of my wife's health. In early 1964 she began to complain about pains in her side. She kept shrugging it off, but eventually she was persuaded to go and see her doctor. The doctor said there was nothing to worry about, that it was just nervous tension, and that it would go away naturally. The pain got steadily worse, however, and on 11 August she was admitted to our small cottage hospital in Dulwich. She had an operation the next day and was back home again two days later. Nevertheless, she felt fit enough to join me at the official opening by the Queen of the New Forth Road Bridge on 4 September.

In October, Joan spent a few days with me towards the end of my General Election campaign in West Fife. Polling day was on 15 October and Joan joined me in going round all the polling stations on that day. But by the 18th, almost as soon as we had returned home, she had to be rushed into Dulwich hospital again, where we were advised that another operation was necessary. Unfortunately, because there was a shortage of beds, she would have to wait, and meanwhile she was allowed home. On 30 October we were told that a major operation was now imperative, and she was admitted to the hospital on 4 November. All kinds of tests, including x-rays, were undertaken and she had her operation on the 9th.

Meanwhile, our good friend and neighbour, Mr Ellison Nash, had been kind enough to suggest that I might like to have a second opinion on Joan's state of health. Mr Nash was a surgeon and Dean of the Faculty of Medicine at the St Bartholomew's Hospital in London. Immediately after that operation on the 9th, Mr Nash and Mr McCrae, the surgeon who had performed the operation, invited me to come and talk to them. I did so, and they told me what I had long dreaded. Joan had incurable cancer of the liver. The operation may have prolonged her life, they said, but for an unknown length of time. Joan was then lying in the ward and the two consultants advised me on what I might like to tell her. They said I could either be absolutely frank, or that I could hide the truth from her. By this time I was emotionally drained and found it hard to say anything at all. I was troubled by the thought of telling my wife a lie, but I couldn't possibly tell her the truth. I managed to tell the two consultants of my dilemma and they suggested that it would be credible if I told Joan that she had had a hysterectomy. I went along to the ward and did as they had advised. Afterwards, I was unhappy about what I had done. I talked to my own doctor, Dr Michael Fisher, about my worry. He was also a great family friend, and he gave me advice which comforted me quite a lot. He suggested that Joan was probably aware of the truth, and that we were both putting up a pretence for the best possible reasons, each trying to protect the other.

On 28 November Joan was allowed home again. Our daughter Sheila was doing her nursing training at Guy's Teaching Hospital in East London. I told her the truth of the matter because I guessed that she would already know. But we decided not to tell my son, Ian. He would only worry, and he still believed that because his mother kept coming home from hospital she must be on the mend. I saw no point in disillusioning him.

Only three days days later, on 1 December, I made my speech in the House of Commons on CADCO – whilst my wife was lying in great discomfort at home. The following weekend she was in such intense pain that on the Saturday she begged me to ring for help. I tried in vain to contact our own doctor. When I failed she implored me to go down to the local chemists to get an enema. I did so and then Joan asked me if I could administer it. By this time I was sweating with fear. There I was, all alone with Joan. I was clumsy and panic-stricken. I tried and tried and tried, and failed. Terrified, I phoned Dulwich hospital, explained who I was and my predicament, and within about half an hour Joan was rushed in again for yet another emergency operation.

In the meantime, I had to cancel a meeting with Brigadier Paddy Doyle, the General Manager of Glenrothes Development Corporation. He had been very concerned over what I had said about CADCO and I in turn had been very angry about his handling of the matter. It was made clear in the Board of Trade Report that he had been deceived by Loraine, Roe and Sanders from the beginning. He had visited their Partridge Green factory and had been led to believe that it was highly profitable when it had in fact lost £134,000 in 1961. Paddy later accepted a CADCO invitation for him and his wife to go to Italy to look at their proposed factory there, with a view to his becoming the manager.

He was subsequently acquitted in the Board of Trade Report of any corruption or malpractice. Though Paddy and I had our differences, we both had the long-term interests of Glenrothes at heart and we ended up the best of friends.

Joan left hospital on 20 December. We were all glad to see her home for Christmas, and we were fortified by a flood of letters, cards and visits from friends and well-wishers.

Early in the New Year, I got an invitation to attend Winston Churchill's funeral on Saturday, 3 January, but I chose to stay with my ailing wife. I still have that invitation in my files. I am sure my order of priorities was right.

All this time I was trying to keep contact with Fife and Parliament, and deal with my constituency correspondence. The Labour Party having won the 1964 Election with a tiny majority, I had to be in constant attendance at the House, but I explained my position to the Party Whips and they were very understanding, as was my Party in Fife.

As for Joan, she was now on regular monthly hospital check-ups, and by May she was well enough to attend the House of Commons to hear me introduce my bill to end the delaying powers of the House of Lords.

17

War Damage Bill

One of the first bills introduced by the new Labour Government of 1964 was the War Damage Bill. Its purpose was to invalidate the claims for compensation made by the Burmah Oil Company for the loss of their oil facilities in Burma in the last war. Those facilities had been destroyed by our own retreating forces, to stop them from falling into the hands of the advancing Japanese Army.

The company had been claiming since 1947, and had been resisted by all *six* British Governments, Labour and Tory, between then and 1965.

Various estimates were made of the actual amounts of the compensation claimed but the generally accepted figure was £84 million, including the smaller claims of another eight companies.

When the general *principles* of the bill were debated in the House of Commons in April 1965 there was a majority of ninety-three in favour. In the House of Lords the principle was also agreed to, by forty-five to twenty-two. Note the figures: a *total* of only sixty-seven peers bothered to vote, with two to one in favour of the bill.

But on 13 April the House of Lords, on the same bill in committee, voted *against* the Government by 144 to sixty-nine. The twenty-two who had voted against HMG on the second reading had increased to 144 shortly afterwards. Why the sudden conversion?

I decided to investigate. I asked the House of Commons Library staff to get me a list of all the titled shareholders of the Burmah Oil Company. The Librarian doubted if the information would be available. But they succeeded. It was a very long list – fifty foolscap pages. Thrilled, I then asked the Library to ascertain which of the 144 peers who had voted for Burmah Oil were on that list. I also asked for voting records of those same peers on other matters, and I asked for their other business interests.

Regarding their business interests, I tabulate below the details as supplied by our very thorough, objective and reliable Library researchers. As for their voting records, fifty-four of the 144 had not voted at all in that session of Parliament. One, Lord Strathalmond, had actually taken his seat for the first time in the Lords for that session. He hadn't spoken on anything for at least ten years. But he had been a director of Burmah Oil until December 1964 – just a few months before he voted. The 144 who voted for Burmah Oil shared 415 company directorships – an average of nearly three apiece.

Of these, there were 110 company chairmanships. There were twenty-one directorships of banks. Fourteen had directorships in chemicals. Eleven had directorships in property. Seven were directors in the steel industry, six in oil, and six in the 'beerage'. Thirty-eight out of the 144 were known shareholders of Burmah Oil.

On 4 May 1965, on introducing my bill to abolish the delaying powers of the Lords in respect of legislation, I quoted all these facts to the House of Commons.

I said: 'It seems to me, on the evidence I have been able to collect, that the House of Lords was not so much acting as a Chamber of Parliament, and debating matters of fundamental principle, but as a shareholders' meeting discussing future policy. Indeed, I would say that at the last general meeting of the Burmah Oil Company there were probably fewer shareholders than there were in the House of Lords.' (Hansard column 1118, 4 May 1965.)

Several times in the course of my speech I was rebuked by Mr Speaker for impugning the honour of Their Lordships. I protested I was doing no such thing. Norman Shrapnel of the *Guardian* summed it up: 'It was entirely by chance that one of them [a Tory peer and Burmah Oil shareholder] had taken his seat that day.' And: 'It was for the best of reasons that another had never opened his mouth [in the Lords] for ten years.' *The Times*' Parliamentary correspondent was equally objective about my speech. 'Tongue in cheek, he [I] was prepared to believe that these thirty-eight [i.e. the noble Burmah Oil shareholders] had been motivated by nothing more than their regard for the rule of law,' and, 'by a supreme effort, he was even prepared to believe that their presence in the House that day was coincidental.'

My own Labour colleagues relished every minute. The Tories walked out, scowling and grunting. I noticed one Tory who did not walk out. Ted Heath stayed to listen to me. I wondered whether he was secretly agreeing with my description of this 'unacceptable face of capitalism'. That was an expression Mr Heath was himself to use in another context some years later.

Nobody voted against my bill. They thought I was on a 'propaganda stunt', and that the bill would proceed no further. But I got a lot of national publicity. It lifted the morale of my own Party. And it alerted the public to the menace of vested interests in Parliament when they are put before the national interest. That menace remains today, in the 1990s.

On 12 May 1965, the same War Damage Bill was back in the Commons – there to deal with the amendments made to it by the

House of Lords. That gave me a further opportunity to say my little piece. This time I raised a point of order with Mr Speaker. All MPs had received, that morning, an *'aide-mémoire'* from the Burmah Oil Company, which contained these words: 'A stockholding in a company does not preclude a Member of either House of Parliament from voting where matters affecting that company are concerned.' (Hansard column 524, 12 May 1965.)

The Speaker confirmed this, saying that as the bill dealt with 'general public policy', any Member could vote on it. Just as farmers in the Government can vote themselves millions of pounds of subsidies, and it's all legal, above board, and 'honourable'.

Long debates ensued and Selwyn Lloyd made a pathetic attempt to justify his about-turn on the bill. As Chancellor of the Exchequer in the Tory Government of 1963, he had opposed the claims of Burmah Oil. Now he supported them. As I smiled at Selwyn's gyrations, he said, kindly, 'I see the Honourable Member for Fife West smiling. We know that despite that very winning smile he is of a perverse and contrary nature. Although the Honourable Member was for long a thorn in my side, I grew to be quite fond of him, which is one of the odd things that happen in this House. I can predict for him an assured future and can say that one day, as Lord West Fife, he will be a respected Leader of the Opposition in another place. That is the psychological and biological explanation of the Honourable Gentleman. He has an incurable love-hate complex for the other place that always colours his arguments.' (Hansard column 550, 12 May 1965.)

I managed to put on record the names of all the peers who voted for Burmah Oil (Hansard column 566, 12 May 1965). I also reminded the House that Burmah Oil had already received £4,750,000 in compensation – about the same as the total sum paid to 100,000 prisoners of war.

Though the debate as a whole had been dominated by lawyers, a few of us laymen concentrated on one simple question: namely, would it be seen as fair or just to give one major company large sums of public money for damage caused to its property in wartime – damage deliberately inflicted as a matter of Government policy – while at the same time tens of thousands of men, women and children who had suffered the loss of life and limb, received derisory financial compensation. Our arguments won the vote that day by a majority of ten. Ironically, one of the Burmah Oil supporters was Mrs M. Thatcher. The fact her husband had a vested interest in the company could not invalidate her own vote on the matter.

The War Damage Bill, and especially its treatment in the House of Lords, was greatly influenced by powerful vested interests, though in the end they conceded defeat. Peers represent nobody. They have no constituency responsibilities to worry about. They are not answerable to anybody. They are not even subject to any kind of Party discipline as can be practised in the elected House of Commons. There, the Party Whip can be withdrawn. A Member can be reported to his CLP for unsatisfactory behaviour, and he can be expelled from the House itself. The contrast with the Lords could scarcely be more stark.

As I tried to show in the debates on the War Damage Bill, there are powerful and commercial interests in the House of Lords, and when the occasion arises they can be mustered for the critical votes.

I remember in the early days of the Thatcher Government meeting a poor old soul shuffling along the corridor towards Mr Speaker's office. He must have been ninety, give or take a decade, and he was obviously lost. He asked me to direct him to the House of Lords. I did so. That day there was to be a critical vote in the Lords on the question of rural transport services. The Government was in danger of losing, so it was whipping in its supporters from all the highways and byways. That old boy could have been one of them. Maybe I should have misdirected him!

In the House of Commons, there has been a Register of Members' Interests since 1975. It is voluntary. 'The purpose of the Register is to provide information of any pecuniary interest or other material benefit which a Member may receive which may be thought to affect his conduct as a Member or influence his actions, speeches or vote in Parliament.' The information it provides is scanty and not very informative. It is better than nothing – but only just. There is no similar Register for the House of Lords. I believe there should be. All who take their seats in the Upper House should have to declare what their outside financial interests are, and such interests should be published in an annual report, as happens in the House of Commons. The outside financial interests of MPs have increased over the last ten years to an alarming degree. Some MPs have publicly touted for business contacts, like political prostitutes. The rules on acceptable behaviour for local councillors are far more stringent than those pertaining to Members of Parliament. Such a situation is indefensible. It should be comprehensively examined – perhaps by a Royal Commission.

MPs are all presumed to be Honourable men and women. They are no more so than the average man or woman in the street. But the temptations and opportunities for engaging in activities which can be very profitable are infinitely greater for an MP than for most other citizens. The standards governing MPs' conduct must therefore be far more stringent than they are now.

18

1966 to 1979, or Joy to Disaster

Labour's victory in 1966 was the biggest since the heady days of 1945.

Just four years later our delight turned to dismay, then joy again in 1974, followed by disaster in 1979.

The details of this political see-saw have been analysed by countless commentators, and I will not repeat them.

For as long as I could remember, expenditure on defence had been regarded by my Party as something to be attacked and cut, the better to spend more on services like health and education. As a former pacifist myself, I had a ready ear for any talk of defence cuts. But I was never a member of the Campaign for Nuclear Disarmament. I was never convinced that if Britain disarmed unilaterally, others would follow our example. That view, however sincerely held, was wrong-headed and unrealistic. When, unfortunately, it became the official policy of the Party, we paid a high price in the form of three heavy electoral defeats, the consequences of which will be with us for generations to come.

PERSONAL HEALTH AND FAMILY TRAGEDY

Early in 1967 I had a heart attack which put me in a West London hospital for three weeks, wired up to an ECG machine. For those three weeks, Joan visited me unfailingly twice a day, with wonderful support from Sheila and Ian. At that time Ian was playing soccer for the England under-18 eleven, as well as for Crystal Palace Juniors, and Joan was one of his most enthusiastic supporters!

I was discharged from hospital on 29 January, but had to convalesce at home for another three weeks at least. In the meantime, Ian had been selected to play for England against Scotland at Aberdeen. I desperately wanted to go there with Joan, but my doctor, Michael Fisher, wouldn't hear of it. Michael, who was a good Labour supporter and friend, fixed up a lady nurse to look after me while Joan went off to Aberdeen to see her son playing against 'the auld enemy'. She was looked after by two of my Scottish colleagues, Donald Dewar and Norman Hogg. Both are now Members of Parliament.

Shortly after my convalescence ended Ian got a month's trial with Sunderland, and Joan and I went up there to stay for a week. But Ian didn't make the grade. We had a talk with Mr Ian McColl, a Scot, who was Sunderland's manager at the time. He told us that Ian had the ability and the physique, but he took size 11 football boots and 'was slow on the turn', and 'a first-class footballer must be able to turn and accelerate at speed over five or ten yards.' We were as disappointed as Ian, but he continued to enjoy his amateur football and eventually became a qualified school games master. His sister Sheila qualified at Guy's Hospital as a State Registered Nurse in 1967.

On 20 March I was allowed to return to the House of Commons, and I appreciated a heart-warming welcome by Mr Speaker and by MPs on all sides. The House of Commons can be a kind place, which is as it should be.

Ominously, in late April, Joan became unwell again and had to take to her bed. By early July we were busy preparing for Sheila's wedding, which took place on 22 July. Joan put on a brave face, although she was in considerable discomfort. However, in early August, she spent a week with me in Fife, combining relaxation with political activities, and in mid-September we went off to Yugoslavia for a fortnight. That was to be the first – and last – time my wife had a holiday abroad. I think she was too ill to enjoy it, and within a few weeks of our return she had to go to bed. The harsh truth was daily becoming more obvious. Joan was fighting valiantly, but the struggle was being lost. Our doctors, Ida and Michael Fisher, probably knew more than they would tell. They were visiting every day and were a great comfort to us all, but it was heartbreaking all the same. I was still making my regular visits to Fife and attending to my duties at the House of Commons, but my heart wasn't in any of it.

The final chapter of this family tragedy began on 29 April 1968, when Joan was taken, in agony, to Guy's, there to die peacefully on 24 September. That was, without a shadow of doubt, the unhappiest period of my whole life. For a few weekends in that glorious summer she was allowed to come home in a wheelchair. I used to collect her by car and take her back on the Sunday evening. But she could scarcely smell the scent of her own garden roses, and couldn't eat anything. The Fishers came in to inject morphia, and that, at least, relieved the pain. At the hospital all the staff were angelic. Joan had her own private side ward, and nothing was ever too much trouble for doctors, nurses or sisters. There was no thought then of terms like 'cost-effectiveness', 'value for money', or 'competitiveness'. You can't put the cost of compassion, kindness and devotion on a balance sheet.

Both Sheila and Ian shared with me the agony and the heartache of those interminable months. Yet it was inspirational and heart-warming, too.

The similarities between Joan's death and that of my mother were uncanny. Both died prematurely of cancer. Both died in NHS hospitals. Both died peacefully, thanks to the use of morphia by the doctors. Our families were grateful for all that was done by the staff at both hospitals.

During the last few years of her life, Joan had worked virtually full-time as a voluntary worker in the East End of London, helping poor families with their problems. I used to travel to Westminster by train every day so that she could have the use of our car. I worried about her personal safety. She was working in an area of great poverty and deprivation where there was a lot of violence and vandalism, but also much kindness. I remember Joan telling me a story about one of her families. The family was being visited by some religious gentleman who was advising Mum to pray. Joan was gentle, good-living, and good-natured. Her words to me as she told the story went something like this: 'That man told Mrs X to pray, when all she wanted was a pair of knickers and a warm coat for Mary and a pair of shoes for Johnny.' Prayer is no good when what is needed is a pair of knickers.

For the next thirteen years, I led the life of an aimless widower – bitter, unhappy, lonely, and vulnerable. I began to think God was not on my side.

Within a month of Joan's death, the Prime Minister, Harold Wilson, offered me the post of Deputy Chairman of Ways and Means. That was in effect the job of Deputy Deputy Speaker. I turned it down because it meant political purdah. The Speaker of the House of Commons and his Deputies are the only Members who must never make Party political speeches, either inside or outside Parliament. They must always act as non-Party referees in the political battle. I would be silenced for ever. I hadn't gone to the House of Commons to keep my mouth shut. To put it bluntly, I thought the offer was an insult. One of my most astute advisers felt that Wilson might be trying to gag me. Anyway, I had a lot of domestic problems to solve. I now had to learn how to cook, shop, use the washing machine, iron shirts, keep the house clean and the garden tidy. I did not relish the idea of having a housekeeper. The Tory press would probably have gone to town on that.

Necessity is a stern taskmaster. Soon I was more or less efficient at washing and ironing my own shirts, hankies and bedlinen, and not bad at the cooking of very plain meals. In fact I became a do-it-yourself expert, thoroughly house-trained. It was hard work, though. I found the House of Commons catering arrangements much more convenient and attractive than my own. The bathing and shower facilities were much better too, and the Library a godsend. Soon I found myself spending a lot more time at the Commons than when my wife was alive. She had never liked me sitting around at the House, so I had always been keen to get back home each evening as soon as I could.

Those thirteen years of living alone brought other problems. After my son Ian married and left home, my house was deserted from early morning till very late at night, and was burgled four times in eighteen months. Two of those burglaries occurred on successive nights. I called in the police, but nobody was ever caught. It is a horrible feeling to return to your home and find it has been ransacked. It made me feel very insecure, even though I had extra locks and alarms fitted.

My Scottish colleagues in the Commons knew that I had some problems, and were anxious to help. Knowing that I was a widower, two of them sought to act as marriage-brokers. One offered to arrange a tryst with 'a nice retired school headmistress'; and the other had on offer a spinster lady doctor. In West Fife itself similar concerns for my welfare and future happiness were being voiced. It was all very amusing, and occasionally embarrassing. I was never anybody's pin-up, so I didn't dislike this little bit of ego-boosting, but I never said yes. I slowly began to enjoy my freedom from family responsibilities.

Over the years I had always been an assiduous attender at the Commons. After my wife's death I was one of the most reliable full-time MPs on the Labour benches. For therapeutic, social and political reasons, I couldn't get up to the House quickly enough each morning, and I was reluctant to leave until as late as possible in the evening. I was never a good socialiser. I spent a lot of time in the Library, reading mainly history and biographies. I was never a fast reader, nor did I ever feel any urge to read much fiction. With so much literature to hand, I became a dabbler, picking up one book after another without finishing any particular one, so I cannot pretend that my reading was wide or varied. I envied the erudition of Members like Denis Healey, Enoch Powell, Nye Bevan, Churchill, Michael Foot and others. I long admired, too, Willie Ross and Norman Buchan for their knowledge of the culture, literature and folklore of Scotland. As one of the few Englishmen representing a Scottish constituency, I often felt I didn't deserve the respect and affection I think I enjoyed for so long among my Scottish colleagues in the Commons and among the wider electorate in Scotland. The pride in their own nationality and culture is far stronger, and more pungently expressed, in Scotland than in England. Large numbers of Scots regard Englishmen with the greatest suspicion, which can be carried to dangerous extremes of intolerance. I thought one of my most ardent supporters in Fife was stretching things a bit when she told me she had only visited England once in her life. 'Willie,' she said, 'as soon as I crossed that Border, I knew I was in England. The air smelt different!'

Scottish MPs, and especially Labour MPs, always felt that Scotland got a raw deal from a Tory Government, but until the early 1970s they supported the concept of a United Kingdom and opposed any idea involving the creation of a separate Scotland, as proposed by the Scottish National Party.

The Party had lost what looked like a very safe Labour seat in Hamilton in November 1967. The SNP took the seat and naturally made a big meal of it, boasting that they would make sweeping gains at the next Election.

One of the most traumatic events in these stormy years was the decision in November of 1967 to devalue the pound, and it is interesting now to compare the different versions of that episode as described by Harold Wilson and Denis Healey. In his famous TV broadcast on devaluation, the Prime Minister had said, or implied, that the pound in your pocket would not be worth any less – even though it had been devalued by about 14 per cent. I heard that broadcast, and it sounded reassuring, which was precisely the impression that the Prime Minister had intended to convey. In his book, *The Labour Government 1964–70*, he sought to justify the choice of words he used.

Whatever the truth may have been, by the time the Tory Party and press had dissected and misrepresented the story, enormous political damage had been done, and Denis Healey rubbed it in in *his* version of those events. Denis was never one of Wilson's most ardent admirers. In his autobiography, *The Time of My Life*, he wrote: 'From the moment devaluation took place, the Government was shaken by crisis after crisis, and Wilson's behaviour became steadily more bizarre. He was thrown off balance by the ridicule he provoked with his television statement that devaluation would not affect "the pound in your pocket".'

You pays your money and you takes your choice. From my own observation of these matters, I think Healey's version is correct. Harold Wilson's behaviour *was* becoming more and more bizarre.

NURSES' PENNIES – AND ROYAL POUNDS

Of course, I was interested in other subjects. Perhaps I made the mistake of not specialising enough in my Parliamentary activities. I was an interfering busybody, a Jack of all trades and master of none.

Insofar as I specialised in anything, it was on subjects like nurses' pay and conditions, the NHS in general, education at all levels, Parliamentary reform, and the institution of the monarchy.

Being wise after the event, it is a sad fact that my reputation, such as it was, was that of a publicity-seeking anti-royalist and republican. That may be my own fault. I typecast myself. Yet I spent only a very small fraction of my time in Parliament on the subject. The publicity I got was out of all proportion to the time I spent on matters royal. My incursions into the subject began with the debates on the 1952 Civil List, and climaxed with my own membership of the Select Committee on the Civil List in the 1970–1 session of Parliament, the subsequent report of that Committee, and the publication of my book, *My Queen and I*, in 1975.

Front Street, Shiney Row, Willie Hamilton's home town, in the 1920s.

Willie (left), with brother Tom, 1920.

The local newspaper reports Willie's hitch-hiking expedition from Sheffield to watch the cup final in Wembley, 1938.

SHEFFIELD TO WEMBLEY AND BACK —FREE OF COST

Students' 300-Mile "Hitch-Hike"

Two Sheffield University students have graduated brilliantly in their first attempt at "hitch-hiking," the American art of travelling by begging lifts from passing vehicles.

They left the city on Friday, "hitch-hiked" to Wembley, and returned to Sheffield on Sunday by the same method, walking less than 10 of their 300-mile journey.

Armed with tickets for the Cup Final, and advice on "hitch-hiking" from fellow students, these two football fans, W. W. Hamilton, who is next year's University Soccer captain, and T. P. Cleary, who has just graduated B.Sc., began walking from Sheffield at 9 a.m. on Friday.

Luck was with them all the way. By a series of short "lifts" they reached Stamford on the Great North Road. Here they were picked up by Mr. J. Crawford, of Leeds, also going to the Final, who took them the remaining 90 miles to London by 5 p.m.

Staying with friends in London they saw the match on Saturday, then, in pouring rain, tramped out of London at 9 a.m. on Sunday. They travelled for 90 miles on a lorry and two cars, when they again met Mr. Crawford on his way home.

He took them as far as Retford, from whence a Sheffield bank manager took them back to the University, arriving there at 4.30 p.m.

MR. T. P. CLEARY

Willie's parents, Joe and Jenny, 1945.

Sheffield University football team, with Willie as captain (centre, seated).

With Huw Wheldon in Haifa, 1945–6.

In uniform, 1945.

First election victory in 1950. From left: County Councillor John Sheddon, Chairman of West Fife CLP; Joan Hamilton; Willie; Alex Eadie, later MP for Mid Lothian; Sheila (aged five); County Councillor Archie Steele.

Mrs Thatcher's Victorian values.

With Fife schoolchildren on the House of Commons Terrace, 1953.

With Harold Wilson and other Labour MPs at the Berlin Wall, 1962.

During a visit to Zambia in 1965.

Speaking to young socialists at the Royal
Musselburgh Golf Club, 1965.

Willie, a sponsored member of COHSE, supporting a nurses' pay and conditions campaign in 1974, with (right) Albert Spanswick, then General Secretary of COHSE.

Celebrating publication of *My Queen and I* in 1975.

Marriage to
Margaret in
Newcastle, June 3
1982.

" **PLEASE** come to bed, Willie, I promise I didn't know they'd give you the Royal suite "

The media responds.

Confronting the Queen in 1982. Willie's opinion: 'A bloody waste of time (God forgive me).'

Cartoon following the birth of Prince William in 1982.

WILLIE HAMILTON
Labour's Candidate

Vote
Labour
June 9

Standing for the Labour Party in Central Fife, General Election 1983.

With Labour supporters in Totnes, June 1987.

Willie and Margaret admire the natural beauty of Druridge Bay, Northumberland, mindful of the Thatcher nuclear threat to our national heritage.

A reputation was made, and it still lingers on. I still receive letters from schoolchildren, inviting me to do a bit of their homework on the monarchy, and from universities and schools inviting me to participate in debates on our more ancient and indefensible institutions.

I had many altercations with Harold Wilson on these matters. He was an Establishment man to the very marrow. Others on the phoney Left privately supported me, but declined to put their heads above the parapet. It was ever thus. The history of the Labour Party is strewn with the bravery of chocolate soldiers.

I regarded my continuous campaign on behalf of NHS workers, and especially nurses, as of far greater importance than any other cause I pursued. Since the beginning of the NHS over forty years ago, the nurses working in it have been shamelessly exploited in terms of pay and working conditions. *All* Governments of *all* political persuasions have been guilty. The public, too, have also been guilty in not protesting loudly enough about this short-sighted meanness.

In my years in Parliament, I probably asked more questions and spoke in more debates on these matters than any other MP. I seldom marched through the streets in protest about anything, whether in London, Glasgow or anywhere else, but I did for nurses – in London, Glasgow, Dundee, Newcastle and many other towns and cities.

With the help of the research staff in the House of Commons Library, I dug out information comparing the rates of nurses' pay with those of policemen, firemen and soldiers, at all levels and over a period of years. Without exception, and at every level, the nurses were seen to be trailing behind. I then posed the question that has never yet been answered, namely: 'Who is more important in society, the policeman, the soldier, the fireman or the ward sister?' A Labour Government tried to answer that question by setting up a Committee on Pay Comparability, but soon after she became Prime Minister in 1979, Mrs Thatcher put a stop to that.

My involvement with the nurses led me to other matters concerning women's rights. Nursing is still mainly a woman's job, and women have traditionally been in the lower paid and unskilled jobs, so I got to work on the question of equal pay. In addition, because women are the childbearers, I got immersed in subjects like abortion, birth control, sex discrimination, and violence in marriage. These were down-to-earth domestic issues which I could study and understand and which I felt able to speak about. They were much less complex than, say, foreign affairs questions like the Vietnam War, racial issues like South African apartheid and Rhodesia. I never felt sufficiently well informed on these matters to speak publicly about them.

My interest in birth control began many years ago when I received a complaint about newspapers which were then refusing to accept any advertisements publicising birth control. I asked questions in the

House of Commons, criticising what seemed to me to be censorship. Subsequently, I received a phone call from Marie Stopes, the famous birth-control pioneer, inviting me to lunch at a posh hotel in Piccadilly. I was glad to accept. Marie was a little charmer, witty, voluble, and persuasive. I think she saw me as her John the Baptist in the House of Commons. We had a long talk about the need for birth control, especially in the poorer parts of the world, in Africa, India, South America and China. Marie outlined some of the problems, such as illiteracy, witchcraft, superstition, and especially the belief in the virtue of having large families. Probably the simplest and cheapest contraceptive for women in those countries would be a wad of cotton wool soaked in vegetable oil. The woman was seen as the partner who would have to take precautions, not the man.

I maintained my interest in birth control, but I never became Marie's John the Baptist.

Birth control and abortion were related subjects. The Roman Catholic Church was, as it still is, violently opposed to both, and I was a firm supporter of both. On abortion, however, I never supported the view that a pregnant woman has the 'right to choose' whether or not to have the baby. For me, that carries Women's Lib too far. A woman has the right to choose whether she gets *pregnant* or not, but once pregnant, the prospective father has some rights as well, and the doctor involved must surely have certain rights and obligations, too.

From 1967, when the law on abortion was liberalised and humanised, until I retired in 1987, a ceaseless campaign was waged against that 1967 Act, led by the Roman Catholic Church and by the Society for the Protection of the Unborn Child (SPUC). Bill after bill was introduced, with one aim: to put back the clock. All were defeated by one means or another. We who opposed those bills were subject to the most vile abuse and misrepresentation. I was described as a child-murderer. On one occasion, a Roman Catholic schoolteacher in my constituency brought her class of about thirty ten-year-olds down to the House of Commons on a weary all-night coach journey. I met them there and took them to a room for a very distressing meeting. The use of innocent children to exert pressure on an MP on a highly controversial matter is, in my opinion, unforgivable.

No doubt the Roman Catholic hierarchy feels strongly and sincerely about these matters, but so do those whose views are diametrically opposed. In my view, Roman Catholic bigotry blinds them to the facts. Women will always want, and get, abortions, no matter what the cost and whatever the law may say, so it is just common sense to make the law on the subject as liberal and as humane as possible. Successive public opinion polls have consistently supported the view – with substantial majorities – that the present law is generally satisfactory.

In this same period, I introduced a bill on sex discrimination. Its purpose was to eliminate discrimination against women, mostly in the areas of employment, promotion and pay. The bill was 'talked out' one Friday by a die-hard Tory, to the fury of my women supporters sitting in the Public Gallery. A Labour Government subsequently introduced its own bills on equal pay and sex discrimination, but the problems remain as intractable as ever. Women are still looked on as a source of cheap and unskilled labour. Their job opportunities are still unduly restricted. The House of Commons, the House of Lords, the higher echelons of the Civil Service, the law, the Church, the City and the trade unions are all still regarded as male reserves. The mills of change grind exceeding slowly – and the lawmakers, being mainly men, do little about it.

I was once Chairman of a select committee on sex discrimination, and one of the witnesses who gave us oral evidence was Mrs Margaret Thatcher, who was then a Tory Opposition Front Bench spokesman. She held firmly the view that any woman with the ability and the will-power could get to the top in any job, so there was no need to make any laws about it. She probably had her own experience in mind. She *did* get to the top, though how she got there will be the subject of much dispute for years to come. She might have proved the case that the place of the woman is in the kitchen!

PARLIAMENTARY REFORM

From my earliest days in the Commons I became engrossed in the way the place worked, the rules under which it worked, the facilities provided for MPs, and the 'powers' who pulled the levers and the strings behind the scenes.

I was a nosy parker. I poked my nose into all kinds of places. I loved to wander round the building, alone, late at night, opening doors and cupboards until I was stopped by some watchful or suspicious policeman. I had private talks with officials of the House like senior clerks, the Serjeant-at-Arms, and others.

On one occasion I had a very special dinner with Mr Speaker, Selwyn Lloyd, when he was the host and I was the only guest. The conversation we had must, unfortunately, remain confidential. It was an eye-opener. I served under several Speakers, but Selwyn was the best of the lot. After an unpromising start he and I became very warm personal friends. I had opposed his election as Speaker in 1971. In 1961, he had been Chancellor of the Exchequer, trying to work a prices and incomes policy. He started by imposing a pay increase of only 2.5 per cent on *my nurses*. I was white with anger, and it was a long a time before I forgave him. So, when he was nominated for the job of Mr Speaker in 1971, I opposed it on the grounds that, 1) his nomination for the post was 'fixed' by the leaders of the two main Parties; though it was supposed to be done by all MPs in the House of Commons, we hadn't even been consulted, and 2) if he became Speaker, he would be in the invidious position of having to sit, unable to speak, while I and others lambasted him for his cavalier treatment of the nurses in 1961. We forced a vote, but Selwyn won, and I am glad to say he proved to be an excellent Speaker until 1976, when he retired and wrote his memoirs, entitled *Mr Speaker Sir*. He was a grand man, and I readily forgave him for being a Tory! Of all the jobs available in Parliament, the one I would have most dearly loved to have had was that of Mr Speaker. Harold Wilson might have had that in mind when he made his offer to me in 1968 of Deputy Deputy Speaker. If I had believed that, I would have believed anything. Just the same, I think I could have made a good fist of the job. Maybe the monarch might have had some misgivings about such an appointment!

In 1966, I had used the occasion of the State Opening of Parliament to make a critical appraisal of the working of the place. The Labour Government of the day had agreed with 'the authorities' that, for the very first time the medieval pomp and pantomime of the State Opening should be televised. No matter what MPs thought. They didn't seem to count. After all, they were 'merely' the elected representatives of the common people. All this was enough to raise my hackles. I criticised 'the pantomime, the irrelevant time-wasting slapstick', and 'the slow parade of Black Rod, Gold Stick, red dragons and purple robes'. I ended by saying, 'All this nonsense must go.' Twenty-five years later it is still with us, and likely to remain for the foreseeable future.

I always advocated the televising of Parliament. We have now got it, though the experiment is still in its infancy. There remains enormous potential for further exposure to our people of the Parliamentary processes. Parliament is still a place of mystery and suspicion for far too many of the electorate.

In the 1960s, Sir Barnett Cocks was the Clerk of the House of Commons. Having served the House for forty-three years, he knew the place inside out and was an expert on both its history and procedure. In his book, *Mid-Victorian Masterpiece – The story of an institution unable to put its own House in order*, Sir Barnett describes in vivid detail how reactionary and conservative Members of the House can be when dealing with their own working conditions. He recalled a debate in 1963, and quoted a speech which I made then about the inadequacies of the building itself: 'As an ordinary back-bench Member, I have suffered over the years increasingly from the feelings of frustration, helplessness, and impotence. Those feelings originate in large measure from the environment in which we work.'

I had then urged a wholesale movement of the Government machine to a completely new purpose-built administrative capital city north of the Trent, somewhere midway between the Thames and Clydeside. My idea was that over a period of years a new city would be built – a Washington, a Canberra or a Bern – to which would be transferred Parliament, Government Departments and civil servants. The project could be an exciting challenge to international architects, civil engineers, town planners and others. It would be a powerful and much-needed blow to the idea that we British are hidebound by tradition and conversatism through an undue reverence for anything that is old, musty and riddled with dry rot and woodworm.

In 1964 yet another coruscating debate took place on MPs' accommodation. Our slum landlord was some faceless aristocrat called the Lord Great Chamberlain (LGC). He ran the whole show for us. Like me, Tam Dalyell was a nosy parker, but he was more diligent and arrogant! His speech on that subject was a revelation. In his voyages of discovery he had found a blacksmith's forge, huge workshops and woodwork rooms. He had also found that the Lord Chancellor had twenty-nine rooms in his *private residence* within the building; plus twenty-four for his Department. Clearly, the running of the building was out of control. The LGC had to be evicted, and the Labour Government of 1964 did just that. His control of the House of Commons was terminated in the spring of 1965, largely due to the sterling work of Charlie Pannell, a former engineer who had become Labour's Minister in charge of such matters. Charlie was a great friend of mine. He gave me vivid accounts of his battles with the Establishment then in control of the Palace of Westminster. That Establishment, including Labour peers, put up a fierce resistance, and there was a degree of passive resistance from the 'new broom', Harold Wilson, our own Prime Minister. He did not like the idea of telling the Queen that we were going to take control of *her* Palace at Westminster, so he was content to keep his head down – until the deed was done. Then, when victory was in the bag, brave Harold decided to announce the victory as his own in the House of Commons. In fact, Charlie told me that the Queen couldn't have been more helpful. 'She was quite charming about it,' he told me.

But the LGC retains responsibility for the Lords end of the building, thanks to the determination of the comfortable tenants there. So, once again, a cock-up resulted in a feudal nonentity still controlling half of the Parliamentary building. The House of Commons had won only half a battle.

Now, at the close of the twentieth century, two families share the office of the LGC: the Earls of Ancaster, and the Marquesses of Cholmondeley. From reign to reign, they take their 'onerous' duties in turn.

Their present functions within the Palace of Westminster are restricted to ceremonial duties and the custody of the royal suite of rooms at the Lords end of the building. All control at the House of Commons end was taken away in early 1965 and later that same year even the House of Lords decided to take control of its own accommodation and services.

In the circumstances I don't know what the present Lord Cholmondeley does in his capacity as LGC. At the recent State Opening of Parliament in the autumn of 1990, I watched him, a thirty-year-old whippersnapper in the fancy-dress parade. It is now time the whole lot of them were pensioned off. They have no right to any role whatever in a democratic Parliament. They represent nobody. They do no useful job. After 800 years, it is time they were given the boot.

Of course nothing will happen. Nothing will change, just as nothing is ever likely to be done about my own suggestion for the construction of a new Government city somewhere in the North. Yet, if that was to be put in hand, it could transform the face of Britain. More than any otherr country in Western Europe, we suffer from an ever-increasing centralisation of power and population in London and the South-East – a tendency which is bound to worsen with the opening of the Channel Tunnel.

Bold and imaginative policies must be put in train *now* if London is not to grind to a complete halt within the foreseeable future. Time is not on our side.

WHAT TO DO ABOUT DEMOCRACY

Linked to the idea of moving the whole Government machine out of London, I had made other proposals about the working of Parliament – such as the hours of sitting and the whole Parliamentary calendar. No Parliament in the world has longer working hours than ours. The situation is not as bad now as it was forty years ago. It was a madhouse then. All-night sittings were commonplace, and MPs even felt virtuous about it. They felt it was proof that they were looking after the nation's interests, day and night. The people probably thought they were just daft. In the summer, MPs don't feel guilty about taking a break of nearly three months, from late July to late October. There are other generous breaks, too, at Christmas, Easter and Whitsun. For about twenty weeks in the year, Parliament doesn't meet at all. That doesn't mean MPs are idle. The correspondence still comes in every day, there is work to be done in the constituencies, and many MPs think they must travel abroad to keep in touch with the outside world. All this might sound plausible – to the MPs themselves. Folk outside are more suspicious, and perhaps envious. For a start, nobody else in the country enjoys nearly three months' summer 'holiday' away from the job and, on top of that, another fortnight at Christmas, Easter and Whit.

The alibi MPs and Government put up – that everybody is still working hard – is largely a smokescreen, though not a complete misrepresentation. MPs are their own masters and can sit on their backsides for those twenty weeks. Government Ministers like the set-up, of course. They, too, can do what they like, although they are under much greater pressure from their respective Departmental responsibilities; however, so long as Parliament is not sitting, they do not have to attend daily to answer awkward questions or reply to any debates. It is not surprising that during these long breaks public opinion poll ratings of Governments go up. When I said these things in the House in the 1970−4 Parliament, Tory Ministers laughingly agreed with me − but not when I proposed that the summer break should be shortened to something like a month! I also suggested that we should start our day's work in the morning, instead of at 2.30 p.m. Very few workers in other jobs start in the mid-afternoon. Parliament does it mainly to suit lawyer MPs and company directors, all of whom can make a nice comfortable living by attending the law courts or board meetings in the morning. If the Commons started each day in the morning, it could finish by about 6 p.m., instead of at 10 p.m., as is the normal practice today. Committee work, now done mostly in the mornings, could be done after six.

Such a timetable would have the benefit of encouraging more women to become MPs, because many of them with family responsibilities might be able to get home to their children at a reasonable hour, though this could not apply to those lady MPs with constituencies outside London. It may be argued that women MPs could bring their families to London, as I had done. I would no doubt be accused of being a male chauvinist pig if I asked the question, 'I wonder what their husbands would say?' This is a real hot potato.

A further proposition I made was that one week in every month could be devoted entirely to the work of an increased number of investigative select committees. That would result in a significant increase in the accountability of Ministers to Parliament. It would also mean a dimi-nution of the role of the House of Commons as a theatre where MPs are often tempted to 'play to the Gallery' − to act a part, or engage in yah-boo politics. This might be entertaining, and sometimes exciting, but far too often it is uninformative, and of course the Government of the day always has the last word, and the last laugh.

THE HOUSE OF LORDS

On 26 June 1968, I used the device of the Ten-Minute Rule Bill procedure to introduce a bill to abolish the House of Lords. That procedure allowed me to speak for up to ten minutes at peak viewing time in the early afternoon. Only one other MP may speak, again only for a maximum of ten minutes, and only if he is opposing the bill.

The device is useful only as a propaganda exercise. I cannot think of one Ten-Minute Rule Bill that has ever become law. But, over the years, I had been amassing a lot of information about activities in our Second Chamber, and my bill was simply an exercise to share my knowledge with all other MPs. Ten minutes were enough for me to put a few facts on the record. The *theoretical* membership of the Lords is over 1,000, so it is probably the only institution in the world that cannot work unless there is mass absenteeism. There were then at least ten Lords who were over ninety years old, and more than sixty were octogenarians. As three is a quorum, it meant that three nonagenerians could be deciding the fate of the nation. Only the week before I spoke, an eighty-year-old peer had made his maiden speech. He must have been a late developer.

I had been doing some research on the voting of the Lords over the years, and the results were not surprising. In the thirteen years of Tory Government between 1951 and 1964, the Government was defeated on average once or twice a year. In the first year of a *Labour* Government, in 1964–5, they were defeated nine times, in 1966, fourteen times, and in 1967, twenty-four times. The Tory bias in the Lords has always been blatant.

At the time of my bill, in fact, the Labour Government was trying to defeat the illegal rebellion against the Crown by Mr Ian Smith and his white government in Rhodesia. Tories are tireless humbugs in their declarations of loyalty to the Crown. Both in the Lords and the Commons, a large number of Tories gave support to Ian Smith. On an Order seeking to impose sanctions on Rhodesia 193 peers voted for the rebel Smith. One hundred and forty-one of those were hereditary peers elected by nobody and representing nobody; eighty of them had neither spoken nor voted in that year. Three Dukes voted for Smith. The Duke of Westminster, the wealthiest man in Britain, had taken his seat in the Lords in June 1967. He wasn't seen again until he voted for Smith. Then he disappeared from sight.

The Scottish Duke of Atholl deserves special mention. He had been fairly active in the Lords, speaking on subjects like salmon, birds' eggs, grey squirrels, venison, and Scottish sewerage. One bit of my speech must have been read by the Duke. He later sent me a neat, handwrritten note saying how important these subjects were to the part of Scotland he knew best, and kindly invited me to lunch. It was a short letter, but I counted six spelling mistakes. I sent it to the young lady in our Library who had done a lot of research for me. She returned the letter saying I had miscounted. There were seven. That lady was still in the Library when I retired. She may recall the incident. I did not accept the luncheon invitation. Yet another opportunity missed.

In my speech I pointed out that the proposal to abolish the Lords had had support over the years from far more important politicians than me – like the Duke of Wellington, Joseph Chamberlain, Winston Churchill, Michael Foot and Manny Shinwell, to mention only a few.

My speech was hugely enjoyed by my Labour colleagues, but Mr Norman St John Stevas rose to oppose it. In his amusing little speech he said, '. . . apart from Lord Salisbury, the Honourable Member for West Fife has the record for the number of times he has spoken and written about the reform of the Upper House.' I took great pride in that fact. Of course my bill got no further.

I was refused permission to introduce my bill by 223 votes to 132. No Labour Government Minister supported me – no Harold Wilson, no Jim Callaghan, no Tony Benn, and no Willie Ross. But I got the votes of twenty-eight Scottish Labour MPs. It was the quality that counted.

In 1968 the two major Parties got together to hatch an agreed policy for the reform of the Second Chamber, and in November 1968 the Government produced a White Paper on the subject. To me the proposal seemed crazy. There were going to be first- and second-class peers – like our 1st- and 2nd-class postage stamps! – voting and non-voting. The first-class lot would be paid, though no amount was specified, and they would have to retire at seventy-two. At a subsequent meeting of the PLP the whole plan was ridiculed.

In the two-day debate later in November, the two Front Benches thought that by a clever manoeuvre they had fixed up a nice quiet debate. It was to be on a 'Take-Note' Motion, with no vote at the end. The Front Bench fixers thought they had the agreement of Mr Speaker not to call any amendment to the Motion.

I had other ideas. I tabled an amendment to throw out the White Paper. To the horror of Mr Dick Crossman, the Labour Cabinet Minister in charge of the debate, Mr Speaker selected my amendment for debate. I was tickled. In a few seconds it looked as if I had ditched the Party fixers. That two-day debate was not now going to be a smooth and quiet affair. Instead it became a battleground, with guns firing on all sides, against the unholy and squalid alliance of Labour and Tory Leaders.

Of course we lost the vote. The Labour Government – like all other Governments – could always count on what was contemptuously called 'the payroll vote', that is all Ministers, junior Ministers, Whips and any others in the pay of the Government. Within our Parliamentary system it is a kind of 'rotten borough' in the control of the Government, and it is usually worth 100 to 120 votes. But in that vote very nearly 100 Labour MPs voted for my amendment. It was obvious then that the White Paper proposals would be sunk without trace. Foolishly, the Government ploughed on and a bill was published in early 1969. To cut a long story short, the combination of skilled Parliamentary debaters like Enoch Powell, Michael Foot and others on all sides of the House, ensured that the bill was a non-starter. After eighty-eight hours of debate, spread over nine Parliamentary days, Mr Wilson and his Government had to surrender unconditionally. I was hugely delighted. The Government, *my* Government, had brought the ignominy and ridicule on its own head. Party loyalty can be stretched too far, and so it had proved on this occasion.

On another occasion, I drew attention to the fact that twenty-six dukes – not counting the royal dukes – could sit in the Lords. Four of them were descended from the illegitimate sons of Charles II – the

Duke of St Albans by Nell Gwyn, the Duke of Grafton by the Duchess of Cleveland, the Duke of Richmond by the Duchess of Portsmouth, and the Duke of Buccleuch by Lucy Walters. The House of Fitzclarence springs directly from the amusements of Charles II, who was credited with twelve illegitimate children. Henry I was much more procreative, with nineteen end products. The Duke of Clarence, later to be William IV, had a son by Mrs Jordan, the actress. That son was George Augustus Frederick Fitzclarence, and the Earl of Munster, a descendant of that illustrious line, was now sitting in the Lords.

The House of Lords probably contains more offspring from illegitimate liaisons than any other Parliamentary assembly in the world. Don't get me wrong. I don't condemn illegitimacy *per se*, but to make it almost a qualification for membership of such an august assembly is carrying permissiveness just a little bit too far!

Just think. If the Lords had been bulging with the illegitimate offspring of *Labour* procreators, who sat as *Labour* peers, so that there was a built-in *Labour* majority, what a fertile ground that would have been for all those 'Christian moralisers' of the Tory Party, the guardians of our national morality. A House of Lords with such a built-in Labour majority would have been abolished overnight.

It is true that for some time before my own retirement, I had expressed the hope, half jocularly, that I might be offered a life peerage. So long as the House of Lords existed, I argued, I would love to have been able to use it as a public platform.

As for the future of the House of Lords, in its present form it should be abolished. There may be a case for having a Second Chamber, but none at all for having anybody in it solely because of a hereditary title. Nor could I support any elected element in it. In my view that would put it on a collision course with the elected House of Commons.

One thing is certain. Any Second Chamber must have as its objectives the furtherance of genuine democracy, and an increase in the effectiveness of the challenge to the growing power of the executive arm of Government. If the total membership of a future Second Chamber were to be limited to, say, 300, to be selected by the Parties as represented by their Members in the House of Commons, and in proportion to the votes cast for the Parties in the previous General Election, that would go some way towards achieving these objectives.

Members could be paid an appropriate salary and be appointed for a period not exceeding ten years. Their functions could be largely investigative, that is, with ten to fifteen select committees working on similar lines to those operating in the select committees in the Commons. Such a set-up would have an additional advantage of releasing accommodation which could be taken over by the House of Commons. If all the accommodation currently occupied by the Lord Chancellor for both his private use and his official purposes was also taken over, that would release a substantial number of rooms for the use of the Commons.

CHALLENGES

The problems facing the Labour Government in 1969 were the bread-and-butter issues: wages, prices, strikes and the trade unions, all persistent issues since 1945. No Government has ever solved them.

In early 1969, the Minister most concerned with labour problems, Mrs Barbara Castle, produced a White Paper entitled 'In Place of Strife'. The idea was to inject a bit more common sense and responsibility into the field of industrial relations. It proved to be political dynamite. It led to civil war in the Labour Movement. The trade unions were the Labour Party's paymasters. They paid the piper; they had the right to call the tunes. Barbara had a very rough time. She fought like a tigress. For once I was on her side. I told my own local union branches that if they didn't accept what Barbara was trying to do, then a future Tory Government might dish up even more unpalatable medicine. The unions weren't listening. The White Paper had to be thrown into the dustbin of history before the end of the year. The impression created in the country was that the unions governed Britain.

By now I was elected Senior Vice-Chairman of the PLP. Each Wednesday evening we had a meeting of our Liaison Committee: the officials of the PLP, our Chief Whip, the Leader of the House, and, from outside, the Party's General Secretary. Some of those meetings were fractious and bad-tempered. My relationship with the Party leadership had often been strained; now it was very near breaking point. In May of 1969 I tried to engineer the resignation of Wilson as Prime Minister.

I convened a meeting of about a dozen in my room at Westminster, and we agreed to consult Douglas Houghton, then Chairman of the PLP, about sending a delegation to Wilson to urge him to resign. Douglas thought that course would be unwise. The story would be bound to leak to the press, he said. However, he agreed to convey our views to the Prime Minister and to report back to us. He did so. The Prime Minister had given us short shrift. He had been appointed by Her Majesty the Queen, he said. There was no vacancy. There was no obvious Crown prince, so there would be no resignation. It was very difficult, in fact impossible, to remove a Labour Prime Minister determined to stay put behind the skirts of Her Majesty. Some years later, the Tories showed us how to do it. To hell with the Queen; Mrs Thatcher was given her cards within a week. But my guess is that such an exercise will never be repeated.

Outside Parliament I had other problems to deal with. My father died on the last day of 1969, just fifteen months after I had lost my wife. Father hadn't been easy to live with. He was obsessed with politics, more than any other person I have ever met, either before or since. That, coupled with the grinding struggle against poverty, made our overcrowded house a place nearly always taut with tension. I had been glad to escape from it when I went to university in 1936. That may sound deeply ungrateful. Had it not been for the sacrifices made by my mother and father, I would probably have ended up in the pits.

Back at Westminster, the Labour Party had dug its own grave, and the chief gravediggers had been the trade union leaders. The main beneficiary was Ted Heath when he became Prime Minister in early 1970.

I always found Mr Heath a lonesome, strange, cold man. Though he and I had entered the Commons together in 1950, we had never spoken to one another. We never met except across the Floor of the House. We had nothing in common except, in the 1980s, a deep loathing of Mrs Thatcher.

Nationally, the Conservatives got an overall majority in the Commons of thirty-one – comfortable enough to go the whole distance of a five-year Parliament. Despite the fact that the economy was strong, with a trade surplus for only the second time in the last 150 years, Ted Heath had won a handsome victory.

In that Election campaign, I felt I should spend some time helping Labour candidates elsewhere, so I spent a few days with Donald Dewar in South Aberdeen and with Bob Maclennan in the Highlands. It was quite exhilarating to help colleagues in marginal seats, where the problems were so completely different from those in Fife.

By 1970 the coal industry in Fife and elsewhere was in the process of rapid decline, and the miners were naturally concerned to protect their jobs. When I fought my first Election in Fife, it was the richest coalfield in Scotland, extending right across to the Lothian shore beneath the Firth of Forth.

In 1946, the Tory-controlled Fife County Council had published an interesting report on the future growth of the county. There were more than forty pits in Fife then; by 1987 they could be counted on one hand. The report was written when the coal industry was still privately owned, and only about half the miners enjoyed pit-head baths. Then, as the report said, 'The unsightly coal bings [waste heaps] are a blot on the landscape', but 'no effective means of dealing with them has been found'. In any case, the report went on, 'the refuse may be dumped in the sea'. And it was.

In those days people were not as conscious of the need to protect the environment as they are today. That suited the private mineowners. They took their profits and left their dereliction and filth behind, to be cleared up by someone else. A few years later, under public ownership and with a Labour Government and a Labour-controlled Fife County

Council, every pit had its own pit baths. Public money was provided to level those coal bings, give a soil cover, and sow grass seed and plant trees. The end result was miraculous. Fife County Council made an exciting film of this story. Bulldozers and their drivers are shown working, often on very steep gradients, on those bings of unstable material, where the temperatures at the centre were so high that the whole thing would burst into flames. The film showed those machines and men working in absolutely hellish conditions, surrounded by the flaming fury of that evil-smelling waste with its dangerous, sulphurous fumes. Yet, in a few years, the whole scene was transformed, with sheep grazing peacefully on what looked like green pasture – which is exactly what it was. The problems had been solved by public enterprise, public money and determined Government intervention. Today, in the Lochore area of West Fife, there is a beautiful park with boating and angling facilities where coal bings and unsightly pit ponds once marred the landscape.

Meanwhile, the displaced miners had to be found jobs. Many went south to coalfields in Nottingham, Yorkshire and other places. Others got work in the new industries attracted to the new town of Glenrothes – another example of public enterprise. I often asked those ex-miners whether they would like to get back to the pits. None did. Although most of them were earning much lower wages, they felt that that was more than offset by working in God's daylight and fresh air. Many of those men had been used to working in coal seams often less than four feet high, and often very wet.

I developed a love of the Glenrothes set-up, with its brand-new factories, its exciting new technologies, its new schools and colleges, houses and shopping centres. There are few towns in the whole of Britain which can boast of being within daily travelling distance of four or five universities and having their own technical college and superb recreational facilities. I was greatly privileged to be the Member of Parliament there as it grew from a wee village into a town of nearly 50,000. Naturally it always had an active local Labour Party and good Labour councillors. There wasn't much space for other Parties.

Trouble with strikes, prices and incomes policy and relations with the trade unions, all played their part in the Government's defeat in the 1970 Election, but naturally my own result in West Fife was good.

W. W. Hamilton (Lab):	29,929
G. McLaughlan (Con):	12,837
J. Halliday (SNP):	5,837
A. McMillan (Comm):	855

The Communist Party vote had plummeted from nearly 18,000 in 1945 to 855 in 1970. I nearly felt sorry for them.

By 1970 I was very lucky to have as my Election agent Jimmy
Stevenson, plus his wife and chief adviser, Meg, and their three lovely
daughters, Margaret, Nancy and Helen. I had known them all since
1945. They were one of the kindest and most unselfish families I have
ever met. They treated me like one of their own. They were all staunch
Party workers, ready to do anything for the 'cause', without any thought
of financial gain. Jimmy was a born peacemaker, all for a quiet life, slow
to temper, and always ready to reason and compromise. Meg couldn't
have been more different. Blunt, fearless, sometimes even rude, she had
a heart of gold and was generous to a fault. After my first wife died,
when I was living on my own, Jim and Meg used to come and stay
with me in London. Jim was a handyman around the house. He used
to do any painting, inside or outside, would put up new curtains and
do all kinds of other odd jobs, while Meg washed, cleaned, cooked and
shopped for me. That wonderful relationship flourished until they were
both cruelly struck down by cancer in the early 1980s. Life for me in
Fife could never be the same afterwards, though I still keep in touch
with their three daughters. That friendship was one of many in Fife that
made all my years there so pleasant and rich.

By 1970, however, things were just beginning to crumble at the edges.
At all levels the Labour Party was being infiltrated and taken over by a
canker calling itself the Militant Tendency – an ultra-Left revolutionary
minority dedicated to the overthrow of Parliamentary democracy by
violent methods, by industrial action, by defiance of the law, and by
just plain thuggery and intimidation. It grew like a cancer, especially
in Liverpool and in certain London boroughs. It built up its own
organisation, had its own newspaper called *Militant*, and raised its
own funds. It was a Party within a Party. The official Labour Party
was unable or unwilling to root it out.

In Fife, we saw a little of that problem, but it was not yet more than a
minor nuisance in my constituency. Militant Tendency never took serious
root in Scotland as a whole. Nevertheless, it has persisted into the 1990s
in Liverpool and those London boroughs despite all the efforts of Neil
Kinnock and the Party to kill it.

In the Commons I was busy with more mundane things, problems like
the Common Market, nurses' pay, sex discrimination, battered women,
and the continuing loss of jobs in the mining industry.

The coal industry came into very sharp focus after the rocketing
increase in oil prices in 1973. Overnight, the petrol we were buying
at about 35p a gallon rose to almost £1 a gallon. That soon fed through
to increased prices for everything else, and we in the Labour Party made
the most of that in the 1974 Election.

The Heath Government is stamped on my memory by two major
events. In 1972 Mr Heath took us into the Common Market. On
the critical vote in that year, I abstained, along with sixty-eight other

Labour MPs, which ensured that Mr Heath got a handsome victory. I had always been a supporter of the concept of a united Europe – united not only economically, but politically as well. The debates on those matters will go on for a long time to come, but it was clear in my mind that Britain's role in the world, after the withering of the Empire, had to be one of increasing co operation in Europe. To that end, our national sovereignty would be gradually diminished as our European commitments increased. Just as we played a large part in creating the NATO alliance, thus limiting our independence, so we had to come to a similar recognition of our interdependence in economic, social and political matters. As an international socialist, I found the European venture an exciting challenge. However, I suspected the Tory motives for joining the EEC were different from mine, and that was my main reason for a deliberate and calculated abstention in that critical vote.

The second outstanding event of the Heath era concerned his determination to legislate against the trade unions, which he did in the Industrial Relations Act. The Tory Party has always hated trade unions. The unions were regarded, even then, as the 'enemy within'. In particular, Mr Heath was determined to humiliate and defeat the coalminers, especially after his defeat by them in 1972. His second effort in 1974 led to a national strike, with the consequent imposition of a three-day working week, and a piece of gratuitous advice from Patrick Jenkins, one of Heath's senior Ministers, to save electricity by cleaning our teeth in the dark. A priceless gem, for the Opposition, and a sure passport for Mr Jenkins' exile to the House of Lords in 1984.

Mr Heath was a Thatcherite long before Mrs Thatcher. He was a Mrs Thatcher without the charm. He too had complete faith in 'market forces'; he too believed in slashing public expenditure. And all that made the lady a happy member of his Government – as long as it lasted.

It came to an end with the February 1974 Election. The miners were still on strike and the country was at a standstill, so Heath's Election question, 'Who Governs Britain?', looked as if it might have a powerful appeal.

In Fife I had an army of willing miners working night and day in our campaign, and we had our usual handsome majority of over 14,000, with the Communist candidate losing his deposit. Our Party agent had published an adulatory leaflet about Willie Hamilton. I'd had profiles in the *Sunday Times*, the *Observer*, the Newcastle *Sunday Sun*, the Sheffield *Star*, the *Tatler*, and the *Spectator*. The Tory London *Evening Standard* had described me as 'one of the finest fighters for women's rights since Emma [sic] Pankhurst.' In the *Spectator*, Hugh MacPherson had written that I was 'just about the most feared backbencher on the political scene'.

The story was not all one-sided, however. The *Tatler* profile was less than complimentary, and the local *Dunfermline Press* had produced a long editorial which criticised me in scathing terms for my obsession with the monarchy: 'He has outshone even his ebullient predecessor [the Communist Willie Gallacher] in his flair for catching the focus of national (and even international) publicity ... He has emerged as one of the stormiest petrels within the Labour Party – accepted neither by the "Establishment" coterie of Wilsonites; nor by the "Lefties" led by Michael Foot and, more recently, Wedgwood Benn.' The article went on cuttingly: 'How come a man of his obvious considerable talents has been so conspicuously ignored for Ministerial office of even a junior nature?' It ended, 'Has the time not come when his persistent intemperance of verbal expression on what is, after all, a comparatively minor issue, is completely undermining *any* expression of view he may make on subjects of vastly more importance to the people who should matter most to him – his constituents?'

With hindsight, I must concede that there was some validity in that point of view. Nevertheless, I always fought hard for the interests of my constituency. Nobody could say I ever neglected it. A fervent interest in any one subject did not mean that local problems were forgotten. I was especially conscientious in dealing promptly with every complaint or problem put to me by individual constituents. I always regarded the close relationship between the MP and his electors as one of the most distinctive and vital elements in our democratic system of government. I very often used the daily half-hour Adjournment Debate to raise individual constituency cases, and often with beneficial results.

The *Daily Express* also tried a little character assassination. In the summer of 1973 I had put up for sale my house in South-East London. The estate agent had recommended to me that the asking price be £38,500. The *Express* thought this might be a good stick to beat me with. Unknown to me, they snooped around, took photographs and talked to neighbours. 'He'll make a good profit, will Willie,' and they made a good spread of it. The furore angered me and I withdrew the house from the market, but not before the local Communist Party in Fife had got hold of the story. At each of the next three General Elections they sold that house for me! I eventually *did* sell in 1987, at a very handsome unearned, untaxed and undeserved profit when I retired. Who was I to challenge the working of Mrs Thatcher's market forces? For once in a while I was lucky. I couldn't otherwise have lived in relative comfort on my two pensions from Parliament and National Insurance.

HAPPENINGS IN NEWCASTLE AND THE NORTH-EAST

Following the publication in November 1971 of the Select Committee Report on the Civil List – i.e. the royal pay claim – and my own vitriolic

Minority Report, I received a cascade of letters, and almost incessant media attention. Not all of it was hostile.

The *Newcastle Journal*, in early 1972, was quick off the mark. On 14 February, Bill Doult wrote a profile on the 'Firebrand, republican, arch-socialist, Willie Hamilton'. Doult talked to my brothers, and he even interviewed Dixie Crawford, my old schoolteacher at Washington Grammar School. Dixie recalled the time I played the role of Grand Inquisitor in our school production of *The Gondoliers*. I loved that part, and I liked it when Dixie was reported to have said that I was 'a good actor with a fair voice' – attributes which were to serve me well in my later life! I would love to have been a professional singer. Dixie Crawford was wrong in one respect. He had expressed surprise and disappointment that I had 'chosen' to leave the North-East for Scotland. The facts were that the Parliamentary seats in Durham were then regarded as the exclusive perquisite of the Durham Miners' Union, and not even miners' sons could be considered. It was the equivalent of the old 'rotten boroughs'. Miners' sons like me who had Parliamentary ambitions just had to seek seats elsewhere. Times have changed since then. With the rapid decline of coalmining in the North-East, the MPs for Durham are no longer solely ex-miners.

In the late summer of 1973, the Newcastle *Sunday Sun* began a series of articles on 'The Life and Times of Willie Hamilton'. Dan O'Neill came down to Westminster to do the long interview. He recalled the speech I had made as one of the guest speakers at the Durham Miners' Gala in July 1973, when 'Willie stole the headlines from Harold Wilson and Miners' leader Lawrence Daly by making an anti-royalist speech about Princess Anne.' I must add that it was about other things too, not least about my own father working for the avaricious Lambtons, and I was delighted to get such a wonderful reception from my own folk. I'm always happy when I am back with them.

In the course of Dan O'Neill's interview for his last article, I mentioned the fact that the first girl I ever went out with was Peggy McKay, when we were both pupils at Washington Grammar School. I used that article to suppose that Peggy was now married, and I invited her and her husband, and any other Washington schoolmates, to write to me at Westminster, saying that I would be thrilled to have them to dinner at the House. None did, but one of Peggy's relations who had seen the piece told her about it and the result was an exchange of Christmas cards for the next few years. And that ends this chapter of that story!

THE SECOND GENERAL ELECTION OF 1974

The Parliament elected in February couldn't last long, and in eight months we were at the polls again. The Labour Party did a little better, and we got a small majority over all the other Parties. We still had less than 40 per cent of the poll, but the Tories did even worse. It was the people's way of saying 'a plague on both your houses', and I couldn't blame them. The results in Scotland were startling. The Scottish National Party got ten seats, and they shrieked that they were going to change the world.

In Fife we had had boundary changes and I lost a number of older mining villages, getting in return some communities who were less strongly Labour, so that my majority went down from over 14,000 to less than 8,000. That was the first time I had ever had a majority of less than 10,000, but our total vote held up well at 22,400 compared with 24,418 in the February Election.

So Harold Wilson was again Prime Minister, with a Parliamentary majority of only three. The passage promised to be very rough, but the roughest passage was reserved for Mr Heath. He had lost a second Election, and the Tory Party doesn't put up with leaders who lose Elections. So, in February 1975, Ted was chopped down by his own MPs, who elected an outsider – Mrs Margaret Thatcher. It was a breathtaking result. For the first time in history we had a woman leading a major political Party, and, moreover, she was the daughter of a small grocer in Grantham. She was to make a lot more history before she, too, was dispatched – while still Prime Minister – not by the electorate but by her own 'gentlemanly' MPs.

In 1974–5 I was appointed Chairman of the select committee on the problems relating to violence in marriage, and we decided to concentrate our enquiry on the 'Battered Wives Syndrome'. We invited written evidence from any interested individuals or organisations. We visited refuges for these women in various parts of the country, including Erin Pizzey's refuge in Chiswick. Erin was a remarkable woman – a large bundle of irrepressible energy, articulate, very loving, and very opinionated. We took oral evidence from her, as well as from the police, individual researchers from Edinburgh University, and not least from the Department of Health and Social Security. After a bit of arm-twisting we eventually got Barbara Castle to appear before us. As the Cabinet Minister responsible, the buck stopped with her. When she turned up, Barbara was dressed as if she was ready to go to some social function – a formal dinner, perhaps. She apologised that as she might have to leave early, in the interests of brevity she would like to read a prepared statement. As Chairman, I bridled. A Minister's responsibilities are first and foremost to Parliament. All other engagements are secondary. So far as I was concerned, the Committee would do its duty in its own way and in its own time. And we did. Barbara was not amused. I hope she got to her dinner in time.

It soon became clear that the DHSS had devoted little time or resources to the problem on hand. It was certainly difficult to quantify: no statistics were available, no research had been done, and none was contemplated.

It was a sorry story. Voluntary groups were left to cope as best they could, and had to rely on local councils for funds.

Our Committee published its report and recommendations in 1975. We estimated that at least 800 refuges would be needed – though in the financial climate of the time there wasn't the slightest chance of achieving that target. Fifteen years later, the problem is still with us, and may even be getting worse. Wife-battering cuts across all class barriers. A doctor or a professor is just as likely to misuse his wife as an unskilled labourer. But nobody seems to care.

It's strange that when a war breaks out, like the Falklands War in 1982, or the Gulf War in 1990, 'No matter what the cost' (Mrs Thatcher's words), it must be seen through to the end. 'Shoot, bomb and kill now, pay later', seems to be the principle. But when it comes to spending money on places for battered wives and children, or shelter for the homeless, or care for the old folk, nobody in Government then says, 'These things shall be done whatever the cost.' It makes you think.

Shortly after the report was published, I resigned the Chairmanship of the Committee when I became a member of our Party's delegation to the European Parliament, where I stayed until the 1979 Election.

In this period, I was active in the referendum campaign on the Common Market. The idea of the referendum was the wheeze which Mr Benn had persuaded the Labour Government to use as a plausible means of consulting the people and at the same time getting the Labour Party off the hook. In earlier days, Mr Benn had been an ardent pro-Marketeer. Now he was just as ardently anti. As an enthusiastic pro-European, I spent an enjoyable ten days motoring, alone, around the South-West, in Devon, Cornwall and Bristol, addressing indoor and outdoor meetings. It was my idea of a perfect holiday, and the referendum result, showing that two out of every three voters were in favour of us staying in the Market, rounded off what was for me the happiest summer since the death of my wife.

There was, however, a squalid episode about that time – I can't put an exact date to it – which still leaves a nasty taste in my mouth. It was known that I had never been one of Harold Wilson's warmest admirers. The Tories loathed him, and in the 1960s and '70s they engaged in a campaign of character assassination, not the least part of which was the spreading of false rumours about Wilson's relationship with his Private Secretary, Marcia Williams. Whispers went round the Westminster corridors and the Members' Tea Room. One day I was approached by a Tory woman Member. I didn't know her too well, and I had never spoken to her before. She handed to me copies of two birth certificates, remarking that they recorded the births of two children to Marcia Williams. The father was Walter Terry, who had worked as a journalist at the House of Commons. The woman MP informed me that one of the doctors who had signed the certificates was Harold Wilson's own private doctor. The inference was obvious and disgraceful. For once in my life I was speechless with horror and disgust. That woman was obviously expecting me to do her dirty work. My views about Harold Wilson were well known, but I have always believed his morals and his private life were above reproach; in fact I think he was almost puritanical in that respect.

Later, it transpired that there had been right-wing forces both inside and outside Parliament, and within the secret services, working for the overthrow, or 'destabilisation', of the Wilson Government, which may have been one of the reasons for Wilson's sudden and unexpected resignation on 16 March 1976, even though he himself said that he had informed the Queen the previous December about his intention to resign.

I had personal reasons for being glad to see him go. I had had high hopes for his leadership in the early days, but he had soon proved that academic brilliance alone doesn't make a good Prime Minister. His final honours list was a sufficient commentary on his Premiership. It reeked.

The non-Party Political Honours Scrutiny Committee usually takes a few weeks to check the list to ensure there is nothing improper about it. In Wilson's case the Committee must have smelt a shoal of stinking fish. They began to query some of the names, and the newspaper gossip columnists had a field day. I name just a few of those on the list. Lord Kagan was best known as the supplier of Harold's raincoats. He was later tried for various criminal offences and committed to a short jail sentence. The new Lord Goldsmith was a wealthy industrial contributor to Tory Party funds. Mr James Hanson got only a knighthood from Harold; he too was a well-heeled industrialist who was a known Tory supporter. Mr Eric Miller was a property millionaire who had been a helpful friend of Mr Wilson's. A Government inquiry had been started to examine his business affairs, and their report charged him with criminal offences. He shot himself in September 1977, some time before that report was published, but after he had been honoured by the Prime Minister.

An Early-Day Motion was put on the House of Commons Order Paper by Labour MPs condemning the list in very forthright terms. If Mr Wilson was using the honours system as a way of thumbing his nose at the Establishment, he had also thumbed it at his own Party.

DIRTY WORK IN PARLIAMENT

MPs are often subject to sneering, curled-lip comment by gutter press journalists and other similar vermin. 'They are all in it for themselves. They are out to feather their own nests.' Now, I have to admit that skullduggery and wheeler-dealing are fixed parts of the furniture at Westminster. I saw it in practice. I could smell it. I engaged in it. I had to if I wanted to survive. And I enjoyed it. It was the spice of life.

If by skullduggery is meant secret plotting for or against somebody or something, then all MPs are involved – and on a large scale. Parliament is a workshop. It is also a battlefield. It is war, a war of words and ideas. Like most wars, any ground rules that exist are there to be bent or circumvented. It's no place for the faint-hearted, or for saints. At least no blood is shed or bones broken. But careers have been ruined, and Governments brought down, by smart skullduggery practitioners. Mrs Thatcher knows all about that. And it was skullduggery inside and outside Parliament that tried to 'destabilise' Harold Wilson's Government in the 1970s.

The 'top-quality' skullduggery occurs at higher levels of Government – in Cabinets, among 'friends'. It is usually revealed by bitter former Cabinet Ministers in the form of their 'diaries'.

I never moved in those exalted circles. I was just one of the Poor Bloody Infantry – the PBI – who did all the donkey-work in Parliament. The only bit of high-level stuff in which I played some part was when I tried to organise a coup to get rid of Harold Wilson when he was a Prime Minister who seemed to have lost his touch. It was a miserable flop.

I attended few Annual Labour Party Conferences, and spoke at only two. MPs were treated as inferior citizens, herded into a particular pen, with no votes, and abused by everybody. The masters of the Conference were the trade union bosses. In smoke-filled rooms, they loved to do their horse-trading, 'fixing' their block votes and brandishing their power in the Conference Hall with cheerful verve and hot rhetoric. Tory Conferences are avoided by Tory MPs for the opposite reason. Their gatherings are like Hitler's rallies. The Leader dictates. The whole agenda is fixed by the Party bosses. Nothing is left to chance, and the standing ovation for the 'Führer' at the end of the proceedings is carefully orchestrated to last at least ten minutes. Party Conferences are an abomination, but those of the Labour Party are at least exciting, because unpredictable.

Wheeler-dealing is a much more respectable activity, and we all engage in it. We have all made deals, whether buying a car or a house, or putting forward a wage claim to tight-fisted bosses.

Making deals is the lifeblood of the democratic process. It's the only civilised way of living with your political opponents. It's the oil which lubricates the wheels of the machine.

In a perfect world, we would all live happily together. There would be no dealing, no skulduggery, no backbiting, no sharp practice. What a dull world that would be. But it is not like that. *C'est la vie.*

THE EUROPEAN PARLIAMENT

By the time Jim Callaghan had become Wilson's successor as Prime Minister, I was already an appointed Member of the European Parliament. As Labour representatives, we went to the Strasbourg Assembly in early 1975, and I stayed there until there were direct elections to that Assembly after 1979.

It was a novel development in my Parliamentary experience. One thing became immediately apparent: the British are the worst linguists in Europe, and perhaps in the whole world. We are linguistic imperialists. We think everybody else should speak English – indeed that they have the *duty* to do so. And if they don't, then they will surely understand if we speak slowly and distinctly to them!

That European Parliament, sitting alternately in Strasbourg and Luxembourg, was like the Tower of Babel. Adjacent to the Parliamentary Chamber itself were what looked like battery-hen cubicles. They were the boxes for the translators – English, French, German, Italian, Danish, Dutch – all highly qualified, and able to translate instantly into other tongues. I found it alarming and disconcerting to watch a Member speaking in a bass male tone, and then listen to the translation coming through my earphones in a high-pitched female voice. All documents were produced in each of those languages, so that every morning we found on our desks a small barrowload of paper. There was a special little factory in Luxembourg which worked all night, churning out those documents. With additional Members in the EEC today like Spain, Portugal and Greece, those barrowloads must have got bigger, and the little factory must have become a big one.

'Democracy' means many things, and so does 'Parliamentary democracy'. In the European Parliament, each nation was represented in proportion to the Parties' respective strengths in their own national Parliaments. When they got to Europe, though, they found that the names of the various parties were different from those at home. In Europe the Christian Democrats were an extreme right-wing party, while the Italian Communist Party consisted of mildly left-wing politicians with little in common with the Communist Party I knew in Scotland. The British Labour MPs joined the Socialist Group, the biggest in the European Parliament, and we fairly quickly got some key positions on the various committees. Each of those committees met two days a week in Brussels, and each Member was expected to sit on two committees.

It was hard work trying to do the two jobs in Westminster and Europe, as well as travelling up to Scotland most weekends, and I must confess to some neglect on all fronts. Luckily, I had a secretary at Westminster who was experienced enough to handle my daily correspondence. When direct elections took place, the Labour Party decided that no one would be allowed to serve in both Parliaments, so we had to choose, and we all chose to stay at Westminster. The Tories chose to allow their Members to continue their dual mandate, and several did.

By our standards, the expenses and allowances in Europe were in the nature of a very full pig trough. The food and drink were excellent, and the Parliamentary proceedings at Strasbourg and Luxembourg were terminated every evening at an early hour to ensure that the 'good life' could be enjoyed to the full. In addition, there were trips to all parts of the globe, and the expenses were so generous that Members could afford, and were allowed, to take their spouses with them.

Meanwhile, at Westminster, the Government was getting into very rough water. It had to seek financial help from the International Monetary Fund, and part of the price for that was a Mini-Budget in December 1976 in which public expenditure cuts of £2,500 million were proposed. This grim story was made worse by the opposition of the trade unions to the incomes policy which the Government was trying to impose. Labour's boat was rocking dangerously, and Mrs Thatcher was smacking her painted lips in anticipation of an early sinking.

In desperation, Jim Callaghan agreed to a pact with the Liberals in March of 1977. It was part of Jim's survival kit. He was filling Ministerial jobs with his personal friends. The appointment of his son-in-law Peter Jay as our Ambassador in Washington was too much for me, and I openly criticised it at a subsequent Parliamentary Labour Party meeting. I liked Jim, but that criticism didn't endear me to him. He annoyed Barbara Castle by giving her the sack, and pleased me by appointing David Owen as Foreign Secretary. David had been one of those who shared my opinion that Wilson should resign away back in 1969, but shortly afterwards he had accepted his first junior Ministerial appointment – from Wilson.

David and I were good friends. On many things our views were similar. He was dedicated to the National Health Service; he had little sympathy with the Left of the Party, and no time for unilateral disarmament. I was very sorry when he deserted us in 1981.

Nineteen seventy-eight was to be a crunch year, and it was Scottish business that forced us into the 1979 Election, defeat, and the beginning of the most divisive decade of the century.

The Labour Party had been frightened by the surge of support for the Scottish Nationalists in the 1974 autumn Election, when the SNP took 30 per cent of the vote, only a few percentage points behind Labour, who had 36 per cent, and well ahead of the Tories, who had 24.7 per cent. Only a small switch from Labour to the SNP could have meant disaster for us in the Labour Party. Yet we got nearly 60 per cent of all the Scottish Parliamentary seats, while the SNP got only eleven, which was fewer than the Tories. If ever there was an example of an indefensible casino-like voting system, that Scottish result was it. It saved Labour's bacon, but nobody could call it fair.

In consequence, the Labour Party found itself committed to the creation of a Scottish Assembly, not out of a conviction that it was *right*, but
that it was *expedient*, a simple case of self-preservation. There is nothing
wrong with that. It's the instinct of all Parties, so let no politician put
on a white sheet. But I didn't like to see my Government caving in to
the ravings of the Scottish Nationalists. I was lukewarm to the whole
idea of a Scottish Parliament, so when the Government produced its
bill, I supported the idea of a *consultative* referendum for the Scottish
people, and I also thought it reasonable to insist that 40 per cent should
be shown to support the concept of a Scottish Assembly. In the end, that
target was not reached. The SNP Members of Parliament were furious,
and tabled a Motion of No Confidence in the Government. The debate
on that Motion on 28 March was one of great excitement and emotion.
When the vote was declared, the Motion had been won by a majority of
one, and the very next day Jim Callaghan announced that there would
be a General Election on 3 May.

That was the only occasion in my Parliamentary experience when a
Prime Minister had been forced to have an Election on a date not of
his choosing. In forcing that vote in March, the SNP MPs cut their own
throats. They showed a complete lack of political guile. The Government
still had seven months to go before it needed to call an Election.
The Assembly building was ready for occupation in Edinburgh. The
referendum had been merely consultative, so the result was not binding
on the Government. If the SNP had held their hand, the Assembly could
have been in place *before* an Election, and the Government of the day
would have found it difficult to abolish it. That is supposition, but by
their reckless behaviour the SNP ensured that there would be a new
Government, probably a Tory one, and that Scotland would be back
to square one so far as an Assembly was concerned.

THE 1979 ELECTION

People still remembered what came to be known as 'the winter of
discontent' of 1978–9, when strikes, mostly by local council workers,
led to dustbins not being emptied, the dead not being buried, and
various other hardships. The Tory Party, led by Mrs Thatcher, naturally
capitalised on these discontents and promised to bring the trade unions
to heel.

Despite these unpleasant memories, and the apparent unpopularity of
the trade unions, the economy was not in such a bad state, given the
huge increases in the price of imported oil and other commodities over
which we had no control. In the event, Mrs Thatcher got less than 45
per cent of the total votes cast, and over the electorate as a whole she
secured about one vote in every three. I recalled that when she was Leader

of the Official Opposition in 1977, she had criticised the then Labour Government on this very point. 'The *right* of a minority Government,' she said, 'the *right* of a *supposed* mandate based on 38 per cent of the votes cast, or 29 per cent of the electorate?' (Hansard column 1285, 23 March 1977.)

She had a valid point. The system did produce absurd results. It was patently unfair and unjust. But what was unfair and unjust in 1977 was no less indefensible in 1979, nor in 1983, nor in 1987. For long periods over that time, she was the most unpopular Prime Minister of the last fifty years, yet she spoke and acted as if she were an elected dictator.

19

The Four Margarets in My Life

In 1979, Mrs *Margaret* Thatcher became Prime Minister.

In 1980, I received my 'usual' Christmas card from Mrs *Margaret* Cogle of Newcastle.

It was *not* usual. She had enclosed a short note telling me that her husband, Stewart, had died suddenly of a heart attack a few months earlier. In such circumstances, the only thing a friend can do is to offer sympathy, and hope that with the help of friends and family the grief can be overcome.

I didn't then know of Margaret's domestic problems. I knew her widowed mother lived with her, and that she herself had retired from her nursing career two years previously. I also knew that her two children, Andrew and Joan, were happily married and living in the North. Margaret and her mother lived in their own house in a Newcastle suburb. That was about all I knew, except her age. She was a year younger than me.

I had then been a widower for over twelve years. I was nobody's oil painting, but there had been no shortage of would-be partners in Fife and among my own correspondents – I had even tried one or two myself in the House of Commons. No names, no pack drill. For one reason or another, nothing came of any of them. There were no takers. I was a 'reject'.

Margaret was different – in every way. She was a Geordie; but as a Wearsider I didn't hold that against her. She had been a schooldays' sweetheart. She was very bright and shiny. She had been in the nursing profession all her working life, and I knew she neither smoked nor drank. I was 'interested', though I suspected she was a vague Tory, and an equally vague royalist.

Over a respectable period of time, we gradually renewed our acquaintanceship. I would break my journeys to and from Fife to spend a few hours or the occasional weekend in Newcastle. We went to local theatres, and enjoyed walking along Tynemouth pier. Margaret came down to London occasionally, and so the friendship ripened. I guess we knew we needed each other. We were married at the fine Civic Centre at Newcastle on 3 June 1982. We had tried our best to keep things private; but that was like trying to keep me quiet in the House of Commons. Waiting for us at the Civic Hall on that glorious June day was an army of journalists, batteries of TV cameras, and local well-wishers. Jim and Meg Stevenson had come down from Fife. Local council employees hung out of their office windows at the Hall, cheerfully waving their Union Jacks.

Inside the Hall, after the ceremony, the local Labour Council leaders presented us with a beautiful gilded plate embossed with the city's coat of arms, which we greatly treasure. We were then besieged by the TV cameras, and interviewed, separately. Margaret had let it be known that she was a royalist in an indifferent kind of way, so the interviewers wanted to know how she would survive living with this vitriolic man. Did she think she would change him? Or would he change her? Had he watched the royal wedding on TV? How did she think her life would change now that she was the wife of one of the most notorious of MPs? All this was televised, and the BBC kindly gave us a videotape of the happy event.

As I expected, Margaret was superb in her handling of the media. Unused though she was to such publicity, she never uttered a word out of place. She had missed her vocation. She should have been a diplomat. Never in her wildest dreams could she have imagined she would have to cope with these media bloodhounds. Her training in all aspects of nursing, and especially in health visiting, had brought her into daily contact with people from all walks of life, so she was able to talk easily – and she has never lost the habit! She has always been articulate, polite, cheerful and had a love of English language and literature. We often talk, still, of the profound influence which Mrs Boyd had on us both as the English mistress at Washington Grammar School.

After a short honeymoon in Guernsey, we had problems to face. We had no 'grace and favour' accommodation. We had no 'hand-out' from the Civil List. And we had Mrs Thatcher as Prime Minister – a very different Margaret.

Fortunately, however, we each had our own house. Margaret decided to sell hers in Newcastle, and her ageing mother, then over eighty but as fit as a flea, resigned herself to moving to foreign parts in the South.

The move to London must have been traumatic for two ladies who had lived in, and loved, Newcastle and the North-East all their lives. That change was difficult enough, but they had me to cope with as well, and my funny way of life. Happily, they took to it all like ducks to water. Old 'Gran' settled in nicely. She had her own room and as much privacy as she wanted. The occasional trip up to Westminster gave her a new lease of life. One evening I was showing Margaret and her mum round the Parliament building when we bumped into Manny Shinwell, then Lord 'Manny' and, later, George Brown. We stood and chatted to Manny, and I said to him I hoped he would invite me to his 100th birthday party, to which he replied, 'I will, if you'll invite me to yours'! That pleased Gran. She was even more delighted when the ever-ebullient George Brown gave her an affectionate peck. Parliament isn't always yah-boo Party politics.

Sadly, in January 1984, Gran died while she was staying for a few days' holiday with her grandson at Cockermouth in Cumberland. She had obviously been a wonderful mother, hard-working, humble and always struggling. For her last twenty years she had lived in dignified comfort with her loving daughter. I was glad to have known her, if all too briefly. Margaret was grief-stricken, but now threw herself into the Parliamentary way of life as if she had been born to it. She had lived a life of hard work and low pay in the nursing profession, in which she had served until she retired. Now she could enjoy a little of the 'good life'. It was all comparative. We both had simple tastes. We occasionally went to the theatre. We liked to go to the Barbican Centre and to the South Bank; not to opera or symphony concerts, which were too high-brow for us, but to listen to the music of Strauss, to enjoy Gilbert and Sullivan's *Mikado, The Gondoliers, Iolanthe, The Pirates of Penzance*, and to see films like Sir Richard Attenborough's *Gandhi*. We liked to stroll in the London parks, and to visit the museums.

Our first holiday abroad together was to Austria, which we booked through the Thomas Cook Travel Office in the House of Commons. Margaret's passport still carried the name of Mrs Cogle, and the nice middle-aged clerk noticed the discrepancy. He didn't say a word, but I detected the raised eyebrow and the knowing gleam in his eye as he handed me my travel tickets. He obviously hadn't been following the news!

On our return home, we fell into a daily routine. Each morning we left our home in South-East London to drive the six miles to Westminster. Margaret was fascinated by the place and soon got to love the routine. We collected my daily mail at the MPs' Post Office; then to the Vote Office to pick up the day's Parliamentary papers; then to the cafeteria for coffee, where Margaret started sorting out the mail, quickly learning what to discard and what to retain. Our partnership fructified rapidly. Margaret was a quick learner, taking phone calls, tidying up my little slum of an office, and filing my constituency correspondence. She would have made a first-class MP – except that she was too gentle, too thin-skinned, too mild-mannered, and too intelligent! She quickly became a super secretary, and my chauffeuse as well. Not least, she loved the new company she was keeping. At lunch-time every day she would meet Members like Lord Donald Bruce, who had been a good colleague of mine in the European Parliament, Lord Elwyn Jones, another good friend who had been Lord Chancellor in a previous Labour Government, Lord Cledwyn Hughes, another former Labour Minister, Lord Jock Stallard, a cheerful Scot who had been a back-bench friend of mine in the House of Commons, other MPs like Frank McElhone, sadly now deceased, and scores of others.

One of the highlights of her time at Westminster was a short trip we had together to Canada. It was a visit to Saskatchewan organised by the Commonwealth Parliamentary Association (CPA). Only two Members of Parliament were on the delegation, it being one of a regular annual series for the purpose of bringing together MPs within the Commonwealth to discuss problems of mutual interest. We were allowed to take our spouses with us, but we paid their fares separately, though the hospitality in Canada was provided. As luck would have it, the wife of the Tory MP and Margaret hit it off right from the start. They both loved the VIP treatment! Everything was laid on, hotels, meals, travel arrangements and entertainment – we were treated like royalty. We were flown to a uranium mine up in the frozen north of Canada, where we were told that the richest uranium ore in the world was being produced.

We then flew off to Ottawa, where we enjoyed the hospitality of the Federal Parliament for a day or two before leaving for home. We had fitted in a week's visit to my son Ian, now in Ohio, before going on to Canada, so by the end of the round trip we were ready for home.

Back at Westminster Margaret never liked going into the Visitors' Gallery in the House of Commons, except when she knew I might be speaking. She had a poor opinion of politicians, and found much more pleasure in walking in St James's Park, shopping in Oxford Street, or, as a member of the Royal Horticultural Society and a keen gardener, going to the regular monthly shows put on by the RHS at their halls within walking distance of the Palace of Westminster.

In those early days of my second marriage we seemed to be constantly on the move, as if we were living on borrowed time, which in a sense we were. We went to the annual conferences of my sponsoring trade union, the Confederation of Health Service Employees, the National Labour Party, and the Scottish Labour Party. We made regular visits to Fife, and in the summer vacation I arranged, through the Scottish Highlands and Islands Development Board, some working holidays on which we could see some of the work the Board was doing to create new jobs in small communities and to preserve existing jobs in traditional industries like fishing, crofting and tourism. A visit to one small factory in particular stands out in our memory. It was on the Isle of Skye. There were less than twenty workers, all escapees from the Glasgow rat race, and many of them well-qualified science graduates. They were *exporting* some of their scientific products to Japan! The atmosphere in the factory was like Utopia, only possible in an isolated small unit operating in a rural community. The quality of life of those men and women was probably far better than that of most big-city workers.

Probably the most unnerving experience which Margaret had after our marriage was her meeting with yet another Margaret in my life – Meg Stevenson in Fife. I had tried to reassure her that Meg's bark was worse than her bite. She was blunt and frank with everybody, and could be rude as well. I, as her MP, was no exception. Meg would tell me when I wasn't properly dressed, or when she thought I had strayed from Party policy. *My* Margaret had no need to worry. What was good enough for me was good enough for Meg. She trusted my judgement, and all was well.

Those last five years in Parliament were, for me, a curious mixture of great happiness on the domestic front, and of growing disappointment and disillusionment politically.

My attendance at the House of Commons became more therapeutic than political. I had voted for Denis Healey in our Party Leadership Election after Jim Callaghan had resigned in 1980. The alternative had been Michael Foot. I had always had a high regard for Michael as an orator and debater. He was one of the most sincere and honest politicians I had the privilege of knowing. He was a cultured, well-read and kindly man, with a wry sense of humour and a cutting turn of phrase. Michael won the Party Leadership because many MPs thought he was the only contender who could unite the warring factions in the Party. In the event it proved to be a disaster; but it is idle supposition to suppose that Denis Healey would have won that 1983 Election, or any other.

I was having my own problems in Central Fife. They had been simmering for a few years before 1979. One or two zealots, some of them newcomers to the Party, felt I should be more forthright in my defence of Clause 4 of the Party's constitution, the clause advocating public ownership of everything. That clause had remained Party Holy Writ since 1918. It was hopelessly out of date, impracticable and a millstone round our necks. When I was harried in Fife about this, I used to compare Clause 4 with the Ten Commandments. All Christians accept the Ten Commandments, but very few obey them all! Our Clause 4 is like that. Nobody takes it seriously except a few ultra-conservatives who think its acceptance is proof of political virility. When Hugh Gaitskell had tried to unload that garbage from the Party's back, he had been howled down by those who still believed in sacred cows. I, too, in the late 1970s, was increasingly suspect of grave heresy, and lacking in socialist principles.

Mrs Thatcher's victory in the 1979 Election instigated within the trade unions and the constituency Labour Parties a vocal minority of activists determined to swing the Labour Party much further to the Left. They planned to do that by changing the Party's constitution, so that the Leader would be elected by the Party Conference. MPs would be the *delegates* of their local Parties, and subject to dismissal if they disobeyed instructions. A multitude of minority left-wing groups began a mushroom growth in the early 1970s. By a combination of inept Party Leadership, and a complete dedication and lack of scruples on the part of these minorities, the above aims had been achieved by 1980. The principal spokesman for the Left was Mr Benn, MP – he of the silver tongue and the pleasant demeanour, the plausible television and platform performer, who had all the self-assurance of the ex-public schoolboy. He more than any other individual was instrumental in the early 1980s in pushing through the Party's Left-controlled NEC, that ragbag of policies which *guaranteed* Mrs Thatcher her two Election victories in 1983 and 1987.

The behaviour of suicidal demagogues within the Party's higher echelons in those two years after the 1979 defeat was almost beyond belief. It was made possible not least by the genial but ineffectual Jim Callaghan, and for a brief moment I was almost tempted to join the breakaway group of MPs – Roy Jenkins, Shirley Williams, Bill Rodgers and David Owen – when they founded their new Party, the Social Democrats, after the Labour Party's Special Conference madhouse at Wembley in February 1981. I hadn't the stomach to attend. I was sick with foreboding, and all my fears about the outcome proved justified. Even by Labour Party standards, all reports indicated that that Wembley Conference was the mother and father of all shambles.

All these rumblings could be heard in Fife, and I was not backward in letting my own views be known within the CLP. The majority there supported me, but a sizeable minority were troubled, confused, and angry.

At the time of the 1979 Election I had let it be known that I would probably retire after another Election. By then I would be sixty-five, or thereabouts. But the new Party rules left the field wide open for any Tom, Dick or Henry to challenge for the Parliamentary candidature in any constituency. That had always been the case. If there was strong opposition to a sitting MP, he could be removed. But *now*, under the new rules of *compulsory* reselection, *every* sitting MP was *compelled* to go through the hoop, like an erring schoolboy.

For over three years, prior to the 1983 Election, work was done to so 'fix' the delegates to the Central Fife CLP that I would be open to serious challenge when the time came. New trade union branches were suddenly created. New trade union delegates began to attend our monthly meetings, and it was clear that dirty work was afoot.

It was held against me that I was pro-Common Market, that I was against unilateral nuclear disarmament, and sin of sins, that I did not toe the trade union line. In addition, I lived in London and was an Englishman, and was therefore remote from Scottish and constituency problems.

It was in that atmosphere that we held a Mandatory Selection Conference on Sunday, 6 December 1981. It was a noisy and bad-tempered affair, and a humiliating experience for me. As the sitting MP, I was made to stand outside the meeting, in a cold corridor, while my opponent addressed the meeting, justifying his claim to replace me. The vote at the end of the meeting was a tie, one of my supporters having been

disqualified from voting because he left the meeting for a few minutes
at a critical moment in the proceedings to have a pee. That absurdity
was defended by the Scottish Council of the Labour Party in a letter to
me dated 8 December.

We were compelled to have a second Selection Conference the following Sunday, when I had a comfortable victory. However, from then until
I retired in 1987, my relationship with the local Party was ruptured. I
had been sickened by the deceit, the double-talk and the plotting. Of
course I continued with my local surgeries and I attended most of the
monthly CLP meetings; but I became increasingly irritated by the absurd
and irrelevant vapourings of the Lefty fringe.

This strife within our Party was not exceptional. It was happening
all over the country. The result was that at the 1983 Election I had a
majority of only 7,794 – the smallest ever in my long Parliamentary
tenure in Fife. Throughout those years, I am happy to think I retained
the loyalty, and I hope the affection and respect, of the majority of my
electorate. I had never tried to hide from them my beliefs and principles.
They always knew where I stood. I hope they felt that I never let them
down. Anyway, I have no apologies for what I did or said. When I finally
left Fife in 1987 I did so with a clear conscience – but with not a murmur
of commendation or congratulation, nor even a farewell dinner. That's
not a complaint. It's just how the Labour Party works.

As I have said, it has been uncanny the way the name Margaret has
threaded its way through my life, both inside and outside Parliament.

My present wife, Margaret, was the first on the scene, at school
in Durham. She was my schoolboy heart's delight. It lasted for at
least a year. She disappeared from my life for over forty years, then
reappeared in the 1980s to rescue me from my political travails. That
rescue operation is still working handsomely.

Margaret Stevenson was the next in line. She, too, was a pretty blonde,
a Scottish girl. I first met her in Thornton, Fife, in 1945. She then had a
lovely young family of three girls and a handsome husband, Jimmy, who
might have made the grade as Scotland's goalkeeper had he not lost two
or three fingers working at a sawmill. 'Meg' Stevenson was as bright as
a button, blazing with integrity, never afraid of hard work, baking cakes
and sausage rolls for almost every organisation in her village, and still
finding time to work like a horse for the Labour Party. I grieved at her
untimely death in the early 1980s.

Margarets three and four couldn't have been more different. My pet
aversion in the royal family is *Princess Margaret*. She more than anyone
else in the family underlines the absurdity and the danger of retaining in
our constitution any trace of the hereditary principle. If the dice had
fallen another way, we could have been saddled with Queen Margaret.
That might have expedited the demise of the monarchy! As it is, the

Princess has become a monstrous charge on the public purse with her languid life of favoured leasure. She has become an embarrassment within her own family and a bad advertisement for the claim that the monarchy is the exemplar of our national morality.

Margaret number four was the one I came to loathe the most. From 1979, and for the *next decade*, Mrs Margaret Thatcher was the real 'enemy within'. The divisions she created in our society, between North and South and between rich and poor, will be very long lasting. And it remains debatable whether the British economy will ever recover from the havoc wreaked by the machinations of this petty dictator. Sheer luck enabled her to remain Prime Minister for over eleven years. No Prime Minister in living memory has ever been so unpopular. Only war, and a divided opposition of two-thirds of the population, allowed her to survive.

20

A Grantham Grocer's Daughter

I had been an MP for nine years when Mrs Margaret Thatcher arrived on the scene in 1959. At the age of forty-two, I was still young enough to appreciate an attractive young blonde – even a Tory. I think she was conscious of her own sensational good looks. God had been very generous with *all* His gifts. The hair was a rich straw colour, and every strand perfectly controlled. The features were well nigh perfect, the complexion didn't seem to need any artificial aids, the adequate bosom was as firm as alabaster, and the rear end was in perfect proportion. All in all, a job to be proud of. But her Creator must have had a sense of humour. He/She gave Mrs Thatcher a funny little walk. It wasn't exactly a walk, more a pigeon-toed bustle, and with a slight forward stoop, giving the impression that the lady was always in a hurry.

All these assets, owned and flaunted by a sparkling new Tory Lady Member, were the topic of much bawdy chat in the Members' Tea Room, especially among my own coarse and earthy trade union colleagues. They believed in calling spades spades. I am sure the lady would have been flattered rather than embarrassed by the testimonials of those rude men.

Within days Mrs Thatcher had her first bit of luck when she drew second place in the ballot for Private Members' Bills. This is an annual lottery in which most MPs take part, and the first six names out of the hat stand a good chance of getting their own Act of Parliament on to the Statute Book. In all my thirty-seven years as an MP I was never in that top six. Yet here was Mrs Thatcher hitting the jackpot the first time round. She took the chance to introduce a bill which was ostensibly to give the public the right to attend local council meetings. In fact it was really a union-bashing bill, handed to Mrs Thatcher by her Party.

She made a good speech in introducing the bill, and that was the first time I heard her speak. The accent, and the voice, were sounds I had never heard in my life. The House of Commons is rich with regional accents – Scottish, Geordie, Liverpudlian, Welsh, Irish, Cockney and Oxford, to name but a few. Mrs Thatcher's was none of these; not even Oxford

BBC. And it was a long way from Grantham. It was indefinably 'posh'. Not only that, the timbre of the voice was harsh, hard, metallic, like the shovelling of coarse gravel. It reminded me of a quote used by my former headmaster at Washington Grammar School: 'A man with a future must of necessity realise that any odious trick of speech or manners must be got rid of.' Mrs Thatcher's speech couldn't be called odious; it was just unusual and unique. I once heard it described by an eminent doctor on a TV programme as being 'like a perfumed fart'. When I had stopped laughing, I could see his point. Nobody had ever heard anything like it. But walk, voice and accent apart, Mrs Thatcher had ambitions as we were to see in the next decade. She hadn't arrived in Parliament with any kind of reputation. She was unknown. No fame had gone before her.

Shortly after she got there, she and I used to 'cadge' a lift in the car of Mrs Freda Corbett, then the Labour MP for Peckham, after late-night sittings. We all lived in South-East London, I in Norwood, and Mrs Thatcher in Keston near Bromley in Kent. I think Charlie Pannell used to travel with us too. Charlie had been an engineer before he became a Labour MP for one of the Leeds constituencies. In later years he spoke highly of Mrs Thatcher's courageous stand against the discrimination practised against Jewish membership of golf clubs in her constituency in Finchley. I had no reason to disbelieve Charlie, and the story impressed me.

Apart from casual chat on those car journeys, and the occasional greeting if we happened to meet over tea and crumpets in the Members' Tea Room, we never had any reason for contact of any kind. We were poles apart, politically and socially.

Apart from her luck and the ensuing publicity over that first bill of hers, there was little in her early years as an MP to suggest, even remotely, that Margaret Thatcher was to carve a permanent niche in history.

As an attractive young woman, she stood out at Westminister. She was in a men's club, surrounded by randy young Tory stallions and older Labour warhorses. She had little competition, intellectually or physically, among the few other female MPs in the House, and certainly not from any on her own side. She soon got a junior Ministerial job at the Department of Pensions and Social Security, but she left fairly quickly, unremarked.

After Harold Wilson's Election victories in 1964 and 1966, Mrs Thatcher found herself on the Opposition Front Bench as the Shadow Minister for Power. Labour's miner-MPs guffawed at that appointment. They relished the prospect of a middle-aged, hoity-toity female Tory from a London suburb lecturing them about coal! They doubted whether she had ever been near a coalmine in her life. Fortunately, she didn't stay long enough in that job to do any lasting harm. She was moved on to Education, but during the whole period of the Wilson Government of

1966 to 1970 she made about as much impression on the Commons as a little boy peeing in the sea.

After Ted Heath's surprising Election win in 1970, Mrs Thatcher must have been thrilled when he appointed her as Secretary of State for Education. She was obviously earmarked for an important role in Ted's scheme of things.

As an ex-schoolteacher with two children, I was always interested in education. I believed in comprehensive education for *all* children, without any segregation through arbitrary selection examinations. I believed it was absolutely right that in 1974 the Labour Government should have modified such an unsound system of educational apartheid as grammar schools, which only helped to confirm and consolidate the class structure of our society. Grammar schools have largely disappeared, though they are not without their admirers still. The divisive class structure remains, reflected and buttressed by our education system. I was glad, therefore, when Mrs Thatcher speeded up progress in the direction of comprehensives. She also preserved another enlightened product of Labour Government, the Open University. She made encouraging noises about the need for more nursery education and for the demolition of thousands of clapped-out old primary schools. It was all exciting stuff, and we in the Labour Party were almost tempted to think we might have a Trojan horse in the Tory stables.

Alas, it all came to nought. Thatcher's fine words turned to ashes. In fairness, it wasn't her fault. Overnight, the Arab oil sheiks multiplied our oil prices fivefold, and that put the Thatcher expansionist plans into a deep-freeze. She became, not Labour's Trojan horse, but our arch-villain. At a stroke she deprived our young schoolchildren of their free school milk to save a few million pounds, and from that day she was branded as 'Thatcher the milk-snatcher'. From being the guardian angel of our children she became the hard-faced enemy. As a mother herself, to rob children of milk was an unforgivable sin.

In other important policy matters she seemed to be an uncritical supporter of everything Mr Heath was doing. For instance, when Rolls-Royce was in trouble, Mr Heath actually *nationalised* it to save it from bankruptcy; and when Upper Clyde Shipbuilders was in financial difficulties, the Heath Government poured more public money into the company, presumably with Mrs Thatcher's agreement. When we eventually get her memoirs, it will be interesting to read her version of these events. She has obviously done more than her fair share of U-turns this last decade. She probably enjoyed her Ministerial work in the Heath Government, and never at any time, so far as I know, expressed disapproval, still less threatened resignation.

In retrospect, Heath's narrow defeat in the 1974 February Election was a blessing in disguise for the Tory Party, and still more so when he lost again in October, though nobody in either Party had any inkling of what was in store. When the victorious Labour Government immediately gave the miners all that they had asked for, I was frankly quite pleased about it. They, the miners, had played a big part in winning those two Elections for Labour.

When we won the 1964 Election, I had coined a phrase which became the quote of the week: 'Nothing quickens the Tory conscience more than finding their ample backsides on the Opposition benches.' From 1974 to 1979 that description fitted Mrs Thatcher. The Labour Government, faced with the effects of the rocketing oil prices, compounded the difficulties by allowing large wage increases which bore no relation to increased productivity. The overall effect of all this was to push inflation to excessive heights.

Meanwhile, Mrs Thatcher, as a Shadow Minister, brought forward proposals which showed an early willingness to bribe the electorate with juicy 'goodies'. She promised to *fix* mortgage interest rates at 9.5 per cent. She promised to allow council-house tenants to buy their houses at knock-down prices, and she promised to abolish domestic rates. None of these ideas originated with her; but it was all heady stuff and, like a good Tory loyalist, she accepted them as part of the price to be paid for Tory votes. She was enticed along these paths on the coat-tails of that wealthy business man and baronet, Keith Joseph. She was an intellectual lightweight compared to him.

HEATH'S DEFEAT

Labour MPs knew that Heath's days as Leader of the Tory Party were numbered, and we smacked our lips at the prospect. The Tories now had to *elect* a new Leader, and the manoeuvring of the various contestants could be sensed all round the building. Of course, we were outsiders, and could not know of the internal struggles within the 'gentlemen's Party'.

With great courage, and not a little conceit, Mrs Thatcher was persuaded to throw her flowery hat into the ring. Rumour had it that the prime mover on her behalf was Airey Neave. We all knew he was very close to her. We also knew that he had a very impressive war record. I personally think he should have had a top job in a Tory Government. He never got there, and it is more than likely that he felt aggrieved. If that were so, it would go some way to explain why he chose to become Margaret Thatcher's vital secret weapon against Heath in the Leadership stakes. We'll never know the truth of that, because Neave was murdered by the IRA at the Houses of Parliament before he had time to tell his story.

To the great surprise of everyone, Mrs Thatcher was the new Leader of her Party before the end of February 1975. She had not expected to win, and she had admitted that she didn't think she was up to the job.

The rank outsider had won against all the odds, and she had a right to be proud.

Already she had several firsts to her credit. She was the first woman to climb to the top of the greasy pole. She was the first ever – man or woman – to defeat a former Prime Minister by democratic election.

Ted Heath never forgave her. For the next thirteen years of my time in the House of Commons he behaved towards her like a growling bear. It was a silly posture; it showed how small-minded senior politicians can really be. Thatcher herself was not blameless in this regard. If she had had any imagination at all, she could have offered him a senior Cabinet post in her Government after she won the 1979 Election. As things turned out, the cat-and-dog fight which went on between the two of them inside and outside the House of Commons was a source of great amusement to us, and of great irritation and anger to the Tories.

Meanwhile, Mrs Thatcher now had to prove herself – to Parliament as an effective Opposition Leader, to her own Party outside, and to the wider electorate. It was a challenging job for a small, relatively untried woman.

Luckily, she had around her men with ideas about how to turn the clock back – how to deal with the unions, how to cut public spending, how to 'roll back' socialism and State control. She herself was a bit of a 'madam', full of innate prejudices and simplistic solutions to all problems, but a workaholic obsessed with the prospect of becoming Prime Minister and prepared to stop at nothing to achieve her objective.

Very quickly, she fell in love with all things American. She soon perceived how easy it was to talk to Americans about the 'evils' of socialism and the tyranny of State control. She aped the American attitude to trade unions, weakening them by legislation or the dole queue. When in America she never hesitated to run down the British Labour Government, and the Americans loved her for it. It was contemptible, but typical.

On the domestic scene the Tories were being helped by the turmoil in the Labour Party. Harold Wilson had suddenly quit as Prime Minister, and Jim Callaghan took his place. Wilson had been a very smart operator, and Thatcher found him hard to deal with. Jim Callaghan was less smart and intellectual, but had a genial, offhand, avuncular attitude which she found irritating and frustrating. He had a wealth of Ministerial experience behind him, and we loved his taunting of her relative inexperience. Jim was the 'don't panic' Prime Minister, even as he stood smiling on the rim of his smoking volcano. He displayed all the craft and credibility of a witch doctor. He created *impressions* of coolness, reasonableness, of a captain in control – of his sinking ship. The winter of discontent finally scuppered it.

Meanwhile Mrs Thatcher's salesmen had been very busy. Her physical attributes had to be capitalised. Image was everything. The good looks;

the lovely figure; the fine head of hair; the glistening teeth and immaculate dress. She was also very photogenic. The majority of the electorate were women, so she was an exciting novelty on the political scene. Never mind the politics, look at the pictures!

But there was work still to do. That hard voice had to be softened, deepened, and made less hectoring. Every hair on her head had to be kept in place, retinted and lacquered into shape. Every tooth had to be honed, ground, polished and straightened. The clothes got more attention than those of the Queen, and the wardrobe was at least as extensive as Her Majesty's. The smile, the right and left profiles, the phraseology, the photo opportunities – nothing could be left to chance, and nothing left in the hands of amateurs. Lies and deceptions were just part of the price to be paid for power. She never had any scruples about lending herself to whatever odious device would put her into Number 10.

In reaching that target she couldn't have had better allies than the unions and the Labour Party leadership. The charge that between them they were leading the country to disaster seemed to have about it some ring of credibility. The Grantham grocer's daughter was ready to run the country like her dad, Alderman Roberts, had run his corner shop, and a lot of people seemed ready to let her try. She must have known that even some of her best friends were frightened of her simplistic and superficial views, so her *package* had to be attractively presented, the better to conceal what was in it.

Her 1979 Election campaign performance was a sickening copy of American-style razzmatazz, contrived photo calls and deception. Few serious speeches on policy were ever made. There were lots of toothy smiles, and always that fussy, mincing walk.

It all paid off. She hadn't *won* as much as the Opposition had *lost*. She won a good working majority of forty-three in the new House of Commons. She now had the chance to show how to run the national shop.

THE NEW BROOM

I was not the only one who had watched and heard her hectoring and lecturing everybody, everywhere, about everything. We feared the worst – and we hadn't long to wait. I was nearly physically sick when I watched her outside Number 10 that first night, mouthing the words of St Francis of Assisi: 'Where there is discord may we bring harmony. Where there is error may we bring truth. Where there is doubt may we bring faith. Where there is despair may we bring hope.' She had to *read* that. Somebody had dug it out for her. Today, twelve years on, it looks like counterfeit coin. At the time it reeked of unctuous humbug. It oozed insincerity. It was the acting of a third-rate con woman.

Little did anyone then realise that we were in for more than a decade

of virtual dictatorship. That 1979 Election result, followed by those of
1983 and 1987, are conclusive reasons for the reform of our electoral
system. For eleven years Mrs Thatcher acted as if she had an overwhelming mandate for what she did. Yet she never had much more than 40 per
cent of the people behind her. And for long periods she was the most
unpopular PM in our postwar history.

From day one she strutted the stage as if she had a life tenure. As she
mouthed her attachment to democracy, freedom, choice and the rule of
law, she ceaselessly strove to throttle democracy; she made freedom a
dirty word; choice, for the millions of unemployed she created, became
a sick joke; and the rule of law was laughed at by many of her dubious
City friends, as fraud became one of our major growth industries.

Democracy was snuffed out in London by the abolition of the Labour-
controlled GLC, thereby making London the only capital city in the entire
Western world without a democratically elected city council. Likewise,
she abolished other Labour-controlled metropolitan authorities up and
down the country.

With the same dictatorial determination she laid into the top civil
servants. Everyone who was even suspected of being remotely opposed
to her and what she stood for was removed, either sideways or out, and
that didn't exclude brilliant servants like Sir Douglas Wass, Head of the
bastion of Whitehall power, the Treasury. Not the least important change
in this context was the appointment of a Mr Bernard Ingham as her Press
Secretary. She needed a man here who could massage the news, to fit
it to her prejudices. Ingham was to be the Rottweiler of the Thatcher
Establishment. Never in our modern history has official Government
'news' been so manipulated as it was by Ingham on behalf of Thatcher.
She even attacked some of her own Cabinet colleagues by using Ingham
as her mouthpiece. That's how she got rid of John Biffen, to name but
one. Biffen was a very able Leader of the House of Commons, but a
known critic of certain aspects of Thatcher's policies. Through Ingham
he was described as a 'semi-detached' Member of the Government. In
effect that was a notice to quit, and sure enough, before too long, Biffen
was out. But such is the sense of loyalty within the Tory Party that Biffen
took his enforced redundancy with scarcely a whimper. It was that kind
of subservience by all members of her Cabinet that enabled Mrs Thatcher
to survive for so long.

Perhaps the best example of this was the Westland affair. Westland
was a fairly small company manufacturing helicopters in Yeovil in
the West Country. In 1985 it found itself in financial difficulties, and
its future depended on either an American or a European link-up.
Cabinet Ministers were divided on the issue, Heseltine favouring a
link with Europe and Leon Brittan favourably disposed to the American
association. It should have been a relatively small problem, but by her
own incompetence, her deception, and her utter lack of scruple, those

two Cabinet colleagues resigned. Heseltine actually walked out of a Cabinet meeting, and Brittan was forced to resign as the 'fall guy' for her suspicious behaviour about a letter which passed between his Department and the Government's senior Law Officer. Here again, luck was on her side. She survived as Prime Minister because of the cack-handed way in which Neil Kinnock handled the issue in the House of Commons. By his inept speech in the House, he allowed her to get off the hook.

THE THATCHER FAMILY AND OMAN

Mrs Thatcher always used to boast about 'batting for Britain' whenever she travelled overseas. However, she also appeared to be batting for her own family when she made her trip to Oman. The story demonstrates her inability, or refusal, to be frank in answering legitimate questions from Privy Counsellors, Members of Parliament and prominent journalists. This behaviour laid her open to charges that she was hiding something disreputable and squalid.

On 4 March 1984, the *Sunday Times* ran a remarkable front-page headline: 'Denis shares Mark's Oman account'. The story was investigative journalism at its best, or worst, depending on your taste. That Oman account was held at Barclays Bank, 415 The Strand, London, in the name of Monteagle Marketing Limited, a company begun in 1979 – note the date – by Mark Thatcher and a friend. Mark acted on behalf of this company in Oman, though what he knew about the place was probably not very much. Anyway, the fees for whatever he did there went into that account in London. Denis Thatcher, the Prime Minister's wealthy husband, was not a director of Monteagle, but his name apparently appeared as a third signatory to the account, though why it was there has never been explained. In 1983, Denis was authorised to sign cheques on his own. Again, nobody was told why this was. It might be said that this was a private matter between Barclays Bank and the husband and son of the Prime Minister. She believed passionately in the free enterprise market where everybody had the right, indeed the duty, to look after him or herself, and to make as much money as possible. And that didn't exclude her own family.

The Mark Thatcher-Oman story had first broken in the *Observer* in January 1984. Mark, poor lad, was not very bright. As the *Observer* cruelly remarked, his career had been 'a model of relentless mediocrity'. It was a career of consistent failure, from his public school days at Harrow to his failed accountancy exams, and, later, to his getting lost in the Sahara Desert.

But in 1979 Mark's luck had changed. His mother became Prime Minister. At once he had a priceless asset – his *name*. Immediately, he resolved to exploit it. So the Monteagle Marketing Company Limited was established in that Open Sesame year of 1979. Long before that, his parents' contacts in the business world and in the Tory Party had ensured for him a lucrative business career. In those quarters, *who* you knew was more important than *what* you knew. So before you could say 'snap', Mark was Chairman of two companies in Hong Kong, one being, appropriately, in the gold trade. Like Dad, Mark preferred to operate overseas, in far-off places like Hong Kong, South Africa and the Middle East.

By the time he was thirty, Mark was working for Cementation International Limited, a subsidiary of the giant Trafalgar House, which in 1981 was awarded the £300 million contract to build a new university for the tiny Sultanate of Oman. A university in such a small place didn't seem to make much sense, but if it made money for a British firm then that was enough for Mrs Thatcher. The contract was won after she had paid an official visit to Oman in April 1981. By a very strange coincidence, Mark 'happened' to be in Oman at the very same time as his mother. Nobody ever explained whether this was a coincidence or whether it had been a carefully planned family operation. The possible conflict between the public interest and private family profit was all too obvious. It was therefore not surprising that in mid-January 1984, the editor of the *Observer* wrote to the Prime Minister and put some very pointed questions on these matters, as follows:

1. When she talked to the Sultan of Oman about the contract in 1981, did she know that her own son Mark was in Oman at the same time, seeking the contract for Cementation, the firm for which he was working?
2. If so, did she not think this might have been improper behaviour?
3. Had she taken any official advice on this possible conflict of interest, and if so what was it?
4. Before her official visit to Oman, had she informed her son about it, and had *he* told *her* that he would be in Oman at the same time, acting on behalf of Cementation?
5. Did she think it wise that her son should be associated with a company likely to benefit from her influence overseas and whose contracts might be underwritten by public funds?
6. Would it not be in the public interest that such arrangements should be widely known?

No attempt was made by Mrs Thatcher to answer any of these questions. Some of us in the Parliamentary Labour Party pursued the matter on the Floor of the House and in correspondence with Mrs Thatcher. The Right Honourable Mr Peter Shaw had been a senior and much-respected Minister in previous Labour Governments. He wrote to Mrs Thatcher on several occasions about these matters and put a large number of questions to her in the Commons. She resolutely refused to answer any of them.

In early March I had put my own *oral* question to her, and in my supplementary question accused her of 'turning Number 10 into a squalid, seedy family casino, where everyone was on the make'. It was a blunt and brutal question and comment, relating to that Barclays Bank account. Mrs Thatcher chose to dodge the issue yet again, not by refuting my charge, but by attacking the *Sunday Times* for using 'methods of impersonation and deception' to get information about a private bank account and then publishing such information. Subsequent letters from me to the Prime Minister were treated with similar contempt, and finally I wrote that I had served in the House of Commons with all postwar Prime Ministers – Attlee, Churchill, Eden, Macmillan, Home, Wilson, Heath, Callaghan, and now her. In my view, I wrote, she was the most superficial and divisive of the lot.

Nothing has happened since then to change my opinion. On this particular Oman episode she deliberately evaded all questions of principle, on the grounds of privacy. A well-known Tory paper commented: 'When public figures take refuge in their rights of privacy, one is normally entitled to be a little suspicious . . . Mrs Thatcher's protective feeling for her children can be well understood, yet their actions, especially here in the case of Mark, can never be beyond the scope of public interest.' Bryan Gould, MP, one of my most respected friends, wrote in the *Guardian*, 'This is not the first time that members of the Prime Minister's family have appeared to think that the true business of Number 10 Downing Street is to promote the interests of what could be called Thatcher Enterprises Limited. It should not be left to Opposition politicians to try to correct that misapprehension.'

That latter observation was not quite accurate. Various journals like the *Observer*, the *Sunday Times*, the *Daily Telegraph* and *Private Eye* had all drawn attention to this squalid affair.

Various estimates were made about how much Mark Thatcher had got out of the deal. It seemed to be anything from £150,000 to £3,000,000. Whatever it was, we shall never know. As his mum said, it was all his private business. Well, wasn't it? Whatever he got, it was far too much. His mother's behaviour was way below the standards normally expected of a Prime Minister.

The episode illustrates once again how powerless the House of Commons is in the face of a Government determined not to tell the whole truth, or even a part of it. In this particular case, Mrs Thatcher could have been pressurised by her own Cabinet colleagues and by her own Members in the House; but, to a man, they kept their mouths firmly shut. Perhaps that was because they believed that Mark Thatcher was doing nothing wrong in seeking to make lots of money, not from his own abilities, but by exploiting the power and influence of his mother as Prime Minister.

Her record deserves a more thorough and critical examination.

21

Sovereignty, Europe and the European Parliament

Margaret Thatcher was always a little Englander. Her activities on the world scene were primarily to play the nationalist card as if it were the ace of trumps. That parochial attitude got her nowhere with our European partners, and finally contributed not a little to her summary dismissal from the Premiership.

She clung to the quaint opinion that our Parliament was 'sovereign'. After ten years of her dictatorship, that was a joke in very bad taste. If the mess we found ourselves in at the end of the 1980s was the result of our Parliamentary sovereignty, then the sooner we end it, the better.

Thankfully, and inevitably, we have been moving in that direction for at least the last seventy years. Our *voluntary* membership of international organisations like the United Nations, the North Atlantic Treaty Organisation, and especially the European Economic Community, to name but a few, has been a realistic recognition of the fact that no nation state, and least of all the UK, can pretend to be sovereign. 'Stop the world, I want to get off' has never been an option open to us for the last 100 years.

Mrs Thatcher herself might have recognised that when, in the mid-1980s, she pushed through Parliament the European Single Act. That Act made nonsense of her prattle about British sovereignty. As we watched her tantrums in the House of Commons on these matters, it was obvious that her own Party was deeply split on Europe. The *coup de grâce* was finally delivered in the brutally brilliant resignation speech of Sir Geoffrey Howe. Nigel Lawson, the Chancellor of the Exchequer, had resigned shortly before Sir Geoffrey, basically on the same issue of Thatcher's authoritarianism, especially on the European problem. Nicholas Ridley was the next Minister to quit the Government, following an intemperate anti-German tirade. He was more Thatcherite than Thatcher. His views on the Germans were similar to hers, but they caused great anguish and embarrassment in the Tory ranks, so he had to go, though it's interesting to note that he was not actually *sacked* by her.

The Prime Minister's mishandling of the European elections campaign showed how far her views differed from those of the electorate. Her humiliating defeat was the only major setback she had had since 1979. It was the beginning of her end.

It is not my purpose here to argue the pros and cons of economic and monetary union within the Common Market. What is clear is that we are in the Community to stay. No major political Party has plans to get out, and most politicians agree that we must play a full part in all future developments towards closer integration, economically, politically and militarily.

The European Parliament's role in these unfolding events opens up a whole can of worms. At the moment, that institution has virtually no powers, and it is held in little esteem. In the UK, I doubt whether one in a hundred could name his or her European MP, or one in a million say what he or she does. The Parliament itself doesn't do very much to project its own image. It is shrouded in secrecy. Perhaps that is because it might be embarrassed if its activities were exposed to too much daylight.

I was a Member of the EP for four years, before the 1979 direct elections. I was *appointed* as a Labour delegate by the PLP at Westminster. My factual information is some years out of date, and there may have been some fundamental changes since then. I give below the facts and figures as I knew them in the 1970s, particularly in relation to my membership of the Socialist Group. It was the largest group, with MPs from all the member states, and with the Germans predominant. We were assisted and advised by a highly qualified multinational staff of about thirty, and all our meetings were attended by a team of interpreters, well-paid and fluent linguists. We were not lacking in technical back-up. All the groups' funds were provided by the Parliament itself, but each group was in full control of how that money was spent.

As a Westminster MP with many years' experience as Chairman of the Estimates Committee, the Group appointed me in 1977 as one of their three auditors. In that capacity, I had access to all the details – or *some* of the details – of the group's income, assets and expenditure.

The figures below, given to me in Belgian francs, have been converted to pounds. The exchange rate I have used is sixty-five Belgian francs to the pound and I have rounded up for the sake of simplicity.

At the end of 1976, our Socialist Group was in receipt of an annual income of about £166,000, of which £140,000 came from the European Parliament. In addition, the Group had assets worth £165,000. Half of that was in current and deposit accounts in five different European banks, whilst £80,000 was invested in loans to the European Investment Bank, the European Coal and Steel Community, one to the Republic of Ireland, and another to Iceland.

Most of the Group's income was spent on 'missions' and 'political activities'. None of the groups were embarrassed by a shortage of funds. Used to the frugality and meanness in the spending of taxpayers' money at Westminster, I was shocked by the attitude in the European

Parliament to the spending of public money. There seemed to be very little accountability to anybody, anywhere. My auditing of the Socialist Group's accounts consisted of a three-hour meeting in Luxembourg in February 1977, when a mountain of paper was put before me. It consisted mainly of bills and receipts, and I was invited to make random checks. The arithmetic seemed to be accurate, but as an audit it was superficial and farcical. I subsequently wrote a report for presentation to the whole Group in which I recommended that we should appoint independent and professional auditors. I also suggested that all members of the Group should have ready access to the accounts and that there should be a full special meeting of the Group to discuss them. Apart from support from my British colleagues, I got little from any of the other European members. I thereupon refused to sign the accounts – and was immediately made redundant.

One item of expenditure puzzled a number of my colleagues. A big German colour TV set suddenly appeared in the Group's offices. The next night – by coincidence – an international soccer match was being televised live, in Germany. I never did find out who authorised the purchase of that machine, but my guess would be that it was our German friends.

On a much larger scale, the Group's money was spent on our regular monthly 'study days'. Allegedly, these were two or three days spent in discussing the agenda of the next session of the Parliament. In effect, they were jaunts, taking us all over Europe to attractive places like Naples, Perpignan in South-West France, Copenhagen, Rome, Paris and Newcastle-upon-Tyne. On one occasion a luxury pleasure boat was hired for a trip on a European lake, and on another 'seminar', we bought a *son et lumière* package at some grotty French castle, which bored me silly. Even so, as one who had led a simple and even puritanical life, I found the European fleshpots luxurious beyond belief. My corruption was complete. There was only one fly in the ointment. Most other MPs could easily afford to take their spouses with them, paid for out of the more than adequate Parliamentary expenses they enjoyed. It was my misfortune that I was still a widower!

The subsistence allowance at that time was around £65 a day. That was in the mid-1970s, and must be substantially more than that now. With the help of a Parliamentary colleague, I got more up-to-date information from the House of Commons Library, but it was not easy. The European Parliament is almost a secret society. Not even our own Government Ministers can get all the information they would like to have. The facts and figures below are based on information which the Commons Library was able to collect, and, conveniently, they are all in pounds sterling and are as up to date as possible.

Salaries Members of the European Parliament get no *salary*, but they don't suffer on that account, because they get 'expenses', which are tax-free; except that in the case of our British MEPs they *seem* to get, in addition to all their expenses, one-third of a Westminster MP's salary, which (in late 1990) is £28,970. The Commons Library information on this is not too clear. Whatever the truth is, this emolument is taxable.

Allowances Here the cornucopia is full to overflowing. This is the real bonanza. In 1990 the *monthly* expenses allowance of £1,626 was to cover office costs, such as telephone and postage, and travel within the MEP's home constituency.

Travel allowance Travelling, by whatever means, *inside* Common Market countries, works out at about 76p per mile, which means that if a Member has a car that does thirty miles to the gallon, he will receive £22.80 for each gallon.

Outside the EC, £1,736 per year is payable for travel in any other part of the world 'in performance of Parliamentary duties'.

Subsistance allowances The £65 a day which we got in the mid-1970s was more than enough to live luxuriously. Today, the flat rate is £113 *per day*, with probably no questions asked and no receipts required. That rate applies anywhere within the EC. Outside, the MEP has to struggle along on a measly £56 a day. Most of the committee meetings are in Brussels. They are held every week. Each MEP sits on at least two committees and the meetings last two days, so in the course of a month each MEP can collect £452 in subsistence allowances, plus two air fares between the UK and Brussels. As I have said, the job is 'unpaid', in terms of salary.

Secretarial allowance At £3,146 a *month*, no further comment is needed.

Communications allowance An MEP needs office equipment, like fax machines, computers, etc, and £694 a year is payable under this heading.

Miscellaneous allowances Here, every other expense seems to be covered; for instance, free phone calls from wherever the Parliament is meeting to anywhere else within the EC. Thus, if a committee happens to be meeting in Rome, free phone calls can be made to London, Paris, Madrid, Athens, Lisbon or Copenhagen. On top of all this, there are severance grants, reimbursement of certain medical costs, life assurance premiums and personal accident insurance.

None of these allowances is liable to UK tax. It's a bit like the royal family.

The fairy tale – or nightmare, depending upon whether you are an MEP or not – doesn't end there. Payments to political groups remain a mystery, a big black hole of obfuscation. In November 1989, a Labour MP asked a question about this in the House of Commons. The answer gave a *total* figure of £25 million, with a footnote that 'No breakdown of the payments to each political group is available.' Our own Treasury can't find out. Nor can anybody else. These groups, Tory, Labour, Liberal or any other, should be compelled to come clean. It is all our taxpayers' money, and we have a right to know how exactly it is being spent.

A further titbit was produced in the House of Lords as the result of a question put by my old friend and colleague from European Parliament days, Lord Donald Bruce. He asked for the emoluments of the European Commissioners. They are the unelected top brass in the EC, appointed by their respective Governments. We have two, one Tory, Mr Leon Brittan, and one Labour, Mr Bruce Millan. In 1990, their basic salary was £99,148. In addition, they receive generous but unspecified allowances for travel, subsistence, pension entitlements, severance pay, etc. The gravy trains in Europe keep on rolling. The mind boggles.

Generally, MEPs are far better off, in purely financial terms, than their counterparts in Westminster. For every committee meeting they attend, be it in Brussels, Rome, or anywhere else, they fill in a claim form for travel and subsistence allowances. Within a few minutes, they are *paid in cash* – and can then clear off, right away. I knew one MEP who flew to Brussels from Sardinia, took his seat in his committee, filled in his expenses claim form, drew his money, never said a word, and flew out again!

The constituency responsibilities of the British MEPs must be very light compared to those of the Westminster Member. All the personal problems of his electors are dealt with by the local Westminster MP – social security, housing, health, education, and tax problems. The MEP has no need to hold regular 'surgeries'. He will have no need to visit individual constituents in their homes. He will have regular contacts with local councils and industrialists seeking advice on Common Market problems, but my guess would be that an MEP's postbag is much lighter than that of his or her Westminster counterpart.

Some Tory MEPs waxed fat on the 'dual mandate'. That is to say, they pretended to be smart enough to do the jobs of two MPs at once, one at Westminster and the other across the water. That was never possible, and it should never have been permitted. Labour MPs like me were given the choice of one or the other, and no Labour Member chose other than Westminster. That demonstrated that financial considerations were not their main concern.

MEPs are rightly concerned about their future role in a fast-changing Europe. They are anxious to extend their powers, and to exert more democratic control over the executive arm of the Community – the Commission and the Council of Ministers. Sympathy for these aims would be greater if they put their own house in order. There is no excuse for the suffocating secrecy about their own monumental extravagance. It's time the top was blown off. I hope I may have loosened a tile or two.

22

1987 and After

The date of the General Election was to be 11 June. That was sad for those MPs who were retiring. It meant we wouldn't be on the payroll for the summer recess. Our pay would stop on 11 June. I attended my last PLP meeting on 13 May, and I have never set foot in the Palace of Westminster since that date. There is nobody so retired as a retired MP. No farewell parties; no parting gifts; no souvenirs. I tried to buy a House of Commons tea set, but was not allowed to do so. The Speaker 'generously' invited retiring MPs to have a sherry with him. I didn't bother. I was sick at heart, sustained only by Margaret. No, that's not quite true. Many months before, I had let it be known to the Party's Headquarters that, whenever the Election might be, I would be willing to stand as the Labour candidate in *any* constituency which, for one reason or another, could not get one. From long experience, I knew there were always constituencies in that category – mostly where there was an overwhelming Tory majority. Nearly all those 'hopeless' seats were in the South. The great divide between the North and South, politically, socially and economically, was sharper in 1987 than it had ever been.

Very soon I was approached by the Central Sussex and Eastbourne CLPs, and I attended meetings there. On each occasion I explained that I should be regarded as a 'longstop' candidate, someone of 'last resort'. In both cases the local Party managed to get their own candidate. At Eastbourne they actually held a Selection Conference at which there were two of us, myself and a young Asian solicitor from London. I had a long chat with my 'rival' before the meeting and was impressed by his intelligence and commitment to Labour. So when I was invited to address the conference, I urged them to go for that young solicitor. It must have been the first-ever Selection Conference where one of the 'hopefuls' urged that his application be rejected. The solicitor was duly selected. The local and national Tory press immediately carried a story about the 'notorious' Willie Hamilton's 'rejection' by the Eastbourne Labour Party. As soon as that 'shock' broke, I was phoned by Mr Ron Brown. I had been a good friend of Ron and his wife. He was an active right-winger and had been the Labour MP for Hackney before he lost the seat after deserting the Party to join the SDP. It was obvious he had been taken in by the press reports about my 'rejection' at Eastbourne. 'It just fits in,' crowed Ron, 'with how the Labour Left has taken over, even in places like Eastbourne!' I was pleased to tell him he was talking rubbish, or words to that effect, and urged him not to be so gullible.

The final CLP invitation came from South Hams in Devon. That was the old Totnes seat, which includes Dartmoor and a beautiful stretch of the South Devon coast. It is a very safe Tory seat. It must also have the most beautiful scenery in the whole of England. The sitting Tory Member later confided that it was not so much a job as a way of life. He was a carpet-bagger from less salubrious parts of the country; I could see what he meant. Why is it that the prettiest and most desirable Parliamentary constituencies are almost invariably Tory, and the ugliest and harshest environments Labour? For make no mistake, poverty in rural areas is just as great as it is in big cities. The wages are often far lower, housing conditions are just as bad, job opportunities are much worse, public transport is almost non-existent, educational facilities are disgracefully inadequate, and health services are pathetic. Almost the only things that were *good* in South Hams were the air, the scenery, and the wonderful folk who were in the local Labour Party. They were the most intelligent, idealistic and hard-working bunch of Party workers I had ever met in the forty-five years I had been in active politics.

Many of them were deeply committed to CND as unilateral nuclear disarmers, and I made it clear from the outset that though I had never agreed with that policy, I would defend it publicly as best as I could. I kept my promise. I argued that no one could ever visualise any circumstances in which a British Government would use its nuclear weapons *unilaterally*. Moreover, I said I could never sanction *any* Prime Minister to press the nuclear button on my behalf. As someone with grandchildren I could never support their deestruction by a Mrs Thatcher – she had already declared her willingness to press that button. Looking back now, I still think that case had considerable force, though the defence problem is far more complex than my emotional responses indicated. However, I hold the view that if a Parliamentary candidate stands for election as an official *Party* representative, he or she has an obligation to propound the policies of the Party, even though he or she may have reservations about some of them.

Before the Election campaign got under way, two national newspapers, one English and one Scottish, ran stories that, as an MP who had announced his retirement, the only reason I was contesting South Hams was to get more 'redundancy' pay from Parliament than I would have otherwise obtained. Just the sort of muckraking we could expect from certain organs of the press. It was a falsehood, so I sued the papers.

I got a small sum of damages, with costs, from each of them. I had never made a libel claim in my life. I innocently thought that an award settled out of court 'with costs' meant that I myself received that sum *net* of legal costs, so I was surprised, and disappointed, when my lawyer deducted his sizeable costs from the total amount awarded. I was ignorant on those matters and I did not pursue it further. Anyway, the trivial sum I eventually received helped to pay my Election expenses in Devon. The local Party had little money, so we ran our campaign on a shoestring. My wife drove me round in my own car. Others, many of them unemployed, were making far greater sacrifices. Margaret had been active with me in my last campaign in Fife in 1983. It couldn't have been more different from what she went through in Devon. In Fife we were on the winning side. There, at a packed public meeting organised by the local churches or by CND and attended by all the Parliamentary candidates, Margaret had found herself sitting next to a prominent lady member of our local Party. *She* recognised Margaret, but Margaret didn't know *her*. She remarked that Margaret had 'won the jackpot', meaning she had married me! Margaret had found it difficult to believe what she was hearing. She wasn't as thick-skinned as her husband. And her sensitivity was greatly tried in South Hams. There, they were hostile, if apathetic. In the Army we used to call it 'dumb insolence'. As we handed out our Party leaflets in the streets of Kingsbridge, Margaret was timid, fearful, but very polite and pleasant. On proffering her leaflets, she was met with rudeness, vicious comments and hostility, as if she were an unwanted enemy intruder, or someone from outer space.

During the campaign I had tried to alert people to the injustice and unfairness of the Poll Tax. The official Tory Election Manifesto had barely mentioned it, and no Tory newspaper, local or national, gave it any publicity. In Devon, I was a lone voice crying in the wilderness, on that and other matters. Earlier, I had introduced a bill in Parliament to set up a South-West Development Agency for Devon and Cornwall, like the one already established in Scotland. I had published the bill, and had had it circulated, but only one Tory MP supported it. Similarly, our campaign warning the Devonport dockyard workers of the job losses that would result from 'privatisation' fell on deaf ears. I got a rapturous reception from a packed hall in the area. The dockyard was outside my constituency boundaries, but we thought the Parliamentary seats of David Owen and Janet Fookes were vulnerable, so I spent some time in the Plymouth area. I had the voice volume to perform very well on a loudspeaker, and I loved that kind of campaigning. 'Never trust a turncoat,' was my bellowed message in Devonport.

In the event it came to nought. Well, not quite nought. For the first time in history, we saved our £500 deposit in South Hams, and the local Labour Party was given a morale-booster – I hope!

POLITICS AND FAMILY LIFE

Confession is good for the soul. So I confess that my Parliamentary work at Westminster and in Fife led to a shameful neglect of my family life. My wife Joan brought up our two children, Sheila and Ian, virtually single-handedly.

Sheila did well at her girls' comprehensive school at Forest Hill in South London. From there she went on to become a trained SRN at Guy's Teaching Hospital, and is now happily married with three grown-up children. She is currently a senior nurse working full-time within a GP group practice at Crawley in Sussex. One of her adopted boys is in the Army; the other, also adopted, is in the catering industry, while her only natural child, Joanne, hopes to go to university in the autumn of 1992.

Ian went to the United States some years ago. He had done sufficiently well at his South London Comprehensive School to go on a teacher-training course at the North London Polytechnic. One of his projects there was the writing of a thesis on sport and politics. I arranged personal interviews for him with Denis Howell, who had been the Minister for Sport in a Labour Government, and with Eldon Griffiths, then the Tory Minister for Sport. I also took Ian to Sweden for a holiday, and fixed up an interview with their Minister for Sport. Ian's final thesis was a knockout. It could be a collectors' piece, if I only knew where it was.

He married a nice young lady from North London who, like himself, was a sports teacher. Unfortunately, the marriage failed after about two years, and it was then that Ian went off to the States, where for a year or two he tried to establish himself as a soccer coach and teacher. After some scarifying adventures he has now finally settled in Ohio, and is happily married to an American. He has no family but is wrapped up in his teaching and coaching. For the last few years he has greatly enjoyed using some of his summer holiday coaching the junior officer ranks of the American Navy how to play soccer.

I don't think Ian will be coming back to the old country to settle again.

Meanwhile, Margaret and I now had to plan an uncertain future. We no longer had the therapy of Parliament to sustain us.

We had already decided to get away from London as soon as possible. The 'big wen' had a lot *not* going for it, including the public transport system, and we couldn't think of a single good reason for staying there a day longer than was absolutely necessary. In any case, the dramatic fall in income made the move essential. So, in October of 1987, we moved to Woodhall Spa in the middle of rural, Tory Lincolnshire. In the following

May I contested a hopelessly Tory seat in the county council elections, and lost handsomely.

It is bliss to garden, to read and write, and to watch the Westminster beargarden on television. My roses respond to feeding and tender care – and don't argue or answer back. Margaret has the green fingers, and I am the enthusiastic but unskilled labourer.

It would be silly to pretend I don't miss the old place and the old faces at Westminster. There is still so much to be done there. Every part of the British Constitution is creaking at the joints, and it will take more than a few drops of oil to put things right. We are rapidly approaching the status of a Third World nation, a process which has been accelerated by the 1980s as a decade of disaster.

My dear Labour Party, having discarded most of the damaging baggage it clung to for far too long, can play a vital part in making our country a more efficient, a more just, humane, *warm* and less divided society than it has been of late.

I live in hope.

23

Miracle or Mirage?

'Oh! what bliss it was
To be alive that day.'

W.W.H.

Nothing epitomised the reign of the Tory 'Goddess' more than the nature of her dispatch. At the drop of a hat, a few Tory 'gentlemen' in dark suits plunged in the knife, and she was gone – appropriately enough on Thanksgiving Day – broken, and with tears in her eyes as she left Number 10 to convey the news to Her Majesty the Queen at Buckingham Palace. Millions of others were in tears, too – tears of sheer joy and relief – including a number of her own Tory MPs whose jobs were threatened as long as she stayed.

For more than a decade she had hawked her prejudices, bullied, shrieked at and lectured everybody like a tinpot dictator, as if she had had the overwhelming support of the British people.

Her long tenure as Prime Minister had less to do with either her own abilities or the will of the electorate, and more with a combination of other circumstances unlikely ever again to appear. An unfair electoral system gave her, in three successive Elections, a numerical strength in Parliament out of all proportion to the total votes cast. It was a Parliament, moreover, whose procedures lent themselves to every kind of manipulation by a Government determined to cling to power *at any cost.*

The Tory Party can draw on unlimited resources of blind loyalty, so long as the Leader is delivering *power.* On the other side of that same coin was a Labour Opposition tragically divided, and with a Leadership, under Neil Kinnock, struggling to bring to the Party some semblance of realism, moderation and common sense. Mrs Thatcher couldn't have wished for a better scenario.

Her luck didn't stop there. The fabulous unearned bonus of the North Sea riches of oil and gas became available to her. They alone amounted to almost £100,000 *million* in that golden decade – or, rather, it *could* have been golden if that wealth had been wisely invested. It *could* have made our country truly great. We *could* have had the best educational system in the world. We *could* have had a modernised manufacturing and industrial economy fit to compete in the international market-place, an ultra-modern transport and communications network, good homes for everybody, a Rolls-Royce National Health Service, and probably the highest standard of living in the world. Sadly, we can all see how far that dream is from being realised. In the 1980s, we watched our housing stock, our schools, hospitals, roads and railways decay and deteriorate, and our industrial policy so mismanaged at all levels that by the early 1980s we were importing more manufactured goods than we were exporting for the first time since the Industrial Revolution. Some miracle!

Within two years, the inflation rate had soared to 22 per cent, and Mrs Thatcher became the most unpopular Premier in modern times. Only the 1982 Falkland Islands War saved her from electoral defeat. That war enabled her to drape herself in the Union Jack and bang the jingoistic drums as she made the specious claim that she was fighting for the freedom and democratic rights of the few hundred Islanders.

So she went on, and on, and on.

In those disastrous 1980s, no political leader excited such a wide range of emotions. She was either loved dearly or bitterly loathed. There didn't seem to be a halfway house. That was probably how she wished it to be. She curled her lip in contempt at any concept of 'consensus' politics. She thrived on *confrontation*. She loved to have enemies. She relished *attacking* somebody or some organisation *all* the time, Church, BBC, trade unions, socialism, society, and 'moaning minnies' everywhere. If you were not 'one of *us*' you were 'one of *them*', the 'enemy within', a 'wet' if not a traitor. There was no room for ditherers or fence-sitters. It was a fight to the death between black and white, between the 'goodies' and the 'baddies'. It had to end in unconditional surrender.

I freely admit, I was one of the 'loathers', though as a lifelong supporter of the rights of women, I was originally far from dismayed when she won the Leadership of her Party in 1975. There had always been a lot of covert anti-feminism in both main political parties. Women were seen as the childbearers, the kitchen maids, the tea-makers or the secretary/typists. Their main service was in bed. The House of Commons itself was like a boys' public school where women were regarded as meddlesome intruders. It was in this atmosphere that Mrs Thatcher made her mark, though it subsequently transpired that when she got real power she didn't do much for the welfare of women.

For eleven of the fifteen years from 1964 to 1979 she was in Opposition, and for much of that time she was a Front Bench spokesman. Her Party had always provided a much better research and briefing service for their Leaders in the Commons than anything the Labour Party could afford. Mrs Thatcher never had much experience as a back-bench Member. She scarcely knew what it was like to do all her own foraging, her own research, or to prepare all her own speeches and questions. However, she always seemed to be very well briefed, and to have done her homework. But she was never an exciting orator. She never brought me to the edge of my seat, except in fury. She had little sense of humour, no original turn of phrase, and no spontaneous repartee. In fact, she was a crashing bore. And that voice ... All the time, she was putting on an act. Throughout her career, she was *acting* and posturing, whether in the House of Commons or on television.

However good the services provided by her own Party, they were trivial compared to those she inherited on becoming Prime Minister. Number 10 Downing Street is not a home, but a vast political power station, infested by legions of experts, advisers and manipulators of the levers of State power. All that was at the disposal of the Prime Minister, in addition to the armies of civil servants in every Government Department in Whitchall. To coin a phrase, she appeared to be 'totally and utterly' unassailable. The propaganda potential of this complex machine was enormous, and she used it ruthlessly in the interests of her own Tory Party – the beauty of it was that the whole thing was paid for by the taxpayer.

As a humble back-bench MP, I could only watch these developments, helpless to stop them, and therefore increasingly angry and frustrated. My contempt for Mrs Thatcher grew by the day. She treated the House of Commons not so much as the great political forum of national debate, but as a battlefield in which she was the General, in full control of an army ready to obey her every whim, and faced with a weak, demoralised and divided Opposition. No wonder she thought she would last for ever. Many of us, and not a few Tories, were appalled and even frightened by the prospect.

HER HOUSE OF COMMONS BEHAVIOUR

A Prime Minister makes at least two compulsory appearances in the House of Commons each week. At 3.15 on every Tuesday and Thursday, the PM answers oral questions for a maximum of fifteen minutes each day. There is great competition to get seats in the Public Galleries, and among MPs there is equally great competition to get a top place in the queue of would-be questioners. It's like a daily Parliamentary raffle, in which the MPs' names and questions are literally shuffled around and drawn out in a random selection by Officers of the House. The most nitwitted Member can find himself top of the list. These days, Prime Ministers Questions nearly all take the same form, namely: What are his or her official engagements for today? That is just the peg on which to hang the devastating, witty or unctuous Supplementary. The last thing the questioning Member is seeking is information! If he were a Tory, he would be on his knees to Mrs Thatcher asking, 'If she is aware that she is performing miracles, and will she please keep on being our Saviour?' A Labour Member would probably engage in some verbal assault about the growing dole queues or hospital waiting lists.

Not only was the PM's Question Time meticulously prepared beforehand in her own Private Office, but the Tory Whips, led by the Chief Whip, organised the 'farming out' to Tory MPs of 'planted' questions – soft balls to be lobbed at the Prime Minister – and, to make sure those Members were 'called' by the Speaker, the Chief Whip made prior representations to him on the matter. It seemed to me sharp practice, but I know on impeccable authority that that happened, and such an exercise could hardly have happened without at least the acquiescence of the Prime Minister.

Nothing substantial was achieved by the infantile prattle of Question Time, except that it gave the Prime Minister *carte blanche* to score easy bull's-eye Party points. Every one of her answers became a little propaganda speech on how wonderfully she was doing; and it was all in order. Nobody could stop the game being played this way; not even an idiot PM could lose it, and Mrs Thatcher was nobody's fool.

Though she had long opposed letting TV cameras into the House, once they were there she used them to parade her undoubted photogenic qualities, and as usual she prepared herself with great thoroughness, including painstaking rehearsals, just like any actress. Her act changed overnight. From being the abrasive, shrill, combative harridan, she became a smiling angel, the crimson-rimmed mouthful of gleaming teeth ever on show, like a piano keyboard, and the tinted face wreathed in a condescending smile, switched on permanently for the benefit of the gawping millions. The expensive couture was changed at least once every day, which must have been good for the rag trade.

As time wore on, however, the image became somewhat tarnished. The 'Iron Lady' showed hopeful evidence of rust and metal fatigue which not even her electrically charged baths could hide. As she became more self-confident and domineering the language grew more absurdly extravagant. The use of the royal 'we' became a national joke. In one brief interview, she used the royal 'we' nineteen times. '*We are a grandmother*' was a universal hoot, but maybe she was delighted that Mark had achieved *something* without her help!

The woman lacked nothing except originality and modesty. When wanting to emphasise a point her repetitive use of the phrase 'totally and utterly' was laughable. She thought football hooligans were totally and utterly wrong. Our law courts were T and U impartial, and reflation was T and U rejected. She became T and U boring and repetitive even in TV interviews, as Sir Robin Day has recounted. Her principle was 'Never mind what the question is, this is the prepared answer you are going to get.' Evasion was her stock in trade both inside and outside the

House. She was a 'conviction' politician to her fingertips, and nobody, anywhere, ever, was going to move her one inch.

Yet, for a woman known to be suffering from chronic verbal diarrhoea, she was strangely reluctant to speak in set debates in the House of Commons – as distinct from the 'quickies' farce of Question Time. Research has shown that in all her eleven years as Prime Minister she made fewer speeches in the Commons than any other Prime Minister in the last 100 years – far fewer than any Labour Prime Minister, and far fewer even than Ted Heath. Her 'Trappist monk' approach to speaking at length to the Commons could only be due to fear, contempt, or a combination of both.

Outside, however, she inflicted some extraordinary lectures on unsuspecting audiences. Not the least objectionable was the one delivered in May 1988 to the General Assembly of the Church of Scotland in Edinburgh. The General Assembly is the Scottish Church's Parliament, and arguably the most radical and progressive institution among all the Churches in the United Kingdom. Mrs Thatcher seemed to be either wholly ignorant of this fact, or determined to ignore it.

In Scotland she was the most disliked of all Tory Party Leaders in living memory. She was an enemy who spoke a foreign tongue. She hectored the Scots in a tone of condescension, as if they were second-class colonials, not intelligent or grateful enough to appreciate how well off they were under her beneficent guidance.

Her purpose at the General Assembly was to play politics with God, to reconcile her beliefs with those of the Christian faith, and to prove her point she made some unfortunate Biblical references. Saint Paul said 'If a man will not work, he shall not eat.' Her audience of clerics could have reminded her that Saint Paul hadn't lived in Scotland! He couldn't have known that thousands of Scots would like to work but couldn't because Mrs Thatcher had thrown them on the scrap heap. Did she then think that these men should not eat? The silent clerics must have been squirming in their seats as they listened to such sanctimonious rubbish.

'Blessed are the poor, for theirs is the kingdom of Heaven.' So that's all right then. Thatcher didn't say that, but her policies were based on the principle of grab all you can while you can, and to hell with everybody else. Those churchmen, and millions like me who watched this bizarre performance, must have been incensed by the sheer impertinence and ignorance of this wealthy woman from the fat cats' provinces of Southern England.

Other targets were in her sights. The official Government Information Services are supposed to be the purveyors of impartial and objective facts on Governmental policies, for example, on pensions, social security benefits and the like. Now the Services were to be used for the dissemination of Government political propaganda. Hundreds of millions of pounds of the taxpayers' money was used to persuade us of the 'benefits' of NHS reforms, to encourage us to buy shares in the big sell-off of our own family silver – *our* gas, *our* electricity, *our* water, *our* Trustee Savings Bank, in fact everything but the crown jewels!

She used her powers of patronage for the same ends. The doling out of peerages, knighthoods and other worthless baubles has been abused by Prime Ministers of all political persuasions. Lloyd George, Macmillan and Wilson were only three of the more notorious practitioners in this murky world, but Margaret Thatcher must take a high place in this role of Prime Ministerial jiggery-pokery. As long ago as 1985 I enlisted the help of the House of Commons Library Research Division to provide me with information on these matters, but I am grateful to Tony Banks for bringing my knowledge up to date. In a speech in the Commons in early May 1991, he was given permission to introduce a bill to abolish these political honours. It was a delightful propaganda exercise, even though Tony knew that his bill would get no further. Since 1979, he said, big-business tycoons who had between them contributed £12 million to Tory Party funds had received a total of seventy-five peerages and knighthoods, and a number of press barons had been similarly rewarded. It was all very reminiscent of Lloyd George.

Yet another target was rife for manipulation. Official Government statistics were often embarrassing to the Government, so something had to be done to 'sanitise' them. Thus, across the board, the figures were fiddled, cooked, massaged, doctored or suppressed altogether. This sinister and unscrupulous practice has been well documented elsewhere, but a few examples may suffice to demonstrate the point.

One of Mrs Thatcher's ways of controlling the trade unions, thereby curbing their ability to engage in damaging strikes, was to create mass unemployment, and so she got over 3,000,000 on the dole. That was backed up by punitive legislation. Few would now dispute that *some* new law was necessary. There was a widely held belief that some trade union leaders had grown too big for their boots, and that they had the power to damage the national interest by irresponsible strike action. Harold Wilson's Government had tried to deal with the problem but was stopped in its tracks by those same trade union bosses. Thus the concept that Labour Governments were ruled by the trade unions gained credibility.

By ransacking our manufacturing industry and putting millions out of work, Mrs Thatcher did more damage to the British economy than all Hitler's bombs. As the dole queues grew, so did the Government's incentive to fiddle the figures. In the lifetime of her Governments, she moved the goalposts thirty times, and each time the effect was to reduce the numbers *counted*. This deception was never meant to provide more jobs, but simply to create the *impression* that the figures were coming down. In February 1981, for example, special employment and training measures were introduced. The idea was that as long as you were being 'trained' you were no longer counted as being unemployed. The effect was to 'cut' the dole figures by about half a million by 1986. The biggest fiddle of all was in June of 1986, just before the General Election. By tightening up the 'availability for work' test and the 'restart' interviews, another quarter of a million ceased to be counted. In September 1988, all sixteen- and seventeen-year-olds were denied all social security benefits, and so, at a stroke, another 100,000 were no longer counted as unemployed.

Statistics relating to the Health Service were similarly doctored. The Tory Party has never liked the fundamental principle on which the Health Service is based. It is Christian Socialism in practice, and Mrs Thatcher vowed to *kill* socialism. 'I am my brother's keeper' had no place in her scheme of things. There was no such thing as 'society' she said. We were all *individuals*, all keen to stand on our own two feet, to pay our own way, whether on pensions, schools or hospitals, and to be fair, when *she* needed hospital treatment, she practised what she preached. She went *private*; she *bought* the privilege of *choosing* her hospital, *choosing* the doctor she wanted, and *choosing* the time she went into the hospital. Her choices were *real*, but only because she was rich enough to put them into effect. The NHS was brought in by a Labour Government *precisely because* it felt that health provision should *not* be based on the right only of the rich to choose. So when Mrs Thatcher said that the NHS was safe in her hands, we didn't believe her. To prove *her* point, she set about fiddling the Health statistics, just as she had done with unemployment.

In 1979, no new hospital building scheme costing less than £5 million was recorded in the official statistics. Under Mrs Thatcher that limit was reduced to £1 million. Hey presto! Without another brick being laid, and without a single extra bed being provided, the recorded number of new hospital building projects soared overnight. To make the figures even better, some schemes were counted even if they were not due to *start* for several years; and if there were two or three phases for a project, each phase was now counted as a new and separate scheme. At a Tory Party Conference in the late 1980s, I watched Norman Fowler, the Minister then in charge of the NHS, unfurl, in front of the television cameras, a long scroll of those hospital building 'achievements' to the ecstatic applause of the gullible audience. They couldn't know how those figures had been arrived at. They couldn't know that Mr Fowler's list included new hospital car parks. It was just another of Mrs Thatcher's 'miracles', and all her Ministers, like Fowler, connived at the manipulation.

The controversial issue of nuclear power was treated in a similar manner. Mrs Thatcher was determined to break the National Union of Mineworkers and to replace coal with electricity generated by nuclear power. So she led us to believe that nuclear power was cheaper, safer and cleaner than any other way of producing electricity. Accidents at our nuclear power stations were either played down or hushed up altogether. This, of course, had happened long before Mrs Thatcher became Prime Minister, but the Government continued to be economic with the truth when it came to the nuclear industry. The Chernobyl disaster in the USSR is still, in the 1990s, giving us all a terrible warning. No one, not even the so-called experts, knows the full extent of the dangers to which future generations may be exposed by the reckless expansion of the nuclear industry. Yet not so long ago, I watched Mrs Thatcher giving a TV interview on these matters where she confidently asserted that the problems of the disposal of nuclear waste had been solved. That was nothing short of glib nonsense. When privatisation of the electricity industry was imminent, Mrs Thatcher was compelled to leave the nuclear industry in the public sector because of its doubtful future concerning costs, safety and profitability. In future, we will all be paying in our electricity bills a hidden special nuclear tax to finance the continuation of this uneconomic industry.

In this brief summary, I haven't even scratched the surface of the indictment. I have made a random selection of some of Mrs Thatcher's lesser offences against our people. She, along with all Ministers who meekly accepted her wildest excesses, and those Tory MPs who were all too willing to cling to her skirts, bears a heavy burden of guilt for the growth of misery, poverty, insecurity and unfairness endured by the British people.

Many of Mrs Thatcher's more indefensible policies – some would call them grave errors of judgement – are less capable of statistical measurement than others. We can *measure* with some degree of accuracy the record adverse trade balance which now bedevils our future. We can count the increasing numbers of companies going bankrupt and the house owners who are being forced out of their homes because of their inability to keep up their mortgage repayments. We can see with our own eyes the dereliction and decay in our towns, cities and countryside. We can see the squalor in our schools, hospitals, and houses, the clutter on our roads, and the rat-run of the London tube network. And all of us must be frightened by the record increases in crime in the last ten years, despite the fact that Mrs Thatcher threw vast sums of taxpayers' money at the problem.

The assaults on democracy itself were no less heinous. As she extolled its virtues, she systematically destroyed it. London is now the only capital city in the Western world without an *elected* council with overall strategic planning powers. The Greater London Council was abolished by Mrs Thatcher because it was a *Labour* council. Other metropolitan councils were also abolished because they, too, were Labour-controlled. Existing local councils have been reduced to the status of mere agents of the central Government. They have been *compelled* to sell their council houses, but have not been allowed to build new ones, not even with their own money. Schools can 'opt out' of the control of democratically elected councils, and be run by non-elected and unrepresentative bodies, answerable to nobody.

Mrs Thatcher's attacks on civil liberties, and the curtailment of individual rights, have occasioned grave concern within respectable national institutions like the BBC, quality newspapers, Churches of all denominations, trade unions, and other non-political organisations. After all her protestations about her belief in democracy and liberty, who would have imagined that Mrs Thatcher's Government could sanction a middle-of-the-night police raid at the BBC studios in Glasgow? Who would have believed that her Government would prohibit decent working men and women at GCHQ in Cheltenham from joining a trade union, and offer bribes to those already in a union to resign? Whatever responsibility the lady may or may not have had for these happenings, the buck stopped with her, and these incidents *did* occur.

She showed how fragile our democracy is, how easily our basic rights can be whittled away and destroyed by a determined and myopic Prime Minister. She may not have done permanent and irreparable damage to our social, economic and industrial fabric, but the wounds and divisions which she inflicted may take generations to put right. In my view, she was never big enough to concede error, and never shrank from being frugal with the truth. The real miracle was that she got away with so much for so long. May God forgive her.

Her booting out by her own Members of Parliament was a fitting end. It was followed by a continuous whingeing and whining by 'moaning Maggie'. 'We was robbed', she proclaimed to her Yankee admirers. The *British* people had got to know her better, and she thoroughly deserved her fate. No tears of sympathy need be shed.

24

What is Your Member of Parliament Worth?

There is no other job like an MP's. For a start, MPs have no boss, except the voters, and they can only sack their MP at an Election. MPs have no set hours of work. They can slog for seven days a week, all the year round, or they can sit on their backside at home or in the tropical sun. The pay cheque comes just the same. They can travel free – and first-class – at any time, between Westminster and home and between Westminster and the constituency. Husbands and wives get fifteen journeys a year free as well.

Constituency work should be hard work, although many may not treat it as such. An MP should act as father confessor, solicitor, welfare officer and Citizens Advice Bureau all rolled into one. The MP has to nurse his or her electorate, please them all if possible, and at all times at least give the appearance of being always active on their behalf.

To be dubbed 'a good constituency Member' can be a double-edged compliment. It can mean that he or she is Lobby fodder at the House of Commons but good at sending letters from his or her constituents to Government Ministers. I think I was a good constituency MP, but I don't think that meant I was inactive on the Parliamentary scene.

From the first day to the last of my thirty-seven years in the House of Commons I never failed to treat my constituency letters as my most important duty. Each one could have, literally, been a matter of life and death, demanding immediate action. Each one had to be judged on its merits. Some were naturally more important and immediate than others. The principal methods of dealing with individual cases were the phone call to a Government Minister or local council official, less often a telegram or urgent letter, or the personal interview with the relevant authority.

I often raised individual cases in the House of Commons itself, either by asking questions about it at Question Time, or in an adjournment debate. There is an adjournment debate, usually lasting half an hour, at the end of each day's business. These are much sought after by MPs and are balloted for weekly. A Government Minister is expected to reply to the case put by the Member concerned. On one occasion I raised the question of a retired miner's pension, and after the debate I sent that miner a copy of the Hansard report in which his name was mentioned. Many months later he came to see me, and proudly took out of his pocket that scruffy and crumpled Hansard and told me he was as pleased as punch to know that *his* name was now permanently in our Parliamentary records.

Another miner was less appreciative. He had been sacked by the National Coal Board for some reason and wanted me to get him his job back. Because his union was Communist-controlled, he was convinced they couldn't or wouldn't help him. When I tried to persuade him otherwise he wouldn't listen, pursuing me for months and months. Finally he came to see me just before one of our regular monthly Party meetings. He didn't say much, but just punched my face and challenged me to call the police. I did just that, and the police were there in a few minutes. I felt sorry for the lad and didn't pursue the case. Neither did he, and I hope he got his job back.

A dear old lady was my most regular customer at my 'surgeries' in the mining village of Kelty. She had leg problems, and every time she came to see me, she insisted on rolling down her stockings to display her tortured limbs. After a while the novelty began to wear off, but I couldn't convince her that her doctor was the man to see. I had to engage in a ploy. The next time she came to see me, I arranged for my good friend Willie Mill to break into our proceedings and announce angrily that there was a big queue waiting to see me. The poor lass had to pull up her stockings and go. That was the last I heard of her.

A similarly persistent old man had a bee in his bonnet about the Social Security. He wasn't getting a fair deal. For weeks he, the DHSS and I engaged in correspondence and got nowhere. Angrily he demanded that I go to visit him in his council flat. When my agent Jimmy Stevenson and I arrived, he had a trestle-table laid out with every letter he had ever received from the DHSS, from me, and from his union, about his case. There must have been over a hundred. He wanted me to go through the lot, and when I told him that that wasn't necessary, he threatened to throw acid in my face. Jimmy and I beat a hasty retreat. A few days later, he wrote accusing me of not winning his case because I was having an affair with the lady at the DHSS office, and also that I had killed my wife.

I was told the story of an old lady who was having trouble with death rays coming through her TV set and threatening her life. The MP kept a straight face and tried to tell her she was imagining things. She wouldn't have that and walked out when she found that her MP wasn't prepared to do anything. But she was back the next week. 'I think I've got the answer,' the MP said. 'What do you have on your feet when you are watching the TV?' 'Just my slippers,' she replied. 'That's it,' the MP replied, 'wear your wellies and they will insulate you from those rays. Try that and come back later and tell me how you got on.' Sure enough, she came back as happy as a lark. The wellies had done the trick. (This tale was told me by one of our lady MPs.)

A more serious case was that of a young man who had been seriously injured in a car accident. He was crippled for life and had been awarded over £100,000 in damages. That was in the early 1980s. He lived in an upstairs flat with his ageing parents. They had to do everything for him, and being upstairs it was hard for the lad to be taken out. In such cases, the Scottish law provides that a solicitor be appointed to safeguard the interests of the injured person. He alone could decide how the money should be spent. The parents asked me to visit them when they wanted to buy a small car to enable them to take their son for an occasional outing. The solicitor wouldn't allow it on the grounds that the car would be used mainly for the benefit of the parents. The same arguments were used when they tried to get money to install central heating in the flat. I visited the family several times, and I judged them to be genuine and honest. I talked about the case to my personal friend, Donald Dewar MP, who was a lawyer himself, and he advised me to be careful. He explained that the law was designed to protect the best interests of the crippled person, who is unlikely ever to work again. He would have to live on that £100,000 long after his parents had died. It was good advice. I followed it up with an interview with the Scottish Office Tory Minister responsible for such matters. He was very sympathetic, but repeated what Donald Dewar had already said. I wrote to the solicitor concerned, and he, too, said he was bound by the law to exercise his discretion.

I later secured an adjournment debate in the House of Commons in which I described the case in some detail. The outcome was a happy one. The Minister had obviously been in contact with the solicitor, and the purse-strings were loosened quite a bit.

I have described this case in a little detail to demonstrate that our democratic processes can sometimes be more humane than a lot of people think.

Constituency work was very exhausting but could be very rewarding. Of course not every complaint that came my way could be dealt with by me. I had to decide, before I took any action, whether there was any Governmental responsibility for the matter in question. Sometimes folk would come with grievances that had nothing to do with Government at either local or national level – marital problems, disputes about wills, car accidents, and even neighbours' cats.

There is no doubt that this work is an invaluable aid to maintaining close contact between an MP and his electors. Many so-called democratic countries do not ensure this contact. Whatever electoral reform may come in the next few years, this intimate relationship between elector and MP must be retained.

MPs' PAY

Should MPs be paid at all? Or should they be unpaid, part-time amateurs? Enoch Powell, one of the clearest thinkers and best debaters in the House, believed that MPs should all feel honoured to serve the people in the great Mother of Parliament, and that should be their only reward.

It is nonsense. The argument today is, not *whether* MPs should be paid, but what the rate for the job should be. And agreement on that is never likely to be found.

Payment of MPs dates back 700 years, when the shires and boroughs allowed their Member certain 'wages' for attending Parliament. In 1296, the City of London MPs were paid ten shillings a day. As late as 1681, a Thomas King presented a petition claiming that he had not been paid his wages by the borough of Harwich, but payment of MPs by their electors had generally ceased by the end of the seventeenth century.

In the eighteenth and for much of the nineteenth century, a seat in the House of Commons was the sure road to wealth in the forms of 'jobs for the boys', pensions and influence. Seats in the Commons were bought and sold for high prices. Democracy was a word neither used nor practised. Parliament was there to be used *by* the rich *for* the rich. Universal suffrage – the vote for every adult in the land – went some way to end that corruption. But even today, at the end of the twentieth century, corruption, the stench of patronage and the lining of private pockets are all with us still in the sacred cloisters of Parliament. With the advent of Mrs Thatcher in 1979, and the great flood of Tory MPs in the 1983 and 1987 Elections, the situation has grown rapidly worse. It must be a source of great anxiety to those who cherish and wish to preserve an incorruptible Parliament *of* the people *for* the people.

For over a hundred years, proposals were made both inside and outside Parliament to pay MPs out of public funds. The People's Charter of 1838 proposed it. It was advocated by Keir Hardie, the great Socialist pioneer, in 1887. Motions or bills supporting the idea were put to the Commons on at least six occasions between 1870 and 1903 and success was finally achieved in 1911.

The first salary was £400. A handsome sum when miners and other workers were lucky if they earned more than £1 a week. But the MP then had to pay all expenses out of his salary. There was no car mileage allowance, no help with secretaries, telephone, stationery or stamps. MPs only got free and unlimited first-class rail travel between Westminster and their constituency in 1924.

In 1913, £100 of that salary was made exempt of tax on the grounds that the MP incurred something like that sum in expenses. That stayed unchanged until 1954, four years after I became a Member.

In 1931, the salary was cut to £360 to encourage other workers to accept similar cuts in their wages. Three years later the salary went up again to £380 and then back to the original £400. Thus there was no increase at all between 1911 and 1937. Then, in a reckless burst of extravagance, the Government of the day put the salary up to £600. There it stayed until 1946, when the Labour Government upped it to £1,000 and gave MPs free travel between their constituencies and their homes.

That was the position when I joined 'the Club' in 1950. With no other source of income, it was not poverty, but neither was it a bed of roses. It has always been an embarrassment to ask for more. The rich men in the House didn't *need* more, though they took whatever was going. The poorer Members, mostly Labour MPs with wives and families to keep on the salary, found it invidious to press for better pay and conditions for themselves when they knew that most of their electors were much worse off. To make the position worse, MPs had to increase their own pay. Nobody can vote on MPs' pay but MPs themselves. They have no trade union to negotiate for them, and even if they had, any agreement would have to be sanctioned by the Treasury and the Chancellor of the Exchequer and then approved by the House of Commons itself. In the last twenty years, various proposals have been put forward to try to take this problem away from Parliament. Ideas like the automatic linking of MPs' salaries to those of comparable professions outside – notably civil servants – or the setting-up of independent bodies to judge what MPs should have. But whatever has been proposed, the final decision has always had to be taken by the Government and approved by Parliament itself. There is no escape from that.

The problem has been juggled with, fumbled, and treated like a hot potato by successive Governments, fearful of a hostile press and public reaction lest Members give even the slightest hint of greed. Over the years they have got the worst of all worlds. Each timid, tardy step taken to improve the lot of MPs has been treated with a mixture of derision, envy and not a little hypocrisy, especially among newspaper and business tycoons who often enjoy vastly fatter salaries and tax-free expenses than MPs have ever had.

The first 'improvement' I enjoyed came in 1953, when the Tory Government of the day thought a £2-a-day allowance could be given, except for Fridays and only when the House was sitting. That worked out at less than £300 a year. It was just a little better than a kick in the teeth. The daily allowance was claimed automatically. The MP who was part-time, or no-time – and there are more of them than folk think – could still claim the £2 a day.

In 1957, that £2-a-day allowance was replaced by an annual £750 to cover Parliamentary expenses. But the whole lot – £1,750 – became subject to tax, though MPs could claim as tax-free any expenses which they could prove they had incurred up to that maximum of £1,750. That meant that those with wealth and private means could use the £1,750 to employ a secretary, for example, and claim it all as tax-free, while MPs like myself, with no other income, had to live on the £1,750, keep a wife and family, repay a mortgage and pay any Parliamentary expenses I might have.

In 1964, the salary went up to £3,250. This was consequent on the findings of an independent outside body known as the Lawrence Committee. That was a great help to me. For the first time in the years since 1952, I was able to give up the part-time teaching and lecturing which I had been compelled to do in London schools and colleges. It was a godsend. My wife thought she had won the pools!

Nothing else was done for the next six years. MPs and Ministers had to live on their fat. Labour Governments were, and always have been, much more sensitive, timid and mean on this problem than any other. The belief in the hair shirt, the hairy chin and cloth cap have been a long time dying in Labour's ranks; they were the symbols of virtue, honour and credibility. One or two back-bench MPs went public in saying that they would donate their salary increases to the pensioners in their constituencies. In politics it is a barren exercise to do good by stealth. If it is worth doing at all, it must be done publicly.

Up to 1964, MPs had no pension scheme at all, of any kind. I recall one off my PParliamentarry ccolleagues fromm Durham dying suddenly. He had been a railway engine driver before he became an MP. When he died, penniless, his poor widow had to go straight away onto National Assistance, as it was then known.

So, in 1965, the first Members' Pension Act was passed. MPs paid an annual contribution of £150, and the Treasury paid a sum equal to the total of all MPs' contributions. Members were to get pensions over the age of sixty-five, or on ceasing to be a Member, if they had served ten years or more. The pension of £600 a year for ten years' service was to increase to £900 after fifteen years' service and by £24 for each year of service thereafter.

As I was then only forty-eight, I wasn't very interested in pensions. Sixty-five seemed a long way off. And selfishly, I gave little thought to ex-MPs who had left the House of Commons before 1965, for whatever reason and after no matter how many years' service, without a penny, and all too often unable to get another job.

THE STORY FROM 1970

There was a pay freeze for MPs from 1964 to January 1972. The Labour Governments of those years were too frightened to do anything. Cabinet

Ministers acted on the principle of 'I'm all right, Jack', and back-bench MPs knew, or thought they knew, that they had little sympathy among their electors.

In that particular matter, at least, it was a blessing that the Tories won the 1970 Election. Mrs Barbara Castle, as the Minister responsible for introducing the Commission for Industry and Manpower Bill in 1970, had proposed to set up a special panel to report on MPs' salaries as well as on other groups' pay. There would be a review every four years. The 1970 Election put an end to that, and on 4 December 1970, the new Tory Leader of the House, Willie Whitelaw, announced that MPs' pay would instead be referred to an independent review body. The final decision, however, would still have to be made by the MPs themselves.

Thus was born the Top Salaries Review Body. Its first Chairman was Lord Boyle, a highly respected one-time Tory MP and former Minister of Education, a liberal, cultivated gentleman, tailor-made for the job – which he held from 1971 to 1981.

The first major report on Members' and Ministers' pay and pensions was published in late 1971. A basic salary of £4,250 was proposed. It sounded a lot – a 38 per cent jump from £3,250. But it would be the first increase in seven years. In that time prices had gone up by 44 per cent and other salaries by 67 per cent.

During its studies, the Boyle Committee tried to sample public views on MPs' pay and other matters, with some strange results. Nearly half of those questioned thought MPs had the free use of a car in their constituencies. Well over half thought secretaries and typists were provided free. Nearly half thought each MP had his own private office, and one in four thought MPs got all their meals free. Yet very few – the numbers being a lot higher among unskilled workers – thought MPs were overpaid.

Willie Whitelaw, the Tory Minister in charge, took the bull by the horns. He proposed a basic salary of £4,500. So, in January 1972, an MP's salary became £4,500. Such generosity couldn't last. And it didn't. The next report of the Review Board, in 1975, proposed an increase in MPs' basic pay from £4,500 to £8,000. The Government – another Labour Government – screwed it down to £5,700. In 1979, the increase, though agreed in full – against the wishes of the wealthy Prime Minister, Mrs Thatcher – was staged over the next three years. By June of 1983, the salary was £15,308, in 1985, £16,900, and in 1987, £18,500.

To pensioners and to millions of low-paid workers and others outside, that sounds a lot. And nothing will convince them otherwise. However, it might be instructive to put the figures in some sort of context.

Take as a starting-point the £1,000 salary which I first received in 1950. Using official statistics, by 1985 the average pay of male manual workers had gone up *twenty-seven times* what it had been in 1950. On that calculation, the salary of an MP would have been not £17,000 but £27,000.

If an MP's pay is compared to the average earnings of men over twenty-one working full-time in manual jobs, in 1950 an MP got over two and a half times what that working man got. By 1985 it was just twice as much.

MPs' EXPENSES

Since 1950 there has been a remarkable increase in the allowances and facilities for MPs. Forty years ago, all telephone calls to places outside London had to be paid for. Likewise every stamp, except when writing to a Government Minister or a nationalised industry. There was no allowance to help pay for a secretary. There was no office accommodation, no private telephone, no private interview rooms. There was no private car mileage allowance. Parliamentary documents were free; so was the drinking water, and a limited amount of House of Commons stationery. You could have a free bath or shower, and there was a cheap barber on the premises.

Things have improved since those hair-shirt days, though facilities are still miserable compared to those for MPs in most other modern Parliaments.

MPs now get free stationery, in unlimited quantities (for Parliamentary business). They can phone free anywhere in the UK. They have free postage as well, so long as it is used only for Parliamentary business. And there is the rub for all these free services. They are all wide open to abuse, and are difficult to check. Everything is left to the integrity and judgement of the MP. All MPs are assumed to be 'Honourable Members'. That is what they must all be called anyway, at least in the Chamber itself. What is said outside is often more robust, and more truthful! A former Tory Minister was found using official postage-paid postcards to contact all new young voters, inviting them to call and see him. Another Tory MP in Scotland used the same device to send congratulations to all those newly wed or newly born and commiserations to all those bereaved. The Births and Deaths columns in the local papers were required reading for that MP. And to keep the Party balance, I know of one prominent Labour MP, a former Minister, who *admitted* to using the free postage to send out all his Christmas cards. All were 'Honourable Gentlemen'!

There is no means of knowing how widespread the abuse is. In fact, the MPs just quoted justified their practices as legitimate political and Parliamentary activities. What do you think? Similar comments can be made on the other allowances, like car mileage payments and the secretarial and research allowances.

By 1984 there were suspicions – to use no stronger language – that the car mileage allowances were being abused. An independent inquiry was set up under Lord Peyton, who had been an acerbic Tory Minister of Transport. Its main recommendations were:

1. The bigger the car engine, the larger the car mileage payment should be.
2. After 20,000 miles had been clocked up, the mileage allowance should be cut. After 25,000 miles, the MP would have to give details of all the journeys covered by his claim.

The Tory Government agreed with all that. So did the House of Commons, with its big Conservative majority. So, in late 1985, the MP who ran a small car of less than 1300 cc could claim 18p a mile, whereas an MP with a big car, a Jaguar or a Rolls, could claim 39p a mile. Thus, a claimant for 20,000 miles a year would receive £3,600 if he was a little-car man, while the big-car MP would get £7,800.

At a time when the Government was urging everybody to economise on fuel, this policy of encouraging MPs to use bigger, petrol-guzzling cars was a nonsense in economic terms, as well as being wholly unjustified on political and social grounds. The big cars are owned mainly by well-off Tory MPs. The smaller cars are run by Labour MPs. Most Tories are businessmen in their spare time – or MPs in their spare time. The car could be a company car, used for company purposes as well as for Parliamentary purposes. The scope for abuse is enormous. Three or four MPs could use one car for a long journey from Westminster and then claim the mileage allowance as if they had travelled separately.

SECRETARIAL AND RESEARCH ALLOWANCES

At the beginning of this chapter I referred to the Rt Hon Mr Enoch Powell. He didn't like the idea of MPs being paid at all. Nor did he think that they should get any financial help to pay for their secretaries or research assistants. He had a point when he said that a Member could get all his research done by the staff in the House of Commons' Library. They are superbly efficient, hard-working, accurate, painstaking and unfailingly courteous. But if Powell's principles were accepted and every MP sought to get all his research done by the Library staff, their workload would become impossible.

Neither the Government – *any* Government – nor the House of Commons has ever accepted Powellism. On the contrary, the argument has always been not about *whether* MPs should get financial help to pay their secretarial and research assistants, but *how much*.

The principle was accepted only in 1969. From October of that year, up to £500 could be claimed as expenses for secretarial and research help and general office expenses. The sum had gone up to £12,000 by April 1984. In July 1984 it was decided that for the year ending 31 March 1985 the amount should be the amount obtained by increasing the £12,000 to four-fifths of the Civil Service salary increase for that year of a senior personal secretary. In late 1985 the figure for secretarial expenses was

£12,437. In 1986 it jumped to £19,000.

There are various other financial arrangements. For instance, provincial Members – that is, those with constituencies outside Inner London – can claim extra expenses for staying away from home overnight while on Parliamentary duties. The maximum claim up to 31 March 1986 was £6,696 a year.

On pensions, too, there have been some improvements. In its Twentieth Report, published in May 1983, the Top Salaries Review Body recommended that in view of the uncertainty of Parliamentary careers, MPs should be able to earn a full pension in a shorter period. The MP now pays a 9 per cent contribution towards his pension, and the scheme gives a degree of satisfaction to most MPs. But it is not extravagantly generous.

SUMMARY

There is keen competition to be a Member of Parliament. And once you have those two magic letters after your name, you fight like a tiger to keep them. Money and tax-free expenses may not be the only reason for the fierce competition to be a member of the Westminster Club. Surely there are other reasons, more honourable and less materialistic ones. Not the least important, I hope, is the desire to serve your fellow-citizens, to help folk who cannot easily help themselves. The satisfaction obtained from a letter of thanks from an old-age pensioner, or from a sick man or woman after you, as their MP, have helped sort out a pension problem or a social security payment matter, cannot be measured in cash terms. I have often been moved by such gratitude.

There is a feeling, too, of being at the centre of things, of being where the political power lies – or seems to lie. Having seen Parliaments at work all over the world, from America to Australia, I have seen none better than ours. Overall, with all its faults, none is less corrupt, closer to its electors, more sensitive to the rights of minorities, more vigilant over the right of free speech, and (dare I say it?) few, if any, are more efficient. That sounds complacent, smug, uncritical. It's none of those things. I have loved the House of Commons as a father loves his son, but sometimes I have felt as if I could be another Guy Fawkes!

The great excitement of seeing and hearing the great men and one or two great women is a priceless experience. In my years as an MP I have watched nine Prime Ministers in action: Attlee, Churchill, Eden, Macmillan, Home, Wilson, Heath, Callaghan and Thatcher. Greater and abler men never reached that high office: Ernest Bevin, Aneurin Bevan, R. A. Butler, Iain Macleod, Sir Stafford Cripps, Enoch Powell and Denis Healey, to name just a few. The wheel of fortune is an unpredictable piece of machinery.

Throughout all those tumultuous years since 1950, the question of

MPs' pay has been small beer. But it never seemed to be like that at the time. The wages and working conditions of MPs should be a matter of concern to everybody. British MPs are among the worst paid and endure worse working conditions than almost any other MPs in the Western democracies. The system as it is lends itself to dangers of increased temptations and corruption, to continued frustration and inefficiency, and much more importantly, to a widening of the gulf between the executive arm of Government and the legislative. Ordinary back-bench MPs have little power or influence on the Government. Perhaps they should accept that position philosophically, as a fact of life. They might be able to do that more easily if they were provided with worthwhile facilities in their constituencies to enable them to get on with their job as social worker and adviser.

Modern government is complex and often too remote from the man in the street. Decision-making is far too centralised in Westminster and Whitehall, in top politicians, top civil servants and top faceless men in the City of London. They all can, and do, cook the books, massage official statistics, and are sometimes 'economic with the truth'. A Home Secretary from leafy Tory Oxfordshire takes decisions about the squalor and deprivation of industrial conurbations in Birmingham and Liverpool. A Prime Minister from a genteel suburb of London knows nothing, and cares less, about the manifold problems of Glasgow, Newcastle or Sheffield. The decision-makers are too remote from the people most affected by their decisions, and the ordinary MP can do little to change that.

What could and should be done is to try to humanise, to professionalise, and to make more efficient, this over-centralised, too remote and too cold form of government. A step in that direction could be made by establishing in each Parliamentary constituency an office, or a small suite of offices, for the use of the MP and the local councillors.

The office, or offices, need not be on a lavish scale. They could be equipped with the most modern office machines and staffed with a full-time complement of three or four people with specialised skills, including, for instance, a qualified legal adviser, a trained social worker, a telephonist and a computer operator.

When the NHS was inaugurated, Nye Bevan visualised the key role which could be played by the local health centre, to which everyone would automatically go with all their health problems. The centres which I visualise would be the governmental, political counterpart of the health centre. The cost need not be excessive. Even if it were, say, £500,000 per constituency, at a total of £325 millions a year, that is 1.5 per cent of the cost of what we spent on defence in 1990. The benefits to the MPs, councillors, and, more importantly, to the local people of such a network of political centres, would be incalculable. The knowledge that anyone could go to the centre with any problem, at any time, and get expert guidance would mean that for the first time we would have a professional advice and guidance service to deal with the manifold problems of the ordinary man and woman. And at the same time it would reduce, if not entirely eliminate, the embarrassment of MPs when they are forced to seek, and argue over, increased payments for secretarial and office expenses. The present system is archaic, amateurish, inefficient, inhumane and susceptible to dishonesty. It is time for a complete overhaul.

A final thought. Up to the end of 1986, my salary earnings over thirty-six years as an MP were much less than £200,000. My dad's earnings as a miner over forty years would have been less than £5,000. In 1984, Prince Charles got £934,505 from the Duchy of Cornwall – and every penny tax-free. Taking account of the value of money and inflation over all those years, these figures don't convey too many messages. But one thing is certain, Prince Charles gets far too much for doing far too little of any consequence, while miners and MPs get far too little for doing a job which could be lost overnight. Who dares claim we have a classless society, still less a just one?

25

Prince Charles, and Other Things

On 26 June 1981, I sent a memorandum on 'The Future of the Monarchy' to the ruling body of the Labour Party, the National Executive Committee, which was then controlled by the 'Left' and the likes of Mr Benn and Mr Heffer. The NEC had already published proposals to abolish the House of Lords and to reform the honours system.

In my memo I accepted that it was unrealistic to propose the abolition of the monarchy. Instead, I suggested that a new Royal Department of State be set up, with its own Government Minister controlling all expenditure on the monarchy. All employees of the new Royal Department, from the Queen downward, would be regarded as civil servants, with perhaps special rates of pay for the Queen and her immediate family. All other questions of pay and conditions of work would be decided by the House of Commons.

The two duchies of Cornwall and Lancaster, plus the 140 grace and favour residences and the Crown Estate, would be amalgamated into one Public Estate within the control of the new Government Department. I concluded: 'These proposals may be too revolutionary for some of the more squeamish members of the NEC, but I hope they may be considered as a serious attempt to modernise, democratise, and make more accountable, one of our more ancient and hereditary institutions.'

After a reminder from me, I got a letter from Geoff Bish, the Party's Research Secretary, dated 15 October 1981, saying that 'The question of the financial arrangements for the royal family is already on the agenda for the future programme of work of the Government Study Group', and full and detailed consideration of my proposals would be given.

Nothing more was heard until July of 1982, when I wrote asking for a progress report. On 26 July Mr Bish replied, saying that 'The NEC feels that it must tread rather carefully in handling this subject – but please rest assured that your Memorandum has not been forgotten, and that I will let you know when there are any further developments.' Complete silence until 1983, when I again pressed Mr Bish in a letter dated 30 January, which I ended by saying, 'Both in questions of its constitutional role and in the absurd and indefensible financial provisions for it, the monarchy is ripe for radical reform. The Party has never been eager to do anything at all. It's time we did.'

A full three years went by, and on 4 February 1986 I wrote again to the NEC and received a reply from Mr Bish dated 12 February. Nothing had been done about my memo, 'But it is, of course, quite possible that the Party will wish to look again at various aspects of constitutional reform at a later date.'

It is quite clear from this correspondence that the Labour Party is terrified of doing anything about such reform. Yet there is abundant evidence that public opinion today is ready to accept change, especially on the subject of royal taxation, but also on the constitutional role of the monarchy, the whole question of the royal prerogatives, and the rather tatty hangers-on.

Among Parliamentarians, also, the worms are beginning to turn. In the middle of 1991, two Private Members' Bills were introduced on these matters, and even polished Tory MP, Norman St John Stevas, now Lord Something or Other, that most ingratiating of all royalists, has conceded that the taxation question might be something worth considering.

The British public are in no doubt. The great majority wish to see the Queen and her family taxed like everybody else.

In the UK today, we have two kinds of taxpayers, Pay As You Earn – PAYE – and Pay As You Like – PAYL.

PAYE covers most of us, with our tax deducted at source, by the employer, so that tax avoidance is almost impossible. PAYL, on the other hand, constitutes a hidden gold-plated Welfare State. It includes all those who can grow fat on tax avoidance or evasion by means of tax-free expenses, perks like company cars, private health schemes, top-hat pension schemes, golden handshakes, secret accounts in overseas tax havens, and a multitude of other tax-fiddling devices costing thousands of millions of pounds annually in lost revenue. This 'wide-boy' sector of our society has mushroomed in recent years. Many of our larger industrial and commercial companies pay no tax at all, or very little. All of them seem to have a highly developed acquisitive instinct. To put it bluntly, they are just plain greedy.

Regretfully, our royal family comes into the PAYL category, and judging by results they have been more brilliantly successful at it than most others. To be fair, their phenomenal wealth has been made possible by deliberate decisions of Parliament and Government rather than by any clever scheming on the part of the Queen and her advisers. The position was made clear in the Treasury's memorandum to the 1971 Select Committee on Taxation of Members of the Royal Family, which stated: 'As part of the Royal Prerogative, the Queen is not liable to pay tax unless Parliament says so, either explicitly or by inevitable inference. There is no distinction for this purpose between the private and public aspects of the Sovereign.' The memo continued: 'The tax immunity extends to the Duchy of Lancaster.' It described how the Crown became liable for the payment of local rates at Sandringham and Balmoral, but went on: 'The Queen is not liable to assessment to income tax or surtax, and is entitled to claim repayment of any income tax suffered at source (e.g. on company dividends). She is not liable to capital gains tax, nor is any of her property liable to estate duty.'

That's not the end of the story. 'The Queen is not liable to indirect taxation (whether in the form of import duties or internal indirect taxation), in the absence of any special statutory provision to the contrary. Where however (as in the normal case) the indirect tax is levied on goods before they are purchased by The Queen there is no relief from tax.' Put shortly, it is Klondyke – by the will of Parliament.

From time to time 'guesstimates' have been made of the Queen's private wealth. The latest have quoted astronomical figures of up to £6,000 million. In 1971 the Queen's official spokesman told our Select Committee that the estimate of £50 million then being made was 'wildly exaggerated'. He must have been told to use these words by the Queen herself. Pressed to be more specific, he refused to go any further. That Committee was probably the most powerful ever set up in Parliament. The Chairman was the Chancellor of the Exchequer. The membership consisted of a former Prime Minister, Ministers and ex-Ministers, Privy Counsellors and senior MPs. The Crown refused to supply that Committee with information which it felt it had the right to have.

Parliament meekly accepted the rebuff. Unless and until *some* Government and *some* Parliament has the courage and the guts to deal with the financing of the monarchy based on principles of openness, fairness and honesty, the present unsatisfactory situation will remain. Indeed, in the last twenty years it has got worse. No longer is the royal cash investigated by a select committee of Parliament. No longer can MPs debate these matters against any background of adequate information. The royal wealth, and the financing of the institution of monarchy, remain among the most tightly guarded secrets in the world, and this makes the nurturing of myths on the subject so much easier.

The mythology surrounding the Crown Estate is one of the more obvious examples. Here we are asked to believe that virtually the whole of Central London is the private property of the Queen. We are further asked to believe that the profits made are 'voluntarily' surrendered by her in exchange for the Civil List, and because the profits of the Crown Estate are greater than the publicised cost of the monarchy, we, lucky us, are actually making a profit out of our long-suffering royals. The Establishment has brainwashed us into accepting this bunkum.

I went into these matters in a little detail in *My Queen and I*. Put briefly, over the last two centuries, the monarch has got a damned good bargain. At any rate, none of her family seems to be too unhappy with the present set-up.

That is not quite true. The Prince of Wales, for one, appears, still, to have an unquenched thirst for more wealth. In 1990, from an estate of 130,000 acres, £1 million was peanuts, especially with a wife and two kids to keep. After all, there were 180 tenant farmers on the estate who could pay more rent, and there were about 1,300 living in Duchy houses and flats, especially in Kennington in South London. Then there were about 160 miles of foreshore in the South-West, and 11,000 acres of riverbed for which charges could be, and are, made, at not less than £1 to £2 per foot for boat moorings. In 1984, investment in stocks and shares by the Duchy had a market value of £11,964,238, yielding dividends of £770,966.

By any standards, the Duchy is Big Business; but when Prince Charles took it over in 1969, he was advised that it needed a shake-up. More juice could be squeezed out of it, but care and stealth were vital. After all, he was the heir to the throne, so he mustn't be too *obviously* greedy and grasping. A pleasing public image was crucial. 'Softly, softly, catchee monkey' seemed to be the order of the day. Top advisers were hired: John Higgs, a United Nations agricultural expert; Lord Franks, a former British Ambassador to the United States; and Sir John Baring, a financial wizard and head of Barings Bank. Their job was plain. They had to make more money for His Royal Highness, and any obstacles in the way had to be removed.

So, in 1982, with the help of Mrs Thatcher's Government, the Duchy of Cornwall Management Bill was introduced in Parliament. The original bill was debated in the House of Commons after 10 p.m. on 5 July. The first speech was made by Barney Hayhoe, the Treasury Minister then in charge of these matters. Barney was one of the nicer Tories, but one of their soporifics, kept back for bedtime debates. He droned on for thirteen minutes about bringing the Duchy into the twenty-first century. Most MPs had sensibly gone home or were otherwise engaged. I was the first back-bench Member to speak. I recalled how the Government had originally planned to prevent the bill from being debated at all on the Floor of the House by treating it as a private bill. When that failed, the Government had tried to have it pushed into a small committee of the House. These two procedural tricks having failed, they were now playing the third − starting the debate in midsummer at the fag-end of a day's work, and a week or two before MPs went on their summer holidays. Only one other MP spoke, Bob Cryer, the ever-present Labour Member for Keighley, and like myself, no fan of the monarchy.

Mr Hayhoe dismissed us as 'sour', 'pathetic', and a 'discordant refrain'. We thought that was praise indeed. We forced a vote on the bill. Only 105 MPs voted: 101 for the bill and four against. The rest were deserters. It would seem that four out of every five of the 650 MPs had no interest in the Duchy of Cornwall or the Prince of Wales. Not even the Prime Minister herself bothered to attend.

THE COMMITTEE STAGE OF THE BILL

This dealt with the details of the bill, and lasted for only two sittings, that is, a total of about five hours' debate. I had made sure I would be on that committee, along with ten Tories, one Liberal and six Labour colleagues. Victory in any vote was assured for the royal establishment, but not before one or two of us had blown the gaffe on a few of the feudal and tyrannical practices within the Duchy. For instance, the Duchy accounts were not available to the local folk, not even to the public libraries, though they *must* be published for Parliament. Nor is the Duchy subject to the law of the land like the rest of us. Everything depends on the goodwill of the landowner, i.e. Prince Charles, which means, in effect, those who run the estate on his behalf. I cited a case in which the Duchy had to retreat when caught red-handed trying to take away from people their right of access to common land at Poundbury Camp in Dorchester.

Earlier that year, on 10 February my good friend, Dr David Clark MP had introduced a bill in the Commons about public access to common land and open country. In his speech he said that the Duchy of Cornwall had applied to 'deregister' Poundbury Camp, which meant that the public would no longer have access to it. I had immediately written a strong letter of protest directly to Prince Charles, and I enclosed a copy of Dr Clark's speech. In that letter I said: 'A day or two after Dr Clark spoke, you yourself made a speech about liberty and freedom. It made me smile. The cheek of it, while you are in the process of seeking to deny those very rights and freedoms to folk in Dorchester. Perhaps you were unaware of what was being done; but you are accountable for what is done in your name by your estate managers. Can you please explain?'

A reply came from the Honourable Michael Adeane. Of course my letter would be seen by His Royal Highness, and the reply went on: 'There may, I think, be some confusion in Dr Clark's mind (and possibly even yours)'. Note the sarcastic, aristocratic, condescending brush-off. It might have deterred one of their tenant farmers in Cornwall or Dorset. They wouldn't have dared to protest anyway. But neither David nor I had been confused. We both knew what we were up to. If anyone was confused, it may have been the Honourable Michael Adeane. Anyway, the Duchy beat a hasty retreat, and for the time being at least Poundbury Camp was safe for all those who wanted to enjoy it.

Following the passage of the 1982 Act, the Duchy is now managed as a compassionate capitalist outfit, if that is not a contradiction in terms. It can invest anywhere, and it can borrow money if it needs to.

But the Prince is not yet satisfied. Recently he suggested that the Civil List should be abolished, and that, instead, his family might live on the income from the Crown Estate. He complained that having to live on an income fixed by Parliament made them little more than paupers. He added that he thought that this might be a 'sensible' suggestion. *I* thought that it was interesting as well, so I wrote to the Prince on 10 April 1987, asking him a few questions:

What did he mean by the Crown Estate?

Did he include the two Duchies, the 140 grace and favour residences, and the rest of the Estate, as established under the 1760 Crown Lands Act and subsequent legislation?

Would his family then be responsible for the running of all the estates without recourse to the public purse?

Would they also be responsible for the financing and maintenance of all the royal palaces, the royal yacht, the royal train, the Queen's flight of planes and helicopters?

Would all members of the royal family be willing, after the implementation of the proposal, to have all their income and investments taxed in the same way as those of all other citizens?

I then suggested that a public debate between the two of us might be a stimulating exercise and a unique demonstration of the real nature of our democratic constitution. I ended by referring to his many recent public speeches in which he had shown great courage and frankness, and hoped that he would now take this chance to continue the good work. I received a short, courteous reply from the prince's Private Secretary. Not surprisingly, there was no attempt to answer my questions, and equally unsurprisingly there would be no debate. It's a pity. Such a debate on television could have been very instructive, revealing, and perhaps even entertaining. It would have been an exciting innovation, and a mighty blow for free speech.

When the Prince had made his suggestion, he had obviously done his arithmetic. The net income from the Crown Estate was then about £30 million. In 1990–1, it was over £60 million, whereas the Civil List was £7.9 million. But statistics never tell the whole truth.

The heir to the throne deserves some praise for his many speeches on matters of public concern. His views about our postwar architecture commanded widespread support, more especially since it was a subject with no obvious political overtones. The same couldn't be said about his concern for the millions out of work, or for the homeless living in cardboard boxes. His criticism, too, of our ramshackle educational system seemed to be too near to current political controversies to please the Tory Party. Norman Tebbit, in particular, was incensed. Norman has been dubbed the Rottweiler of the Tory Party. He fumed that the monarchy would be in great danger if politically controversial speeches continued to be made by a man who was himself unemployed. For my part, I say all power to the Prince's elbow so long as he draws attention to the manifest injustices in our society. However, it would come better, and would sound more convincing, if the Prince himself practised what he preached. For instance, his criticism of our educational system would be more convincing if he sent his own children to local council schools.

Just suppose His Royal Highness announced tomorrow that his children would transfer to his chosen council school. Imagine that he then complained about the dilapidated school buildings, with their outside toilets, the tattered books, and the shortage of teachers. In those circumstances, he could then make a powerful and credible speech on our education system, based firmly on his own family experience. You could bet your last penny that the Government would find the extra cash as quickly as Mrs Thatcher found it for her Falklands War.

We all know that that is pure fantasy. It will not happen – on grounds of 'security'. The royal children will continue to be contracted out of an educational system which struggles on to provide as best it can for more than 90 per cent of our children.

It is this lack of exciting, imaginative and inspirational leadership by example which leads many of us to the conviction that the monarchy is built on foundations of myth, humbug and hypocrisy.

Just one more example of what I mean may help to prove my point. A while ago, Prince Charles hit the headlines by actually visiting the homeless sleeping in cardboard boxes on the Thames Embankment – the first time any of his family had done so. He went 'incognito' and was apparently deeply distressed by what he saw. The problem of homelessness, in one of the richest countries in the world, is a disgrace, and Prince Charles did a public service in expressing his concern about it.

However, in 1980 he had bought a mansion for himself – Highgrove House, near Tetbury in Gloucestershire. It is a little more than a cardboard box. It has six bathrooms, nine bedrooms, a nursery wing for the children, and about 350 acres of land. The price paid was said to be nearly £1 million. Duchy of Cornwall money was used to help pay that price. Three of the Duchy's houses were sold for about £300,000 and that contributed towards the price of the Gloucestershire mansion.

A Duchy official said at the time that until then Prince Charles 'hadn't a roof over his head'. Poor soul.

In 1975 I had introduced a Private Member's Bill to take into public ownership, without compensation, the Crown Estate, the Duchies of Lancaster and Cornwall, and all the revenues therefrom. The sponsors of my bill included such present-day celebrities of the Parliamentary Labour Party as Robin Cook, Dennis Skinner, John Prescott and Bob Cryer, as well as Jack, now Lord Dormand. Sadly my bill, although published, did not become law. So the royal pillage continues unabated.

When Prince Charles eventually becomes King, he will presumably inherit the astronomical untaxed wealth of his mother. He will then surely be the richest man in the world. He will also be the most powerless and probably the least exciting head of State in the universe.

Why, oh why, do we, a normally rational people, go on putting up with this expensive, irrelevant luxury?

26

An Urgent Message to Her Majesty the Queen

Your Majesty,

I wrote an open letter to you in 1975. Though now sixteen years older, my views on the institution of the monarchy remain unchanged.

As you know, *My Queen and I* was published in that year, and for a while topped the list of best-sellers. It was subsequently published in Spain and Japan.

During the following year or two, I probably visited Canada more often than you yourself did, there to discuss and debate on TV and radio the role and worth of the monarchy. I declined invitations to visit Australia.

In the United Kingdom, I took part in a large number of TV and radio programmes, not only for British viewers, but also for French, German, Swedish, American and other nationalities. Nothing seems to titillate the international fancy more than tales about the British monarchy.

Our own BBC ferried me up to your private royal home at beautiful Balmoral. There we had to climb a steep hillock in order to get a glimpse of your castle over the high protecting walls. From that vantage point, we discussed the 'Us and Them' theory of democracy, and your own fabulous wealth. Of course we couldn't know then anything about the Poll Tax. You will recall that one of your predecessors, Richard II, introduced a Poll Tax in 1379, to finance a war against the French. You will know that that tax and other hardships inflicted on poor people at the time led to the Peasants' Revolt, the murder of many of the Establishment figures of the time, and the eventual murder of the King himself. No one would wish that fate on you. You can bear no responsibility for the modern version of that tax abomination. Its blatant unfairness was underlined by the way in which you yourself benefited. When the Scottish Poll Tax law was being debated in a House of Commons Committee on the 27 January 1986, the Government Minister in charge of the debate revealed that Balmoral Castle would fall into the standard Community Charge category. That meant that instead of paying annual rates of about £3,300, you would only have to pay something between £160 and £320. You were to save over £3,000 a year. In the same Highlands region, a married old-age pensioner couple living on State benefits faced an increase in their annual bill of anything between £60 and £100.

I quote these figures not to criticise you, Ma'am, in any way. A paltry few thousand pounds is peanuts to you; but to that old couple, an extra pound or two a week could literally be a matter of life and death. Your wealthy Prime Minister, Mrs Thatcher, benefited, just like you, on her Poll Tax payments for her new retirement house in Dulwich. In the House of Commons she promised to donate her windfall to charity, and no doubt you have done the same. However that may be, our Labour MPs in Scotland deserve your accolade for highlighting so graphically the obscene unfairness of the new tax.

After publication of *My Queen and I*, some well-known booksellers in London and the provinces refused to stock it. My brother tried to buy it in Newcastle, but was told by the bookseller that he had no intention of selling it. At the time, that shop was still selling Karl Marx's *Das Kapital* and Hitler's *Mein Kampf*.

In the next year or so, thousands of letters poured in from all over the world. I couldn't possibly cope, so I carried suitcases full of them up to Fife. There my agent and friend Jimmy Stevenson, his wife Meg, and their three daughters, set about the job of opening and reading them and sorting them out into pros and cons. A few years later Mr Philip Ziegler, the well-known author and biographer, asked me if he could have access to those letters. I readily agreed, but told him that he would have to take a small van up to Fife to collect them, which he did. In his subsequent book, *Crown and People*, published in 1978, Mr Ziegler devoted a whole chapter to 'The Hamilton Letters'. He revealed that a significant majority supported my views, but I didn't attach too much importance to that fact. Years of experience as an MP had taught me that people who feel strongly *against* something tend to write to MPs in greater numbers than those who are for it. But there was, and still is, a very substantial majority of our people who firmly hold the view that all members of the royal family should be taxed in exactly the same way as everybody else. I had made that very recommendation in my own Minority Report submitted to the House of Commons Select Committee on the Civil List in 1971, but at that time I got no support whatever, not even from my own Party.

By your refusal to disclose the extent of your personal wealth to that all-Party select committee, you effectively thumbed your nose at *your* Parliament. The supposed 'Sovereignty of Parliament' meant nothing to you and your advisers. It was a constitutional outrage, and you, Ma'am, were the principal instigator.

After a lapse of twenty years, the taxation of your considerable private assets is again high on the political agenda. At least two Private Members' Bills have recently been introduced to bring this about. The secrecy which surrounds the finances of the monarchy cannot go on.

Your repeated denials about various estimates of your private fortune cut no ice with the general public. The present position, in which all documents relating to the finances of the royal family are closed to the public gaze for a hundred years, must be ended. A new Freedom of Information Act introduced by a new Labour Government after the next Election would, I hope, make this explicit. Your plea that you might have to sell Balmoral Castle if you have to be taxed rings hollow, and I would guess evokes little sympathy among ordinary people struggling to keep a roof over their heads. One thing is certain — none of your family will ever have to sleep in a cardboard box.

A different matter which may have exercised your mind in recent years is the possibility of your abdication. A recent public opinion poll showed that almost half your people thought you should do so. Not, I think, out of any personal animosity, but because of a feeling that you must be almost worn out, though to do you credit, you seem to wear well. Yet another consideration may have crossed your mind. You are understandably anxious to preserve the succession. You all know when you are on to a good thing. When you came to the throne, you were young and glamorous, and the nation swooned with delight and anticipation. But now the caste is changing. Your heir and successor is ageing, balding and thickening perceptibly. He may be growing a little impatient as he waits in the wings, fearful that the glamour might be wearing off. You must have noticed how people got really sick of the sight of Mrs Thatcher after ten years. Is there not a message there for you?

Despite your promise to keep on in your 1991 Christmas broadcast, might it be that those who would like you to abdicate think that a change now would make good sense for everybody?

I have sometimes heard the view expressed that a new incoming Labour Government would have a youngish and inexperienced Prime Minister who would be leading a minority Government with no overall majority in the House of Commons. In those circumstances, the new Prime Minister might need an elderly Queen's advice, encouragement and warnings. If, however, you should abdicate before that event, there might be two inexperienced men as Prime Minister and King respectively. The result could be a recipe for constitutional instability and uncertainty at the very time when Europe could also be in a considerable state of upheaval and change.

In my view such a scenario need cause little concern. You, Ma'am, have *your* advisers, mostly right-wing. An incoming Labour Prime Minister would have his left-wing advisers. And you are too long in the tooth not to realise that any attempt by the sovereign to thwart the will of an elected Prime Minister would spell danger for the monarchy itself. The Bagehot dictum that the monarch's role of advising, encouraging or warning the PM is as dead as Queen Victoria.

However, you do have your own ways of influencing our affairs, as I shall now show. The *Sunday Times* on 20 July 1986 published what they claimed to be a royal scoop: 'Queen dismayed by (uncaring) Thatcher?' was the blaring front-page headline. That would surely sell the paper like hot cakes. The story was that you were deeply concerned about: the long-term damage done to our country's social fabric by the miners' strike of 1984–5; your Prime Minister's 'caving in' to the Reagan Government's bullying on the use of British air bases for American bomber attacks on Libya; the handling of the South African issue; and the whole divisive thrust of all Mrs Thatcher's policies.

There was much more on the inside pages, with the shrieking headline, 'The African Queen at odds with Number 10'. You, Ma'am, must have been furious – or were you? Had you really blown your top? The editor of the paper was in no doubt. Your advisers had blabbed to him, and with deliberate intent. The story was filled out the following week by the paper's political editor, Michael Jones. He knew that Mrs Thatcher was 'depressed' by the story. Her guests at her country home at Chequers 'could see that she was not herself'. But then she seldom was, as you must have noticed. Mrs Thatcher was always acting a part, whether as the Iron Lady, the compassionate caring mother of a dull family, or the bustling, hectoring busybody, ready to lecture anybody about anything.

Of one thing we can be certain. Like much else about your family, we'll never know the truth. Whether or not you *had* voiced your misgivings about the Prime Minister's policies, I find it hard to believe that as a highly skilled practitioner in the art of personal survival, you would be capable of such political ineptitude as to allow these misgivings to be leaked to the *Sunday Times*.

Yet I know from a little incident in which I was personally involved that you have other ways of letting your views be known. Some years ago your sister, Princess Margaret, was alleged to be sowing some middle-aged wild oats. Apparently you were irritated and concerned about the potential damage being done to the monarchy by her supposed behaviour. So, through a high Court official, you let it be known to a wealthy Tory MP at a top-class London club that you would welcome some publicly expressed alarm at your sister's behaviour.

The Tory MP subsequently conveyed that message to me. Always ready to oblige, I recounted this story in a recorded interview at a TV studio in the Midlands in the late summer of 1980. There were horrified gasps of incredulity, and soon the wires between Buckingham Palace and Granada TV were humming. The programme never got on the air. I protested to Granada, accusing them of having been 'got at' by the Palace. You, Ma'am, will know the truth of that. The producer of the programme wrote to me on 6 August 1980 denying my charge and gave other reasons for not transmitting the programme. Once again, a royal mystery remained unsolved.

There was an amusing sequel. Journalists had had a preview of that programme, and Mr Winston Churchill had been present. He crossed my path in the Members' Lobby at the House of Commons next day. He was apoplectic with rage. He had obviously seen the film. 'You've made a fortune out of peddling your anti-monarchy views,' he foamed. In the insults that followed I commented unfavourably on his intelligence and compared him no less favourably with his ancestor. The exchanges became more heated and I raised my fist to the aristocratic brat, threatening to 'knock his block off'. He wisely took a few hasty steps backwards. Greatly heartened by the retreat of a Churchill before a Hamilton, I followed. The class war was about to start, for real. Alas, it was not to be. The Great Warrior had had enough. The scene had been watched by one or two bemused Lobby correspondents. They were puzzled to know what it had been about, and I was glad to fill in the details. Thus do Parliamentary tales and tittle-tattle reach the political columns of newspapers.

The very next Sunday, a newspaper sleuth buttonholed me in Fife with his paper's front-page story, which included a photograph of a Tory MP. 'Is that him?' I refused to confirm or deny. A few days later that Member went public. The media had all but called me a liar. Now they were left with egg all over their faces. I don't think the MP concerned was harmed by the incident. I hope not, because I had some sneaking admiration for his courage and independence.

The tale has little importance, Ma'am, but it does show that you do have various ways of airing your views. It was small beer compared to the *Sunday Times* story, in which you seemed to challenge the policies of your own Government. In recent times, most members of your family have done the same, notably the Prince of Wales. One newspaper has commented: 'The Prince of Wales as monarch ... might be a saving counterweight to the materialistic greed and short-term thinking which lie so close to the heart of Thatcherite values ... The Prince, in this sense, is the acceptable face of Her Majesty's Opposition.' But 'That is a delusion. The days when Buckingham Palace can appreciably change, or even substantially temper, what elected Governments decide, are very rightly dead ... Those who believe that the present imperious freedom of elected politicians to do very much as they please ought somehow to be constrained, must look elsewhere for solutions.' An excellent summary.

As a good constitutional monarch, I am sure you would agree with it. It must have been very wearying to have endured for so long a time a Prime Minister who acted as if she were you, and used the royal 'we' as if she were. I wouldn't have been surprised if you had blown your top. Privately, you must have been glad to see the back of her.

Just one more comment before ending this lengthy screed. The claim that your institution is a unifying force in our society, that you and your family magically give us all moral uplift, political stability and continuity is, to put it bluntly, just so much codswallop.

POSTSCRIPT

I have sometimes been criticised for concentrating too much on the finances of the monarchy and engaging in personal abuse in the process, instead of dealing with the political and constitutional problems associated with it.

Nevertheless, the need to tax the royals now attracts some surprising adherents. Twenty years ago I appeared on numerous TV and radio programmes with Mr Norman St John Stevas, MP. Norman and I were good personal friends, but I think he regarded himself as the self-appointed royal shop steward, the apologist *par excellence*. Now, even he regards the tax privileges of the Queen and her family as indefensible. The revolution cannot be long delayed.

No one should doubt the difficulties of finding an acceptable way of dealing with the matter. Both major political Parties are terrified of it. Moreover, the public and private wealth of the institution are so entangled and intermixed that it is almost impossible to separate the two.

Perhaps the best way of tackling the problem would be for a newly elected Labour Government to set up a high-powered all-Party select committee charged with letting the full glare of daylight into the monarchy's finances. The committee would have full and unrestricted access to all royal papers pertaining to the Queen's investments and all other sources of private wealth. The hundred-year rule would be repealed, as well as any legislation dealing with the secrecy of royal wills. The committee would have the power to call for any persons and papers, it would sit in public and be televised. The full report of the committee would, naturally, be published.

A separate select committee might be established to inquire into the constitutional role of the monarchy. This is imperative in view of the fluidity of the European situation. Increasingly over the years, much of the law affecting the United Kingdom will be made in Europe, and the British monarch's signature will be superfluous.

The absurd pretence that the British Government is the *Queen's* Government, that our Navy is the *Royal* Navy, our Air Force the *Royal* Air Force, that all Army officers hold the *Royal* Commission, that our Prime Minister is *Her* Prime Minister, and appointed by Her, that she alone has the 'prerogative' to dissolve Parliament and to call an Election, that she is the Fount of Honour, that MPs must take an oath of allegiance before they can be paid one penny piece – all those cobwebs must be swept away.

Her Majesty's Government can get away with anything by calling in aid the 'Royal Prerogative'. The 'Crown' can bug our telephones without any of us knowing. The 'Crown' can send our sons and daughters to war without consulting Parliament. The 'Crown' can detain any prisoner 'At Her Majesty's Pleasure'.

It's not difficult to see how, far from being an institution *safeguarding* our liberties, the monarchy actually threatens them. The time is overripe to end this monstrous nonsense.

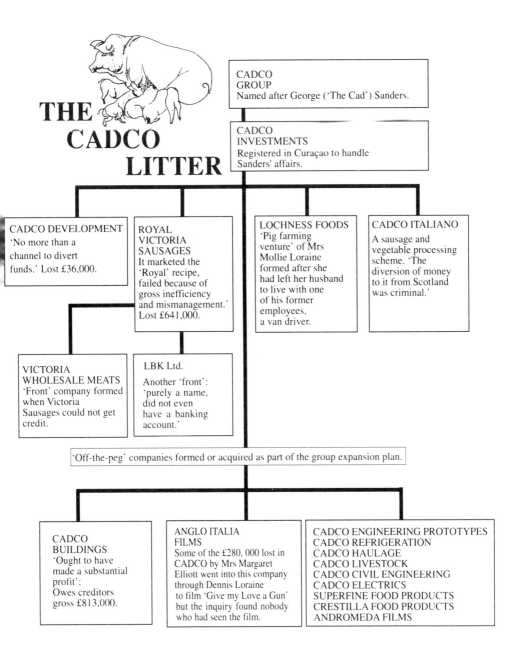

THE CADCO LITTER

CADCO GROUP
Named after George ('The Cad') Sanders.

CADCO INVESTMENTS
Registered in Curaçao to handle Sanders' affairs.

CADCO DEVELOPMENT
'No more than a channel to divert funds.' Lost £36,000.

ROYAL VICTORIA SAUSAGES
It marketed the 'Royal' recipe, failed because of gross inefficiency and mismanagement.' Lost £641,000.

LOCHNESS FOODS
'Pig farming venture' of Mrs Mollie Loraine formed after she had left her husband to live with one of his former employees, a van driver.

CADCO ITALIANO
A sausage and vegetable processing scheme. 'The diversion of money to it from Scotland was criminal.'

VICTORIA WHOLESALE MEATS
'Front' company formed when Victoria Sausages could not get credit.

LBK Ltd.
Another 'front': 'purely a name, did not even have a banking account.'

'Off-the-peg' companies formed or acquired as part of the group expansion plan.

CADCO BUILDINGS
'Ought to have made a substantial profit': Owes creditors gross £813,000.

ANGLO ITALIA FILMS
Some of the £280,000 lost in CADCO by Mrs Margaret Elliott went into this company through Dennis Loraine to film 'Give my Love a Gun' but the inquiry found nobody who had seen the film.

CADCO ENGINEERING PROTOTYPES
CADCO REFRIGERATION
CADCO HAULAGE
CADCO LIVESTOCK
CADCO CIVIL ENGINEERING
CADCO ELECTRICS
SUPERFINE FOOD PRODUCTS
CRESTILLA FOOD PRODUCTS
ANDROMEDA FILMS

Index

Aberdour, 72
abortion, 123, 124
Acton, Lord (1st Baron), 46
Adamson, Willie, 50
Adeane, Michael, 7, 201
Africa, 84–5, 98–9
Ancaster, Earls of, 127
Anne, Princess, 139
anti-semitism, 157
apprenticeships, 47
Armenia, 91–2
Atholl, Duke of, 130
Attlee, Clement, 54, 71, 75, 77, 81

Bainbridge, Mr and Mrs, 38
Baker, Bill, 24–5
Baldwin, Stanley, 14, 32
Bangor, 36–7, 49
Banks, Tony, 181
Baring, John, 200
Barry, John, 108
Batley Technical College, 59
BBC, 184
Begin, Menachim, 56
Bence, Cyril, 75
Benn, Tony, 131, 141, 152–3, 197
Bethlehem, 57
Bevan, Aneurin (Nye), 69, 71, 81, 82, 103, 121; and NHS, 70, 85, 195–6
Bevin, Ernest, 71, 195
Bevin Boys, 52
Biffen, John, 162
birth control, 123, 124
Bish, Geoff, 197–8
Boyd, Mrs, 20, 24, 25, 149
Boyle, Edward, 77, 191
Braddock, Bessie, 71, 76
Brendon, 34–5
Brezhnev, Leonid, 92
Brier, Mr, and family, 42, 55
Brittan, Leon, 162–3, 170
Brown, George, 103, 149–50
Brown, Pat, 94, 95
Brown, Ron, 171–2
Bruce, Donald, 150, 170
Buccleuch, Duke of, 132
Buchan, Norman, 121
Buchanan-Smith, Alex, 88

Burmah Oil Company, 114–16
Bury, 42
Bush, George, 96
Butler, R.A. (Rab), 70, 82, 101, 195

CADCO, 4, 104, 108–11, 112–13, 211
Callaghan, James, 103, 131, 145, 146, 153, 160
Callow, Joan, see Hamilton, Joan
Campaign for Nuclear Disarmament, 87, 118, 172
Cardington, 39, 40
Castle, Barbara, 74–6, 133, 140, 145, 191
Catholic Church, 62, 124
Cementation International, 164
censorship, 124, 205
Central Fife Labour Party, 152, 153–4; see also West Fife Labour Party
centralisation, 69, 128, 195
Chamberlain, Joseph, 130
Channel Tunnel, 128
Chaplin, Charlie, 110
Chapman, Arthur, 31–2
Charles, Prince, 196, 200, 201–3, 206, 208
Chernobyl, 183
Chicken, Mr (grandfather), 9
Chicken, Annie (aunt), 9
Chicken, Jack (uncle), 9
Chicken, Jennie, see Hamilton, Jennie
Chicken, Mary (aunt), 9
Chicken, Ralph (uncle), 9, 10
Chicken, Tom (uncle), 9
Chicken, Willie (uncle), 9
Chiswick Women's Aid, 140
Cholmondeley, Marquesses of, 127–8
Church of Scotland, 180
Churchill, Winston (PM), 32, 54, 69, 71, 113, 121; and House of Lords, 130
Churchill, Winston (MP), 208
Civil List, 122, 139, 199, 201–2
civil service, 162
Clark, Alan, 207–8
Clark, David, 201
class system, 8–9, 29, 35–6, 158, 196; armed forces and, 45–6; see also inequality
Cleator Moor, 54–5
clothing, 14, 23
CND, 87, 118, 172

Cocks, Barnett, 126
Cogle, Margaret, *for earlier life see* McKay, Margaret; *for later life see* Hamilton, Margaret
COHSE, 151
common land, 201
Common Market, *see* European Community
Commons, House of, *see* House of Commons
Commonwealth Parliamentary Association, 84, 151
Communist Party, in West Fife, 50, 52, 61, 62, 71, 72, 88, 138; campaigning tactics, 52, 53, 61, 138; support for, 50, 62–3, 72, 88, 136, 137
Communist Party, Italian, 144
compensation, 116, 187; *see also* War Damage Bill
Conservative Party, 14, 54, 70, 74; conferences, 143; and European Community, 137, 166–7; leaders, and means of choosing/deposing them, 82, 101, 107, 134, 159, 160; attitude to MPs having dual mandate, 145, 170
Cook, Arthur, 14
Cook, Robin, 203
Cooper, Frank, 106–7
Corbett, Freda, 157
Coulson, Rev. John, 30–1, 34
councillors, 117
CPA, *see* Commonwealth Parliamentary Association
Crawford, Dixie, 24–5, 139
crime, 162, 183
Cripps, Stafford, 71, 195
Crossman, Richard, 71, 131
Cryer, Bob, 200, 203
Cuban crisis, 93
Cummings, Bob, 19–20

Daily Express, 138
Daily Herald, 21
Daily Record, 109
Daily Telegraph, 165
Daily Worker, 50
Dalry, 43
Dalton, Hugh, 33
Daly, Lawrence, 72, 88
Dalyell, Tam, 127
Dartford, 73
Davies, Harold, 75
Day, Robin, 179
Defence of the Realm Act, 33
devaluation, 122
Devon, 5, 34–6, 37, 57, 172–4
Devonport, 173
Dewar, Donald, 119, 134, 187
DHSS, 186; and violence in marriage, 140, 141
Dinsdale, Mrs, 37
Dollan, Patrick, 71
Dolly Pit, 8, 9, 15
domestic violence, 123, 136, 140–1
Dormand, Jack, 203
Dorothea Pit, 8, 9, 15

Douglas-Home, Alec, *see* Home, Lord
Doult, Bill, 139
Doyle, Paddy, 112–13
Duchy of Cornwall, 196, 197, 200–1, 202, 203
Duchy of Lancaster, 197, 198, 202, 203
Dulwich, 89
Dunfermline Press, 138
Dunglass, Lord, *see* Home, Lord
Durham, 139

East Witton, 37–8
Eastbourne, 171–2
EC (Estimates Committee), *see* Estimates Committee
EC (European Community), *see* European Community
Eden, Anthony, 79, 82
Edinburgh Evening News, 108
education, 23, 70, 76–7, 158, 202–3; Thatcher and, 184; working-class, 36–7
Edward VIII, 32
elections: in USA, 93–5, 161; *see also* general elections
eleven-plus, 16–17, 23
Elizabeth II, 7–8, 101, 109, 111, 127; finances, 198–9, 204–6; potential for abdication, 206; and Princess Margaret, 207–8; and Thatcher, 207, 208; *see also* monarchy
environment, 134–5
Estimates Committee, 77, 83, 104–5, 106
European Community, 5, 97–8, 136, 137, 166, 167; Commissioners' salaries, 170; referendum on membership, 141
European Parliament, 144–5; finances, and MEPs' allowances, 145, 167–70; lack of power, 167; secrecy over, 168, 169–70

Falklands War, 141, 177
Fartown, 55
Fatfield, 8
Fernie, John, 61–2
Festival of Britain, 57
Fife Coal Company, 52
Fife County Council, 50, 79, 134–5
Fife Labour Party, *see* West Fife Labour Party *and* Central Fife Labour Party
Fife Socialist League, 88
finance, *see* public spending; *see also under* European Parliament *and under* MPs (pay)
Fisher, Ida, 119
Fisher, Michael, 112, 118, 119
Fookes, Janet, 173
Foot, Michael, 3, 121, 130, 131, 152
forestry work, 34, 35, 37–9
Forth Road Bridge, 111
Fowler, Norman, 182
Francis of Assisi, St, 161
Franks, Lord, 200
Fraser, Don, 94
Fraser, P.W.N., 62
Fraser, Tom, 66
fraud, 162

Freeman, John, 70
Fyfe, J.P., 71, 72

Gaitskell, Hugh, 70, 81, 82, 85, 103, 152
Gallacher, Willie, 50, 52, 61, 63, 71; support for, 50, 54, 62–3, 72
Gambia, 84
GCHQ, 184
general elections: (1945), 48, 49–54, 55; (1950), 59, 61–4; (1951), 70–3; (1955), 79; (1959), 87–8; (1964), 88, 103–4, 111, 113, 159; (1966), 118; (1970), 88, 118, 134, 135; (Feb. 1974), 118, 137–8, 158–9; (Sept. 1974), 140, 145–6; (1979), 118, 145, 146–7, 161, 162; (1983), 154, 162; (1987), 162, 171–4; campaigning methods, 51–3, 61–2, 72, 79, 95, 161, 173; decisions over dates, 79; unfairness of system, 145–6, 147, 162, 176; voting figures, 54, 62, 72, 80, 88, 103–4, 135–6, 137, 140, 154
General Strike (1926), 14, 15
George V, 7
Georgia, 91
Ghana, 84
Glasgow, 62
Glenrothes, 108, 109–10, 112–13, 135
Glenrothes Development Corporation, 109, 110, 112–13
Glenrothes New Town Corporation, 80
Gold Coast, 84
Goldsmith, Lord, 142
Gorbachev, Mikhail, 92
Gosport, 41
Gould, Bryan, 165
Grafton, Duke of, 132
Granada TV, 207–8
Greater London Council, 162, 183
Griffiths, Eldon, 174
Griffiths, Jim, 82
Guardian, 115, 165
Gulf War, 141

Haifa, 55–6
Hailsham, Lord, 71, 101
Hale, Leslie, 71
Halliday, J., 136
Hamilton, Arthur (brother), 2, 14, 47, 139; war work, 16, 27, 47
Hamilton, Ian (son), 58, 112, 118–20, 121, 174
Hamilton, Jack (brother), 2, 14, 15, 47, 139
Hamilton, Jennie (mother), 7, 9, 12, 14, 19–20, 23, 27–8, 31, 37, 47, 86; family, 9; and politics, 15, 16, 49; death, 16, 85–6, 120
Hamilton, Joan (first wife), 43, 51, 118–19; family, 43, 50, 54–5; early married life, 50, 54–5, 57–8; birth of children, 54–5, 58; life in London, 66, 84, 88–9, 174; and politics, 73, 80, 102, 103; and religion, 120; voluntary work, 120; final illness, 104, 111–12, 113, 119; death, 119–20
Hamilton, Joe (father), 2, 7–8, 9, 12, 14, 23,

38, 47–8, 86; parents, 16; childhood, 16; churchgoing, 27, 28; earnings, 47, 48, 196; expectations, 16, 49; and politics, 2, 15, 16, 30–1, 49, 82, 96, 134; extent of fame, 52; speaking, 16; and WH's education, 13, 16, 17, 20, 21, 23, 30–1, 36, 49; and WH's politics, 32–3, 36, 38, 45, 80; WH publicises work, 139; death, 134
Hamilton, Margaret (second wife) (*for earlier life see* McKay, Margaret), 24, 148–52, 154, 171; and politics, 149, 151, 173; work for WH, 150
Hamilton, Peter (nephew), 47
Hamilton, Sheila (daughter), 2, 77, 112, 118, 119–20, 174; birth, 54–5; childhood, 66, 76–7; pen-pal, 93, 95; career, 77, 112, 174; marriage and family, 2, 119, 17
Hamilton, Tom (brother), 10, 15, 19, 20, 46–7, 48; death, 47
Hamilton, Tom (uncle), 16
Hamilton, Willie: family, 9, 10, 14, 22, 47–8, 86, 134; birth, 7; childhood, 9–21; at primary school, 11–17; at secondary school, 22–9, churchgoing, 27, 28; discipline, 15, 24; reading, 13, 20–1; sport, 25, 26, 28, 30, at university, 29–33; joins Labour Club, 32; joins Labour Party, 32–3; as conscientious objector, 33–9, 45, 57; at NCLC summer school, 36–7; first meeting with Fife miners, 36–7; first walk-out, 37; sacked from forestry jobs, 37, 38; in Air Force, 38–42; in the army, 42–6, 49, 54, 55–7; as an officer, 43–6, 55–7; first marriage, 43; family life, 57–8, 66, 70, 79, 88–9, 104, 118–20, 174; decision to stand for Parliament, 49; first general election, 5, 49–54, 55; lectures at Army Formation College in Haifa, 56, 57; demobilisation, 57, 58; teaching work, 57–9, 76, 88, 190; with NCLC and WEA, 58; organises mock election 59; in 1950 election campaign, 59, 61–4; first visit to mine, 59; becomes MP, 64; early experience as MP, 64–9, 105; first meeting with Cabinet Minister, 64–5; in 1951 election campaign, 70–3; on parliamentary committees, 77, 83, 104–5 106, 122–3, 125, 139, 140–1; in 1955 election, 79, 80; parliamentary activities, 83, 102, 121, 122–5; visits West Africa, 84–5, 92, 98–9; visits USSR, 90–2, 98; visits USA, 93–9; non-promotion 104, 111; coins quote of the week, 159; gets Chairmanship of Estimates Committee 104–5, 106; gives up teaching, 190; assists new MPs, 105–6; on TV and radio, 106, 204; and CADCO, 108–11, 112–13; introduces bill concerning House of Lords, 113, 115–16; heart attack and recovery, 118, 119; death of first wife, 119–20; offered post of Deputy Chairman of Ways and Means, 120, 126; life as widower, 120–1, 136; house burgled, 121; introduces bill on sex discrimination, 125; introduces bill to abolish House of Lords, 129–31; and

White Paper on House of Lords, 131–2; elected Senior Vice-Chairman of PLP, 133; attempts to engineer Wilson's resignation, 133, 143, 145; helps other candidates in 1970 election campaign, 134; appointed chairman of select committee on violence in marriage, 140; and attempts at legislation on monarchy, 197, 200–1, 203; campaigns on EC membership referendum, 141; appointed to European Parliament, 141, 144; work in European Parliament, 144–5, 167–8; second marriage, 148–52, 174–5; visits Canada, 151; working holidays, 151; problems with constituency party, 152, 153–4; required to go through Selection Conferences, 153–4; and Oman affair, 165; introduces bill to set up South-West Development Agency, 173; last general election, 5, 171–4; libel case, 172–3; retirement, 138–9, 153, 154, 171, 174–5
    acting, 139; on the armed forces, 40–1, 57, 64; articles on, 137–8, 139; on autobiography, 1; on class, 2; and constituents, 76, 89, 105, 124, 138, 154, 185–6, 187; dancing, 63; and drink, 91; on European Community, 97–8; finances, 4, 30–1, 64–5, 79; houses, 58, 66, 76, 89, 138, 174; journalism, 104; on divisions in Labour Party, 152–3, 154, 176; on Labour Party policies, 118, 123, 133, 136, 152–3, 161, 172, 175; on lawyers, 67; on parliamentary politics, 1, 3, 4–5, 67; on patronage, 104–5; on political classifications, 80–1, 103; on power, 3, 45–6, 68, 69; proposals for reform of Parliament, 126–33; on public speaking, 51; on punishment, 15; reading, 121; and religion, 28, 41, 62; on Scotland, 121–2, 153; singing, 139; on socialism and communism, 28, 96, 97, 182; on war and weapons, 2–3, 33, 75, 87, 98, 118, 141, 172; and women, 12, 17, 23, 28, 32, 156; on women, 47, 86, 123–5, 129; and women's rights, 123–5, 136, 138, 140–1, 177

Hanson, James, 142
Hardie, James Keir, 71, 188
Harrower, Bob, 53
Hayhoe, Barney, 200
health/ill health, 11
Healey, Denis, 121, 122, 152, 195
health services, 10–11, 30–1, 59, 70, 76, 85, 96, 103, 119–20; Thatcher and, 180–1, 182; in USA, 96; *see also* nurses
Heath, Edward, 69–70, 107, 115, 134, 137, 180; and Thatcher, 137, 158, 159, 160; demise as PM, 140
Heffer, Eric, 197
Herrington, 7, 8, 9
Heseltine, Michael, 162–3
Higgs, John, 200
Highlands and Islands Development Board, 151
Hogg, Norman, 119
Hogg, Quintin, 71, 101

Holden, William, 110
Holland, Mr, 105
Home, Lord (13th Earl), 101
Home, Lord (Sir Alec Douglas-Home), 100–2, 103, 107
homelessness, 202, 203, 206
honours lists, 142–3, 181
Houghton, Douglas, 133
Houghton-le-spring, 8
House of Commons, 64–6, 69, 105–6, 125–9; adjournment debates, 83, 185–6, 187; committees, 77–8, 83, 122–3; Library, 65, 105, 114, 121, 123, 130, 168, 169, 181; PM's powers in, 79; Private Members' Bills, 156; Question Time, 83, 177–8, 180, 185; Register of Members' Interests, 117; Ten-Minute Rule Bills, 129–30; *see also* MPs *and* Parliament
House of Lords, 113–17, 127–8, 129–32
housing, 7, 9–10, 18–20, 38, 41–2, 52, 55, 58, 79–80; Thatcher and, 159, 183, 184; *see also* homelessness
Howe, Geoffrey, 166
Howell, Denis, 174
Huddersfield, 42, 55, 57–9, 65, 79; council, 59
Hughes, Cledwyn, 150
Hungary, 88
Hunter, Adam, 36–7

Iceland, 46–7
illegitimacy, 43, 132
income tax, 7, 10
inequality, 2, 3, 7–9, 15–16, 24, 88–9; centralisation and, 195; cheating and, 111; educational, 23; North/South divide, 88–9, 171, 180; in USA, 95, 96, 97, 98
inflation, 177
Ingham, Bernard, 162
Inter-Parliamentary Union, 84, 90
interest rates, 159
IPU, *see* Inter-Parliamentary Union

Jay, Peter, 145
Jenkins, Patrick, 137
Jenkins, Roy, 102, 153
Jerusalem, 56, 57
Johnston, Tom, 71, 100
Jones, Elwyn, 150
Jones, Len, 34, 35, 57
Jones, Michael, 207
Joseph, Keith, 159

Kagan, Lord, 142
Kelty, 50, 51, 59, 61, 63, 186; mining disaster at, 86
Kennedy, Edward, 93–4
Kennedy, John F., 93, 95
Khrushchev, Nikita, 93
kibbutzim, 56
King, Horace, 64
Kingsbridge, 173
Kinnock, Neil, 136, 163, 176
Kirkwood, Davie, 71

Labour Party and Labour governments, 59, 63, 70, 160; conferences, 143, 153; constitution, 152; and House of Lords, 131–2; leaders, and means of choosing/deposing them, 81–2, 133–4, 152; and the monarchy, 197–8; and MPs, 143, 152, 153, 154; attitude to MPs having dual mandate, 145, 170; and MPs' pay, 190; National Executive Committee, 197–8; and Palestine, 55–6; Parliamentary Labour Party, 70, 74–5, 80, 81–2, 85, 87, 133; and Scottish Assembly, 146; Scottish Council, 154; selection of parliamentary candidates, 139, 153–4, 171–2; and trade unions, 133, 181; *see also* West Fife Labour Party *and* Central Fife Labour Party
Lambton, Viscount Antony, 8–9
Lambton, Hetton and Joicey Coal Company, 8, 26, 139
Lauchlan, William, 71, 72, 79, 80, 88, 90
Lawson, George, 104
Lawson, Nigel, 166
Lawther, Will, 30
Lenin, V.I., 92
libraries, 20–1; *see also under* House of Commons
Libya, 207
Lincoln, 43
Lincolnshire, 174–5
Lister, John, 51
Lister, Mrs, 51
Lloyd George, David, 10, 181
Lloyd, Selwyn, 116, 125–6
local government, 82, 117, 162, 183–4
Lochore, 53, 62, 135
Lodge, George, 93–4
London, 34, 128, 162, 174, 183; royal ownership, 199, 200
London County Council, 82
Loraine, Denis, 108, 109, 110, 112–13
Lords, House of, 113–17, 127–8, 129–32
Loudon, Miss, 24, 25
Lumphinnans, 52, 62

McCarthy, Joseph, 97
McColl, Ian, 119
McCrae, Mr, 112
MacDonald, James Ramsay, 100
McElhone, Frank, 150
McKay, Margaret (Peggy), 5, 24, 28–9, 139–40, 148, 154; family, 148, 149–50; *for later life see* Hamilton, Margaret
McKay, Mary, 62
McLaughlan, G., 136
Maclean, John, 71
Maclennan, Bob, 134
Macleod, Iain, 69–70, 71, 85, 101, 195
McMillan, A., 136
Macmillan, Harold, 71, 82, 85, 87, 101; honours lists, 181
MacPherson, Hugh, 138
Manchester, 42–3
Margaret, Princess, 5, 154–5, 207–8

Marshall, Willie, 50–1, 53
Maudling, Reginald, 69–70, 106
Maxton, Jimmy, 71
MEPs, *see under* European Parliament
Militant Tendency, 136
Mill, Mary, 36, 50
Mill, Willie, 36–7, 50, 52, 61–2, 186
Millan, Bruce, 170
Miller, Eric, 142
miners, 14, 15, 36, 50, 135; Conservatives and, 137, 183; and Labour Party, 159; loss of jobs, 135, 136; pay, 47, 48, 196; working conditions, 12, 48, 59–60, 135; *see also* mining
miners' unions, 14, 30, 36, 50, 52, 62, 72; and selection of parliamentary candidates, 139; Thatcher and, 183
mining, 8, 9, 10, 12, 16, 47–8, 134–5; accidents, 86; nationalisation, 59, 102–3; in Nigeria, 84; pit ponies, 11, 12, 15, 26–7; Rothes (Glenrothes) colliery, 109; *see also* miners
Mitchum, Robert, 110
Moffat, Abe, 52
Moffat, Alex, 52
monarchy, 3, 32, 41, 122–3, 139, 196–210; and parliament, 133–4, 208, 209–10; shedding of German titles, 7; *see also* Elizabeth II
Monteagle Marketing, 163–5
Morrison, Herbert, 81–2
Mount Carmel, 55–6
MPs, 67–8, 194–5; facilities, 64–5, 67, 125, 185, 192–3; foreign trips for, 83–4, 93; other employment/interests, 4, 67, 117, 129, 188, 193; pay, 4, 64–5, 79, 88, 188–94, 195, 196; pensions, 190, 194; powerlessness of backbench, 82, 110–11, 126; selection, 153–4, 171–2; serving also in European Parliament, 144–5, 170; treatment after defeat/retirement, 63, 154, 171, 190–1; work, 4, 67–8, 69, 78; constituency work, 4, 68, 76, 128, 185–8, 194; working conditions, 66–7, 69, 78, 89, 127–9, 185, 195; freedom, 67, 185, 189–90, 192–3, 200; *see also* House of Commons *and* Parliament
Munster, Earl of, 132
music, 9, 27, 28, 139, 150
My Queen and I, 3, 123, 204, 205

Nash, Ellison, 111–12
Nasser, Gamal Abdel, 82
National Council of Labour Colleges, 36–7, 49, 51, 58
National Health Service, *see* health services
National Insurance, 10, 59
nationalisation, 59, 102–3, 158
NATO, 70, 75, 137, 166
NCLC, *see* National Council of Labour Colleges
Neave, Airey, 159
Newbottle, 8
Newcastle Journal, 139

Newcastle Sunday Sun, 138, 139
Nigeria, 84
Nixon, Richard, 94–5
North Queensferry, 52–3
nuclear power, 182–3
nuclear weapons, 75, 77, 87, 118, 172
Nuneaton, 42
nurses and nursing, 29, 42–3, 123, 125, 136

Observer, 108, 138, 163, 164, 165
oil prices, 136–7, 147, 158
Oman affair, 4, 163–5
O'Neill, Dan, 139
Open University, 158
Orr, Mary, 12–13
Owen, David, 145, 153, 173

PAC, 77, 106
Paddock Stile School, 11–17
Palestine, 55–6
Pannell, Charlie, 127, 157
Parliament, 64–9, 74–8, 105–6, 125–33, 143–4, 194–5; 'sovereignty', 5, 67, 166, 205; televising, 78, 126, 179; vested interests in, 114–17; *see also* House of Commons *and* House of Lords
Pay Comparability, Committee on, 123
Penshaw, 8
pensions, 190, 194
Pentland, Norman, 91
Peyton, John, 193
Philadelphia, 8
Philadelphia Cricket Club, 26, 28, 30
Philip, Prince (Duke of Edinburgh), 80, 109
Pizzey, Erin, 140
Plebs, 49
PLP, *see* Parliamentary Labour Party *under* Labour Party
Political Honours Scrutiny Committee, 142
Poll Tax, 173, 204–5
Poundbury Camp, 201
poverty, 58–9, 84–5, 172; *see also* inequality
Pow, Mr, 26–7
Powell, Enoch, 69–70, 101, 121, 131, 195; on MPs' pay, 188, 193
Prescott, John, 203
Private Eye, 102, 165
privatisation, 181, 183
Public Accounts Committee, 77, 106
public meetings, 51–3, 72, 79
public spending, 77–8, 105, 106, 141, 145, 158, 176–7, 203

Quinn, Mrs, 62

religion, 41, 62, 120; Thatcher and, 161, 180, 182; *see also* Catholic Church
retirement, 7, 190, 194
Rhodesia, 130
Richmond, Duke of, 132
Ridley, Nicholas, 166
Roberts, Alfred, 161
Roberts, Margaret, 73; *for later life see* Thatcher, Margaret

Robinson, Miss, 12
Rodgers, Bill, 153
Roe, Thomas, 108, 109, 110, 112–13
Rolls-Royce, 158
Roosevelt, Franklin D., 96
Ross, Willie, 104, 121, 131
royal family, 15–16, 32, 196–210; *see also* monarchy
Rushton, Willie, 102
RVS, *see* CADCO

St Albans, Duke of, 132
St John-Stevas, Norman, 131, 198, 209
Salisbury, Lord, 131
Sanders, George, 108, 109–10, 112–13
Schofield, Mr (headmaster), 23, 24, 157
Scotland, 75, 121–2, 146, 153; Thatcher and, 180
Scottish National Party, 62, 122, 140, 145–6
secrecy, 168, 169–70, 199, 201, 205–6, 209
sex discrimination, 123, 125, 136
Shaw, Peter, 164
Sheffield Star, 138
Sheffield University, 29–33
Shiney Row, 8, 18, 20, 31; St Oswald's Church, 27, 28
Shinwell, Emanuel (Manny), 71, 104, 130, 149–50
Short, Ted, 104
Shrapnel, Norman, 115
Sierra Leone, 84
Silkin, John, 104
Skegness, 40
Skinner, Dennis, 203
Skye, 151
Smith, Ian, 130
Sneddon, John, 63, 79–80
Social Democratic Party, 153, 172
South Africa, 207
South Hams, 172–4
Spanish Civil War, 32
Spectator, 138
sport, 25, 26, 28, 30, 118–19, 174
Spring Gardens, 9–11
SPUC, 124
Stalin, Joseph, 92
Stallard, Jock, 150
statistics, 181–3, 202
Stevenson, Helen, 136, 154, 205
Stevenson, Jimmy, 136, 149, 154, 186, 205; death, 136
Stevenson, Margaret (Meg), 5, 136, 149, 151–2, 154, 205; death, 136, 154
Stevenson, Margaret (daughter of Meg), 136, 154, 205
Stevenson, Nancy, 136, 154, 205
Stevenson, R.S., 54
Stewart, William, 33–4
Stopes, Marie, 124
Strathalmond, Lord, 114–15
strikes, 14, 15, 18, 137, 146
Suez crisis, 82, 85, 87, 88
Sunday Mail, 104
Sunday Sun, 138, 139

Sunday Times, 108, 138, 165, 207, 208
Sunderland, 8, 10, 31
Sussex, 171–2
Swaffham, 41

Tatler, 138
taxation, 7, 10, 198–9, 202, 205–6, 209; *see also* Poll Tax
Taylor, Albert, 25–6
Tebbit, Norman, 202
television, 51, 78, 126, 179
Tennessee Valley Authority, 96
Terry, Walter, 142
Thatcher, Denis, 116, 163, 164
Thatcher, Margaret, 5, 81, 96, 97, 155–67; appearance and manner, 156–7, 160–1, 178, 179–80; career, 73, 137, 140, 156, 157–63, 177–8, 180; demise as PM, 97, 101, 107, 134, 176, 184; and education, 158; finances, 163–5, 191, 205; honours lists, 181; influences, 156, 159, 160; and mining, 59; and monarchy, 200; and pay comparability, 123; political methods, 160, 161–6, 176–84; and the Queen, 207; and religion, 161, 180, 182; on right of minority government, 147; and war, 141, 155, 177; and War Damage Bill, 116; and women, 125, 177
Thatcher, Mark, 163–5, 179, 184
Thomson, Tommy, 26
Tillicoultry, 36
Times, The, 115
Totnes, 172
trade unions, 133, 137, 146; and Labour Party, 143, 151, 181; Thatcher and, 156, 160, 181, 183, 184; *see also* miners' unions
truth, 1, 4, 30, 32, 33, 184; *see also* statistics

unemployment, 88, 181–2
United Nations, 166
Upper Clyde Shipbuilders, 158
USA, 93–9; and Cuba, 93; elections, 93–5, 161; submarines in Scotland, 75; and Suez crisis, 82; Thatcher and, 160, 207; WH visits, 93–9
USSR, 7, 38, 61, 75, 88, 90–2, 97, 98, 99; Chernobyl, 183; and Cuba, 93; WH visits, 90–2

vermin, 19–20, 58
violence in marriage, 123, 136, 140–1

wages/incomes, 10, 45, 65, 123, 125, 168–70, 192, 196; *see also under* MPs (pay)
War Damage Bill, 4, 114–16
Washington, 17
Washington Secondary School, 17, 20, 22–5, 67, 139, 149; headmaster, 23, 24, 157
Wass, Douglas, 162
weapons, 75, 77, 87, 118, 172; costs, 106
Weekly Scotsman, 111
Wellington, Duke of, 130
West Africa, 92, 98–9
West Fife Communist Party, *see* Communist Party
West Fife Labour Party, 36, 50, 51–2, 59, 61–3, 71–2; selection of WH as candidate, 49–50; Women's Section, 52, 53, 62; *see also* Central Fife Labour Party
Westland affair, 162–3
Westminster, Duke of, 130
Wheatley, John, 71
Wheldon, Huw, 56–7
Whitelaw, William, 191
Williams, Marcia, 142
Williams, Shirley, 153
Wilson, Harold, 70, 81, 102–3, 122, 127, 141–3, 160; on devaluation, 122; honours lists, 142–3, 181; and House of Lords, 131; and the monarchy, 123; offers WH post, 120, 126; right-wing campaigns for overthrow, 141–2, 143; WH attempts to engineer resignation, 133, 143, 145
Windsor, House of, 7; *see also* royal family
Winterton, Lord, 76
Women's Aid, 140, 141
women's rights, 123–5, 136, 138, 140–1, 177
Wood, John, 36
Woodhall Spa, 174–5
Workers' Educational Association, 58
World War One, 7, 9, 26
World War Two, 33, 36, 37, 41, 46–8, 54, 57, 75, 92; *see also* War Damage Bill
Wrotham, 43
Wylie, Norman, 79, 80

Ziegler, Philip, 205